PRAISE FOR *THE VIRTUE OF NATIONALISM*

"Yoram Hazony's book is profound as well as accessible and well-crafted, reflecting years of inquiry and reflection into a subject of unparalleled importance. Political figures, scholars, and the broader public will have to think carefully about this remarkable book."

—NATAN SHARANSKY, author of
The Case for Democracy and *Defending Identity*

"In a time when nationalism is all too often conflated with racism and authoritarianism, Yoram Hazony reminds us that democracy and liberty can flourish only in a world of sovereign nation-states."

—MICHAEL LIND, author of
The Next American Nation

The
VIRTUE
of
NATIONALISM

ALSO BY YORAM HAZONY

God and Politics in Esther

The Philosophy of Hebrew Scripture

The Jewish State: The Struggle for Israel's Soul

The
VIRTUE
of
NATIONALISM

———

Yoram Hazony

BASIC BOOKS
New York

Hachette Book Group supports the right to free expression and the value of copyright. The purpose of copyright is to encourage writers and artists to produce the creative works that enrich our culture.

The scanning, uploading, and distribution of this book without permission is a theft of the author's intellectual property. If you would like permission to use material from the book (other than for review purposes), please contact permissions@hbgusa.com. Thank you for your support of the author's rights.

Basic Books
Hachette Book Group
1290 Avenue of the Americas, New York, NY 10104
www.basicbooks.com

Printed in the United States of America
First Edition: September 2018

Published by Basic Books, an imprint of Perseus Books, LLC, a subsidiary of Hachette Book Group, Inc. The Basic Books name and logo is a trademark of the Hachette Book Group.

The publisher is not responsible for websites (or their content) that are not owned by the publisher.

The Library of Congress has cataloged the hardcover edition as follows:

Names: Hazony, Yoram, author.
Title: The virtue of nationalism / Yoram Hazony.
Description: First edition. | New York : Basic Books, 2018. | Includes bibliographical references and index.
Identifiers: LCCN 2017060188 (print) | LCCN 2018002030 (ebook) | ISBN 9781541645387 (ebook) | ISBN 9781541645370 (hardcover)
Subjects: LCSH: Nationalism—Philosophy. | Nationalism—History.
Classification: LCC JC311 (ebook) | LCC JC311 .H374 2018 (print) | DDC 320.5401—dc23

LC record available at https://lccn.loc.gov/2017060188

ISBNs: 978-1-541-64537-0 (hardcover), 978-1-541-64538-7 (ebook)

LSC-C

10 9 8 7 6 5 4 3 2 1

This book is dedicated with love to the members of my tribe:

AVITAL

TECHELET

EFRAIM

YARDENA

HADAR AHIAD

GAVRIEL

BINYAMIN ZE'EV NETZAH

YOSEF

ELIAHU

CONTENTS

PART THREE

Anti-Nationalism and Hate

Introduction

A RETURN TO NATIONALISM

POLITICS IN BRITAIN AND AMERICA have taken a turn toward nationalism. This has been troubling to many, especially in educated circles, where global integration has long been viewed as a requirement of sound policy and moral decency. From this perspective, Britain's vote to leave the European Union and the "America first" rhetoric coming out of Washington seem to herald a reversion to a more primitive stage in history, when war-mongering and racism were voiced openly and permitted to set the political agenda of nations. Fearing the worst, public figures, journalists, and academics have deplored the return of nationalism to American and British public life in the harshest terms.

But nationalism was not always understood to be the evil that current public discourse suggests. Until only a few decades ago, a nationalist politics was commonly associated with broad-mindedness and a generous spirit. Progressives regarded Woodrow Wilson's Fourteen Points and the Atlantic Charter of Franklin Roosevelt and Winston Churchill as beacons of hope for mankind—and this precisely because they were considered

1

expressions of nationalism, promising national independence and self-determination to enslaved peoples around the world. Conservatives from Teddy Roosevelt to Dwight Eisenhower likewise spoke of nationalism as a positive good, and in their day Ronald Reagan and Margaret Thatcher were welcomed by conservatives for the "new nationalism" they brought to political life. In other lands, statesmen from Mahatma Gandhi to David Ben-Gurion led nationalist political movements that won widespread admiration and esteem as they steered their peoples to freedom.[1]

Surely, the many statesmen and intellectuals who embraced nationalism a few generations ago knew something about this subject, and were not simply trying to drag us back to a more primitive stage in our history, to war-mongering and racism. What, then, did they see in nationalism? There have been surprisingly few attempts, whether in the public sphere or in academia, to answer this question.

My own background allows me some insight into the subject. I have been a Jewish nationalist, a Zionist, all my life.[2] Like most Israelis, I inherited this political outlook from my parents and grandparents. My family came to Jewish Palestine in the 1920s and early 1930s with the aim of establishing an independent Jewish state there. They succeeded, and I have lived most of my life in a country that was established by nationalists, and has been governed largely by nationalists to this day. Over the years, I have known a great many nationalists, including public figures and intellectuals both from Israel and from other countries. And while not everyone among them has been to my taste, on the whole these are people I deeply admire—for their loyalty and courage, their good sense, and their moral decency. Among them, nationalism is not some unfathomable political illness that periodically takes over countries for no good reason and to no good end, as many in America and Britain seem to think these days. It is instead a familiar political theory on which they were raised, a theory of how the political world should be ordered.

What is this nationalist political theory about? The *nationalism* I grew up with is a principled standpoint that regards the world as governed best when nations are able to chart their own independent course, cultivating their own traditions and pursuing their own interests without interference. This is opposed to *imperialism,* which seeks to bring peace and prosperity to the world by uniting mankind, as much as possible, under a single political regime. I do not suppose that the case for nationalism is unequivocal. Considerations can be mustered in favor of each of these theories. But what cannot be done without obfuscation is to avoid choosing between the two positions: Either you support, in principle, the ideal of an international government or regime that imposes its will on subject nations when its officials regard this as necessary; or you believe that nations should be free to set their own course in the absence of such an international government or regime.[3]

This debate between nationalism and imperialism became acutely relevant again with the fall of the Berlin Wall in 1989. At that time, the struggle against Communism ended, and the minds of Western leaders became preoccupied with two great imperialist projects: the European Union, which has progressively relieved member nations of many of the powers usually associated with political independence; and the project of establishing an American "world order," in which nations that do not abide by international law will be coerced into doing so, principally by means of American military might. These are imperialist projects, even though their proponents do not like to call them that, for two reasons: First, their purpose is to remove decision-making from the hands of independent national governments and place it in the hands of international governments or bodies. And second, as you can immediately see from the literature produced by the individuals and institutions supporting these endeavors, they are consciously part of an imperialist political tradition, drawing their historical inspiration from the Roman Empire, the Austro-Hungarian Empire, and the British Empire. For example, Charles Krauthammer's argument for American "Universal Dominion," written at the dawn of the post–Cold War period, calls for America to create a "super-sovereign," which will preside over the permanent "depreciation . . . of the notion of sovereignty" for all nations on earth. Krauthammer adopts the Latin term *pax Americana* to describe this vision, invoking the image of the United States as the new Rome: Just as the Roman Empire supposedly established a *pax Romana* (or "Roman peace") that obtained security and quiet for all of Europe, so America would now provide security and quiet for the entire world.[4]

This flowering of imperialist political ideals and projects in the last generation should have sparked a rigorous debate between nationalists and imperialists over how the political world should be organized. But until very recently, a discussion of this kind was largely avoided. Since 1990, when Margaret Thatcher was deposed by her own party for expressing doubts about the European Union, virtually no one in a position of influence in either America or Europe has showed much interest in picking a fight with the broad vision at the heart of these twin empire-building projects.[5] This uncanny unanimity allowed both the

European Union and American "world order" to move forward without triggering an explosive public debate.

At the same time, political and intellectual spokesmen for these projects remained keenly aware that Europeans might not relish the prospect of a renewed "German empire," even one that was nominally governed from Brussels. They were mindful, too, that Americans have often balked at the idea of an "American empire." As a result, almost all public discussion of these efforts was conducted in a murky newspeak riddled with euphemisms such as "new world order," "ever-closer union," "openness," "globalization," "global governance," "pooled sovereignty," "rules-based order," "universal jurisdiction," "international community," "liberal internationalism," "transnationalism," "American leadership," "American century," "unipolar world," "indispensable nation," "hegemon," "subsidiarity," "play by the rules," "the right side of history," "the end of history," and so on.[6] All of this endured for a generation—until finally the meaning of these phrases began to become clear to a broad public, with the results that we see before us.

Whether the outpouring of nationalist sentiment in Britain and America will, in the end, be for the best, remains to be seen. But perhaps we can all agree on this: The time for vacuous talk is past. The debate between nationalism and imperialism is upon us. Imperialism and nationalism are formidable and opposed ideals that have contended with one another in the past, and they have resumed their old conflict in our day. Each of these points of view deserves to be thought about carefully and with due respect, which includes speaking about them in straightforward, unambiguous terms so we can all understand what we are talking about. Let us hope that this debate, so long overdue, is conducted in a manner that is at once frank, reasoned, and clear.

I have written this book so that we have a statement of the reasons for being a nationalist.[7] In the interest of contributing to a discussion that is as clear and comprehensible as possible, I will understand "globalism" for what it obviously is—a version of the old imperialism. And in the same way, I will not waste time trying to make nationalism prettier by calling it "patriotism," as many do today in circles where nationalism is considered something unseemly.[8] Normally, *patriotism* refers to the love or loyalty of an individual for his or her own independent nation. The term *nationalism* can be used in much this way as well, as when we speak of Mazzini as an Italian nationalist or of Gandhi as an Indian nationalist. But nationalism can also be something more than this. There is, as I have said, a long tradition of using this term to refer to a theory of the best political order—that is, to an anti-imperialist theory that seeks to establish a world of free and independent nations. That is how I will be using it in this book.

Once events are seen in light of this long-standing confrontation between two irreconcilably opposed ways of thinking about political order, the entire subject becomes much easier to understand, and a more intelligent conversation can emerge.

My argument will be as follows:

In Part One of the book, "Nationalism and Western Freedom," I offer a basic historical framework for understanding the confrontation between imperialism and nationalism as it has developed among the Western nations. I introduce the distinction between a political order based on the *national state,* which seeks to rule over one nation alone; and one whose purpose is to bring peace and prosperity by uniting mankind under a single political regime, which is an *imperial state*.[9] This distinction is central to the political thought of the Hebrew Bible (or "Old Testament"), and in the wake of the Reformation it inspired the renunciation of the authority of the Holy Roman Empire by national states such as England, the Netherlands, and France. Thus began a period of four centuries during which the peoples of Western Europe and America lived under a new Protestant construction of the political world, in which national independence and self-determination came to be regarded as foundational principles. Indeed, these things came to be viewed as among the most precious human possessions and the basis for all our freedoms. An order of independent nations would permit diverse forms of self-government, religion, and culture in a "world of experiments" that would benefit all mankind.

As late as the Second World War, many still believed that the principle of national freedom was the key to a just, diverse, and relatively peaceful world. But Hitler changed all that, and today we live in the aftermath, in which a simplistic narrative, ceaselessly repeated, asserts that "nationalism caused two world wars and the Holocaust." And who, in fact, would want to be a nationalist if nationalism means supporting racism and bloodshed on an unimaginable scale?

With nationalism thus tarred as having caused the greatest evils of our age, it is not surprising that the old intuitions favoring national independence have been gradually attenuated and finally even discredited. Today, many have come to regard an intense personal loyalty to the national state and its independence as something not only unnecessary but morally suspect. They no longer regard national loyalties and traditions as providing a sound basis for determining the laws we live by, for regulating the economy and making decisions about defense and security, for establishing public norms concerning religion and education, or for deciding who gets to live in what part of the world. The new world they envision is one in which liberal theories of the rule of law, the market economy, and individual rights—all of which evolved in the domestic context of national states such as Britain, the Netherlands, and America—are regarded as universal truths and considered the appropriate basis for an international regime that will make the independence of the national state unnecessary.[10] What is being proposed, in other words, is a new "liberal empire" that will replace the old Protestant order based on independent national states. It is empire that is supposed to save us from the evils of nationalism.

But have supporters of the new imperialism correctly described what nationalism is and where it comes from? Are they right in attributing to nationalism the greatest evils of the last century? And is a renewed imperialism really the solution?

In my view, all these things appear exceedingly doubtful. And in Part Two, "The Case for the National State," I argue for regarding a world based on independent national states as the best political order, in the process showing why we should reject the imperialism that is now so much in fashion. This part of the book offers a philosophy of political order based on a comparison of the three rival ways of organizing the political world that are known to us from experience: the order of tribes and clans that is found in virtually all pre-state societies; an international order under an imperial state; and an order of independent national states.

Most recent attempts to compare a "globalist" political order with a world of national states have been focused on the proposed economic and security advantages of a unified legal regime for the entire world. But according to the view I defend here, arguments based on economics and security are too narrow to provide an adequate answer to the question of the best political order. In reality, much of what takes place in political life is motivated by concerns arising from our membership in collectives such as families, tribes, and nations. Human beings are born into such collectives or adopt them later in life, and are tied to them by powerful bonds of mutual loyalty among their members. In fact, we come to regard these collectives as an integral part of ourselves. Many, if not most, political aims are derived from responsibilities or duties that we feel we have, not to ourselves as individuals, but to an extended "self" that incorporates our family, tribe, or nation. These include a concern for the lives and property of members of the collective to which we are loyal. But we are also powerfully motivated by shared concerns that are not physical in this way: the need to maintain the internal cohesiveness of the family, tribe, or nation, and the need to strengthen its unique cultural inheritance and pass it on to the next generation.

We cannot accurately describe these dimensions of human political motivation in terms of the individual's desire to protect his life, personal freedom, and property. Each of us in fact wants and needs something else in addition, which I suggest we call *collective self-determination:* the freedom of the family, tribe, or nation. This is the freedom that we feel when the collective to which we are loyal gains in strength, and develops those special qualities and characteristics that give it unique significance in our eyes.

In the liberal political tradition, the desire and need for such collective self-determination tends to be regarded as primitive and dispensable. It is assumed that with the advent of modernity, individuals free themselves from motivations of this kind. But I will argue that nothing like this actually happens. British and American concepts of individual liberty are not universals that can be immediately understood and desired by everyone, as is often claimed. They are themselves the cultural inheritance of certain tribes and nations. Americans or British who seek the extension of these concepts around the world continue to give voice to the age-old desire for collective self-determination, which moves them to want to see their own cultural inheritance grow in strength and influence—even if it means destroying the inheritance of others who may see things differently.

My argument points to a number of decisive advantages of organizing the political world around independent national states. Among others, I suggest that the order of national states offers the greatest possibility of collective self-determination; that it inculcates an aversion to the conquest of foreign nations, and opens the door to a tolerance of diverse ways of life; and that it establishes a life of astonishingly productive competition among nations as each strives to attain the maximal development of its abilities and those of its individual members. In addition, I find that the powerful mutual loyalties that are at the heart of the national state give us the only known foundation for the development of free institutions and individual liberties.

These and other considerations suggest that a world of independent national states is the best political order to which we can aspire. This does not mean, however, that we should endorse a universal right to self-determination, as Woodrow Wilson proposed. Not all of the thousands of stateless peoples in the world can or will have political independence, so what place should the principle of national independence have in the affairs of nations? I conclude Part Two by considering what can be the relevance of the order of national states for a real-world international arena in which political independence cannot be applied always and everywhere.

The argument most commonly made against a nationalist politics is that it encourages hatred and bigotry. And there is certainly some truth in this: In every nationalist movement, one finds individuals who are haters and bigots. But what conclusion should we draw from this fact? To my mind, its significance is weakened by the realization that universal political ideals—of the kind that are so prominent, for example, in the European Union—seem invariably to generate hatred and bigotry to at least the same degree as nationalist movements. In Part Three, "Anti-Nationalism and Hate," I investigate this phenomenon, comparing the hatred between rival national or tribal groups that feel threatened by one another, with the hatred that proponents of imperialist or universalist ideologies feel toward national or tribal groups that refuse to accept their claim to be bringing salvation and peace to the world. The most famous example of the hatred generated by imperialist or universalist ideologies is perhaps Christian anti-Semitism. But Islam, Marxism, and liberalism have proved themselves quite capable of inflaming similarly vicious hatreds against groups that are determined to resist the universal doctrines they propose. In fact, I suggest that liberal-imperialist political ideals have become among the most powerful agents fomenting intolerance and hate in the Western world today. This is not itself a recommendation for nationalism. But it does suggest that hatred may be endemic to political movements in general, and that the dispute between nationalism and imperialism should be decided on other grounds.

In the Conclusion, "The Virtue of Nationalism," I offer some brief remarks on the relationship between nationalism and personal character. All my life, I have heard it said that nationalism corrupts the human personality. This is an opinion I have heard from Christians and Muslims, liberals and Marxists, all of whom consider nationalism to be a vice because it seeks to raise barriers among people, when we should be tearing them down. My own understanding is different. In my father's house I was taught that to be a nationalist is a virtue. I explain how this can be so, showing that an orientation toward an order of independent nations can pave the way for certain positive traits of character that are more difficult, if not impossible, to attain so long as one remains committed to the dream of empire.

———

MUCH REMAINS UNCERTAIN ABOUT the exact course that the revived nationalism in Britain, America, and other nations will take. But whatever direction the political winds may yet turn, it is certain that the fault line that has been uncovered at the heart of Western public life is not going away. The politics of nations are rearranging themselves along this fault, dividing those who wish to retain the old nationalist foundations of our political world from educated elites who have, to one degree or another, become committed to a future under an imperial order. At this time, then, there can hardly be a subject more worthy of careful attention than that of nationalism and imperialism.

In addressing this subject, I will employ and develop political concepts such as *nation, empire, independence, national freedom, self-determination, loyalty, tribe, tradition,* and *toleration.* Many of these terms have a somewhat antiquated feel to them, but I ask the reader's patience in this regard. It is true that these and related concepts have been largely sidelined in recent years in favor of a discourse that seeks to understand political problems almost entirely in terms of the *state, equality, personal freedom, rights, consent,* and *race.* But this constriction in our political vision is itself one of the principal difficulties facing us today. The political world cannot be reduced to these terms, and the attempt to do so induces blindness in crucial areas—blindness, followed by disorientation when we begin colliding with things that are still quite real, even if we cannot see them any longer. A broader range of political concepts, updated for use at this time, can do much to restore the full range of our vision and dispel the confusion that has overtaken us. Once we can see the roads clearly, deciding which way to go becomes easier as well.

Part One

NATIONALISM
AND
WESTERN FREEDOM

I: Two Visions of World Order

FOR CENTURIES, THE POLITICS of Western nations have been characterized by a struggle between two antithetical visions of world order: an order of free and independent nations, each pursuing the political good in accordance with its own traditions and understanding; and an order of peoples united under a single regime of law, promulgated and maintained by a single supranational authority. In recent generations, the first vision has been represented by nations such as India, Israel, Japan, Norway, South Korea, Switzerland—and of course by Britain, in the wake of its turn toward independence. The second vision is held by much of the leadership of the European Union, which reaffirmed its commitment to the concept of an "ever closer union" of peoples in the Treaty of Maastricht in 1992, and has proceeded since then to introduce EU laws and currency into most member nations, as well as requiring the free movement of populations among most member states.[1] The United States, committed from its founding to the ideal of an independent national state, was for the most part able to maintain this character until the Second World War. But in the face of competition with the Soviet Union, and especially after the end of the Cold War, it has deviated from this model of national independence and has increasingly sought the establishment of a worldwide regime of law that would be enforced upon all nations by means of American power.[2]

The conflict between these two visions of the best political order is as old as the West itself. The idea that the political order should be based on independent nations was an important feature of ancient Israelite thought as reflected in the Hebrew Bible (or "Old Testament").[3] And although Western civilization, for most of its history, has been dominated by dreams of universal empire, the presence of the Bible at the heart of this civilization has ensured that the idea of the self-determining, independent nation would be revived time and again.[4]

Why is the Bible so concerned with the independence of nations? The world of Israel's prophets was dominated by a succession of imperial powers: Egypt, Babylonia, Assyria, and Persia, each giving way to the next. Despite their differences, each of these empires sought to impose a universal political order on mankind as a whole, the gods having sent them to suppress needless disputes among peoples and to create a unified international realm in which men could live together in peace and prosperity. "None hungered in my years or thirsted in them," Pharaoh Amenemhet I wrote a few centuries before Abraham. "Men dwelled in peace through that which I wrought."[5] And this was no idle boast. By ending warfare in vast regions and harnessing their populations to productive agricultural work, imperial powers were in fact able to bring to millions a relatively reliable peace and an end to the threat of starvation. No wonder, then, that the imperial rulers of the ancient world saw it as their task, in the words of the Babylonian king Hammurabi, to "bring the four quarters of the world to obedience." That obedience was what made salvation from war, disease, and starvation possible.[6]

Yet despite the obvious economic advantages of an Egyptian or Babylonian peace that would unify humanity, the Bible was born out of a deep-seated opposition to this very aim. To Israel's prophets, Egypt was "the house of bondage," and they spared no words in deploring the bloodshed and cruelty involved in imperial conquest and in the imperial manner of governing, its recourse to slavery and murder and its expropriation of women and property.[7] All of this, the Israelite prophets argued, stemmed from Egypt's idolatry—from its submission to gods who would justify any sacrifice so long as it advanced the extension of the imperial realm of peace and kept the production of grain running at maximum capacity.

Was there a viable alternative to universal empire? The ancient Near East had much experience with localized political power in the form of city-states. But for the most part, these were helpless before imperial armies and the ideology of universal empire that motivated them. It is in the Bible that we find the first sustained presentation of a different possibility: a political order based on the independence of a nation living within limited borders alongside other independent nations.

By *nation,* I mean a number of tribes with a common language or religion, and a past history of acting as a body for the common defense and other large-scale enterprises.[8] The Bible systematically promotes the idea that the members of a nation should regard one another as "brothers," and Mosaic law offered the Israelites a constitution that would bring them together in what would today be called a *national state.*[9] The king of such a state would be drawn "from among your brothers." Its prophets, too, would be "from among you, from among your brothers." And so would its priests, appointed to guard the traditional laws of the nation and teach them to the king "so that his thoughts should not be lifted above his brothers."[10] Moreover, Moses sets boundaries for Israel, instructing his people to keep their hands off the lands of neighboring kingdoms like Moav, Edom, and Ammon, which deserve their own independence. As he tells them in God's name:

> Take good heed of yourselves therefore. Meddle not with [the children of Esau], for I will not give you of their land. No, not so much a foot's breadth. Because I have given Mt. Seir to Esau for a possession. . . . Do not harass Moav, nor contend with them in battle, for I will not give you of their land for a possession, because I have given Ar to the children of Lot for a possession. . . . And when you come near, opposite the children of Ammon, harass them not, nor contend with them, for I will not give you of the land of the children of Ammon any possession, for I have given it to the children of Lot for a possession.[11]

Nor are these passages unique. Throughout the Bible, we find that the political aspiration of the prophets of Israel is not empire but a free and unified nation living in justice and peace amid other free nations.[12]

The Bible thus puts a new political conception on the table: a state of a single nation that is united, self-governing, and uninterested in bringing its neighbors under its rule. This state is governed not by foreigners responsible to a ruler in a distant land but by kings and governors, priests and prophets drawn from the ranks of the nation itself—individuals who are, for just this reason, thought to be better able to stay in touch with the needs of their own people, their "brothers," including the less fortunate among them.

In addition, because the Israelite king is one of the people, and not the representative of some abstract universal ambition, his powers can be circumscribed to prevent abuse. Unlike the kings of Egypt or Babylonia, the Israelite king under the Mosaic constitution is not empowered to make the laws, which are the heritage of his nation and not subject to his whim. Nor does he have the power to appoint the priesthood, thereby making law and religion subservient to him. Moreover, the Mosaic law limits the king's right to tax and enslave the people, just as the limitations on Israel's borders prevent the king from embracing the dream of universal conquest.[13]

It is important to notice that the Israelites' conception of the nation has nothing to do with biology, or what we call *race*.[14] For biblical nations, everything depends on a shared understanding of history, language, and religion that is passed from parents to children, but which outsiders can join as well. Thus the book of Exodus teaches that there were many Egyptians who attached themselves to the Hebrew slaves in fleeing Egypt, and that they received the Ten Commandments (more accurately translated as the "Ten Precepts") at Sinai with the rest of Israel. Similarly, Moses invites the Midianite sheikh Jethro to join the Jewish people. And Ruth the Moabite becomes part of Israel when she is ready to tell Naomi "your people is my people and your God is my God," her son being the forefather of King David himself. But the ability of Israel to bring these foreign-born individuals into its ranks depends on their willingness to accept Israel's God, laws, and understanding of history. Without embracing these central aspects of Israelite tradition, they will not become a part of the Israelite nation.[15]

II: The Roman Church and
Its Vision of Empire

THE JEWS WERE NOT the only people to recognize the potential of a national form of political organization as a bulwark against the tyranny of universal empire. The Greek historian Polybius blamed the Greek city-states for not having acted as a unified nation in their lost struggle with Rome. A Greek national state had never existed in history. But Polybius had before him the examples of the Armenians and the Jews under the Maccabees—two nations that, in his lifetime, revolted successfully against the Seleucid-Greek empire and established themselves as independent national states—and he apparently hoped for a united Greece one day as well.[16]

Throughout much of the history of Western peoples, however, the ideal of national independence remained largely in abeyance. Christianity eventually succeeded in establishing itself as the state religion of Rome. In the process, it adopted the Roman dream of universal empire, and the project of Roman law, which aspired to provide a single framework for a *pax Romana* ("Roman peace") extending to all nations.[17] For more than a thousand years, Christianity thus aligned itself, not with the ideal of setting the nations free as had been proposed by the Israelite prophets, but with much the same aspiration that had given rise to imperial Egypt, Assyria, and Babylonia: the aspiration of establishing a universal empire of peace and prosperity.[18]

Regarding itself as the "Catholic" or universal church, the Roman church was allied, in theory and often in practice as well, with the German Holy Roman emperors, who were entrusted with establishing the universal Christian empire. In this, Roman Catholic political thought paralleled that of the Muslim caliphs and the Chinese emperors, who likewise believed they had been charged with bringing peace and prosperity to the world under the rule of a universal empire of their own.[19]

But Christian political thought differed from that of Islam or China in at least one crucial respect: Christianity had the Hebrew Bible, with its vision of the justice of a world of independent nations.[20] This vision never ceased to cause trouble for the idea of a universal Catholic empire, even if many Christian thinkers were hesitant to embrace the Old Testament too closely. It was the presence of the Hebrew Bible in the Christian canon that shaped the peculiar history of French Catholicism, which took on a national character modeled on the biblical Davidic kingdom and stubbornly resisted the control of popes and emperors. It shaped, as well, the unique national-religious traditions of the English, Poles, and Czechs well before the Reformation.[21]

Thus when Protestantism emerged in the sixteenth century, along with the invention of the printing press and the widespread circulation of the Bible translated into the languages of the nations, the new call for freedom to interpret Scripture without the authority of the Catholic Church did not affect religious doctrine alone. Especially under the influence of Old Testament–oriented thinkers such as Ulrich Zwingli and John Calvin, Protestantism embraced and quickly became tied to the unique national traditions of peoples chafing against ideas and institutions that they regarded as foreign to them. In 1534, Henry VIII asserted the independence of an English-Anglican nation, a status that achieved finality with the defeat of a Spanish-Catholic invasion fleet by his daughter Elizabeth in 1588.[22] The revolt of the Dutch against their Spanish overlords likewise pitted a Calvinist insurrection against Catholic empire, culminating in the Dutch declaring themselves an independent nation in 1581. The Scottish national covenants of the same time, modeled on the Jewish national covenants of the Bible, were similarly motivated. The self-image of these Protestant peoples as rightfully independent in the face of imperial opposition was often explicitly modeled on biblical Israel's effort to wrest its national and religious freedom from the dictates of Egyptian and Babylonian universal empire.[23]

The Thirty Years' War, ending in the peace of Westphalia in 1648, is often said to have been a "war of religion" fought between Protestants and Catholics. But this is not quite right. The war actually pitted the emerging national states of France, the Netherlands, and Sweden (nations that were, respectively, Catholic, Calvinist, and Lutheran) against German and Spanish armies devoted to the idea that universal empire reflected God's will, and that such empire alone could bring true well-being to mankind. It was in the Thirty Years' War that the concept of a universal Christian empire, which had held sway over the West's political imagination for thirteen centuries, was decisively defeated.[24]

III: The Protestant Construction of the West

THE PERIOD BETWEEN THE English Act of Supremacy and the Westphalia treaties gave a new, Protestant construction to the West. By the middle of the seventeenth century, a ring of independent national states on the Western rim of

Europe—England, the Netherlands, France, Switzerland, Sweden, and Denmark—had given what later came to be known as the Westphalian political order its distinctive form. Although the settlement was not officially accepted by the Catholic Church (Pope Innocent X said that it "was, is and forever will be, null, void, invalid, iniquitous, unjust, damnable, reprobate, inane, and entirely devoid of effect"[25]), in practice it refounded the entire political order in accordance with the theory of the independent national state that had been advanced by English and Dutch Protestantism during the preceding century.[26] Under this Protestant construction, the political life of Europe was rebuilt upon two principles, both of them having their origins in the Old Testament:

1. The Moral Minimum Required for Legitimate Government. First, the king or ruler, in order to rule by right, had to devote himself to the protection of his people in their life, family, and property, to justice in the courts, to the maintenance of the sabbath, and to the public recognition of the one God—roughly, the biblical Ten Precepts given at Sinai, which both Luther and Calvin regarded as a natural law that could be recognized by all men. These precepts were seen as providing the minimum requirements for a life of personal freedom and dignity for all. A government incapable of maintaining this moral minimum was one that had failed in its most basic obligations to the well-being of its people.[27]

2. The Right of National Self-Determination. Second, nations that were cohesive and strong enough to secure their political independence would henceforth be regarded as possessing what later came to be called a right of self-determination, by which was meant the right to govern themselves under their own national constitutions and churches without interference from foreign powers. Thus, while it was accepted that there exist natural minimum requirements for maintaining a civilized society, and that, in line with the first principle, these were binding upon all governments, it was not expected that all nations would become as one in their thoughts, laws, or way of life.[28]

The two principles of the Protestant construction were not entirely new. The idea that a ruler must serve as the protector of his people had existed in various forms throughout the history of Christendom. This had already been articulated explicitly in the twelfth century by Catholic political theorists such as Honorius of Augsburg and John of Salisbury, relying on the Mosaic law in Deuteronomy and the descriptions of the Israelite kingdoms in the books of Samuel and Kings.[29]

But the second principle—permitting each nation to determine for itself what constitutes a legitimate ruler, a legitimate church, and appropriate laws and liberties—brought the Christian world directly into dialogue with the biblical vision of an order of independent nations. And it was this principle that set the world free. In the context of post-Westphalian Europe, this meant that some nations would be monarchies while others would be republics. It meant that different nations would have different forms of national religion, as well as varying provisions for the protection of minority religions. It also meant that different nations would manifest different degrees of personal freedom in various areas. An outstanding example of such variety was the English constitution, which, as John Fortescue's *In Praise of the Laws of England* (published c. 1543) emphasized, diverged dramatically from that of the French and Germans, following biblical precedent in removing the determination of the laws from the hands of the king—a crucial characteristic of limited government that was later known as the "separation of powers."[30] The Dutch Republic, as well, offered an exceptional degree of personal freedom of expression, with the result that science, trade, and publishing flowed to Amsterdam from other nations more skeptical of the value of such openness. What made these innovations possible, however, was not a doctrine enumerating a list of "universal rights." Rather, it was the "ancient customs and privileges" of the English and Dutch nations.[31]

In works of Protestant political theory such as John Selden's *On Natural Law and National Law* (1640), the two principles of the Protestant construction are understood as reinforcing one another. This is an intuition drawn from Hebrew Scripture, which emphasizes that a nation whose rulers will protect their people and pursue their well-being will establish mutual loyalty and gain cohesiveness in the face of hardship. Internal brotherhood and justice, the prophets believed, is the necessary prerequisite for national longevity and for the capacity to resist foreign encroachment.[32]

Yet these two principles also stand in tension with each other. On the one hand, the idea that there are natural standards of legitimacy higher than the dictates of any particular government means that nations cannot rightly do whatever they please. They are always subject to judgment by God and man, and this necessarily makes government conditional.[33] On the other hand, the principle of national freedom strengthens and protects the unique institutions, traditions, laws, and ideals of a given nation against the claim that they must be overturned in the name of doctrines being promoted by the advocates of a universal church or empire. While the existence of a moral minimum is recognized, interpreting how this minimum will be expressed is taken to be a right of every independent nation, each approaching the issue from a perspective rooted in its own historical circumstances, experience, and insight.

The tension inherent in maintaining both principles of the Protestant construction imparted a unique dynamism to the nations of Europe, releasing a storm of dormant energies and fostering a stunning degree of experiment and innovation in government and theology, economics, and science. By permitting a diversity of constitutional and religious arrangements within different countries, the Protestant order also provided national laboratories for developing and testing the institutions and freedoms we now associate with the Western world. And the contest among rival national perspectives went far beyond political theory and theology. English empirical science was fueled by outrage over the deductive character of the Cartesian method, which the French, in turn, insisted was the only truly "rational" way to advance science. German philosophy likewise thrived on the belief that British empiricism was a grand catastrophe, and that Immanuel Kant's idealism would save us all. The same could be said for virtually any field in which European civilization made significant advances, including finance, industry, medicine, philosophy, music, and art. In each case, rival points of view, recognized at the time as being distinctly national in character, were proposed as being best for mankind as a whole, spurring others to imitate what they saw as successful, even as they incited renewed efforts to rebuild defeated approaches more intelligently so that they might fight another day.

None of this is to say that post-Westphalian Europe was some kind of idyll. The Christian national states were constantly resorting to war over territories and trade, a habit that cannot but strike us as a willingness to accept gratuitous bloodshed. Moreover, even as the English, Dutch, and French insisted upon the Westphalian principle of national independence and self-determination within the European context, they were all too ready to devise reasons for maintaining colonial empires based on the conquest and subjugation of foreign peoples in Asia, Africa, and the Americas. These states—and later the United States as well—also long maintained unconscionable racialist arrangements and institutions, and placed a variety of barriers before the participation of Jews in national life. One could easily add to the list of practices from that period that we would and should find objectionable.

Yet for all its evident shortcomings, the argument for the international order introduced into Europe in early modernity remains: As an order based on the principle of national freedom, it imparted a remarkably beneficial political and religious form to the Western nations—a form that provided a basis for the eventual remediation of many of its deficiencies. In time, the Protestant principle of national freedom did put an end to Europe's overseas empires. And in so doing, it brought about the founding of new national states around the world, among them the United States of America and a restored Jewish state of Israel.

IV: John Locke and the
Liberal Construction

IN AUGUST 1941, SEVERAL months before America's entry into the Second World War, Franklin Roosevelt and Winston Churchill signed what became known as the Atlantic Charter, which reaffirmed the principle of national freedom ("the right of all peoples to choose the form of government under which they will live") as the very heart of the Western powers' vision for the postwar world. Both leaders continued to speak of their nations as committed to what Roosevelt called "the old ideals of Christianity," which they understood as undergirding the freedom of their own nations, no less than that of other nations. At this critical juncture, the Protestant construction remained the basis for the political order in the West. The great challenge was to defeat the Nazis and the Soviets in their efforts to overthrow this order.[34]

But the defeat of the Nazis, and ultimately also of the Soviets, did not bring about the restoration of the Protestant construction of the West. In fact, in the years since the end of the Second World War, the future of this political order has only grown increasingly uncertain. We can see this in the progressive abandonment of the view that family, sabbath, and public recognition of God are institutions upheld by legitimate government and minimum requirements of a just society (i.e., the first principle). And we can see it in the sharp decline of concern for safeguarding the political independence of nations as the most effective barriers to the tyranny of universal empire, culminating in the reconstitution of Europe under a multinational regime, and the increasing tendency to identify American power with a new world order that will supersede the independence of nations (i.e., the second principle).

This crisis in the Protestant political order is being driven by pressure from an emerging alternative to it—an alternative that can be called the liberal construction of the West. Although its ultimate triumph is by no means assured, the rise of this new liberal order, to the point that it has succeeded in putting the entire Protestant order in jeopardy, is the most significant political development of our time.

What is this liberal construction? I will touch on a few of its most important characteristics, some more familiar than others.

Unlike the Protestant construction, which thrived on the tension between the two biblically derived principles of national freedom and the moral minimum for legitimate rule, the liberal construction of the West assumes that there is only one principle at the base of legitimate political order: individual freedom. A classical and still influential source for this idea is modernity's most famous liberal manifesto, John Locke's *Second Treatise of Government*. Published in 1689, it opens with the assertion that all human individuals are born in "perfect freedom" and "perfect equality," and goes on to describe them as pursuing life, liberty, and property in a world of transactions based on consent. From this basis, Locke builds his model of political life and theory of government.

Locke himself was a product of the Protestant construction, and his work was intended to strengthen it, not to undermine it.[35] Nevertheless, in fashioning his theory, Locke downplayed or entirely omitted essential aspects of human nature and motivation without which no political philosophy can make sense. Every theory involves a reduction or simplification of its material, of course. But a well-framed theory will capture the most consequential features of the domain being studied, while a poorly framed one will let crucial elements slip away unnoticed. And so it is with the *Second Treatise,* which offers a rationalist view of human political life that has abstracted away every bond that ties human beings to one another other than consent.[36] In speaking of "consent," Locke means that the individual becomes a member of a human collective only because he has agreed to it, and has obligations toward such collectives only if he has accepted them.[37] This is flattering to the individual, since it makes it seem as though the important choices are almost always his to decide. However, it is painfully lacking as a description of the empirical political world, in which mutual loyalties bind human beings into families, tribes, and nations, and each of us receives a certain religious and cultural inheritance as a consequence of being born into such collectives. It ignores the responsibilities that are intrinsic to both inherited and adopted membership in collectives of this kind, establishing demands on individuals that do not arise as a result of consent and do not disappear if consent is withheld. And it is oblivious to the effects of a common adversity, which brings inevitable challenges and hardships to families, tribes, and nations, reinforcing the responsibilities to the collective and turning them into the most acutely felt, and often immovable, features of the moral and political landscape. No intelligent account of politics, or of political obligation, can be devised that does not give great weight to these factors. And Locke's account, which elides them, is in effect a far-reaching depreciation of the most basic bonds that hold society together.

Consider the family as an example. Most of us suppose that brothers and sisters born to the same parents have a special responsibility to help one another in a time of need that takes precedence over other obligations. In the same way, we would suppose that grandparents have obligations toward their grandchildren, and that grandchildren have obligations toward their grandparents. But none of these family relationships are the result of consent: One does not choose one's brothers or one's grandchildren. And so these obligations must derive from other sources. Locke's model, however, which seeks to found the family on free choice and consent, generates no such obligations. This is to say that anyone embracing the premises of the *Second Treatise* would be unable even to understand, much less defend, the existence of the family as we know it and the ties of responsibility that give it shape.[38]

Much the same can be said of Locke's theory of the state. The state that is brought into being in the *Second Treatise* is the product of consent alone: Individuals feel that their life and property are insufficiently secure, so they choose to form a pact to defend those interests.[39] But this pact in defense of one's property bears little resemblance to the national states that we know from experience. In real life, nations are communities bound together by bonds of mutual loyalty, carrying forward particular traditions from one generation to the next. They possess common historical memories, language and texts, rites and boundaries, imparting to their members a powerful identification with their forefathers and a concern for what will be the fate of future generations. I am thinking, for instance, of the way in which Fortescue's belief in the superiority of the laws of England resounded through the centuries of his heirs, or of the way in which England's historic dread of domination by Catholic Spain gave life to the institutions and wars in that land over generations. Attachments and dispositions such as these move the individual to serve his or her country, not only for the sake of their lives and property, but even at the cost of sacrificing these very things. Yet in most cases, they are instilled in us in childhood, and are no more freely chosen than the identity of one's brothers and sisters or one's grandparents. A Lockean theory of the state does not enable us to understand, much less justify, the existence of the national state and the ties of obligation that give it shape.

In reducing political life to the individual's pursuit of life and property, Locke did not merely offer an impoverished and unsuccessful account of human motivation and action. His political theory summoned into being a dream-world, a utopian vision, in which the political institutions of the Jewish and Christian world—the national state, community, family, and religious tradition—appear to have no reason to exist. All of these are institutions that result from and impart bonds of loyalty and common purpose to human collectives, creating borders and boundaries between one group and another, establishing ties to future and past generations, and offering a glimpse beyond the present to something higher. An individual who has no motives other than to preserve his life and expand his property, and who is under no obligations other than those to which he has consented, will have little need for any of these things. Without intending to, the dream-world offered by Locke's *Second Treatise* rendered most of the Protestant order senseless and superfluous.

Locke's first readers were deeply troubled by this. It moved the great British statesman and philosopher Edmund Burke, for example, to declare on the floor of Parliament that of all books ever written, the *Second Treatise* was "one of the worst."[40] But the radical deficiency of Locke's account has gradually ceased to be recognized as a problem. Western intellectuals have come to delight in it, until today we are inundated with follow-up works—from Rousseau's *On the Social Contract* (1762) and Kant's *Perpetual Peace* (1795) to Ayn Rand's *Atlas Shrugged* (1957) and John Rawls's *A Theory of Justice* (1972)—tirelessly elaborating this dream-world, working and reworking the vision of free and equal human beings, pursuing life and property and living under obligations that arise from their own free consent. A theory or program that is committed to this rationalist framework is what I will call a *liberal* theory or program.[41]

It is worth paying particular attention to the inability of liberal political theories to account for the existence of borders between nations. Protestant political theory followed Hebrew Scripture in considering national boundaries to be no less important for the peace and well-being of mankind than property boundaries. Locke's attempt to derive the existence of the state from the consent of an arbitrary group of property owners, however, eliminates this understanding of the nation as an intrinsically bounded entity living in a more or less determinate territory. In the *Second Treatise,* there is no in-principle limit to the size of state or the number of people whose property it can propose to protect, and the state is in fact eerily without boundaries or borders of any kind. According to the law of nature, Locke writes, "mankind are one community." The existence of political boundaries among men is, as far as he is concerned, nothing but a product of human "corruption and viciousness."[42] Since the law of nature is for Locke identical with universal reason, this means that men guided by reason, and therefore neither corrupt nor vicious, will have no need for national boundaries at all.

As long as liberal political theories were being promoted in a context still under the sway of strong Calvinist or Anglican Old Testament traditions, the inability of these liberal theories to provide any sense of the nation as a bounded community was of little consequence. Statesmen and philosophers raised on the Bible just assumed that their own nation was, like ancient Israel, a bounded entity that sought freedom and independence from other nations. But as liberalism has detached itself from its biblical and Protestant origins, its non-nationalist character has become ever more pronounced. Since all men are equally in need of having their lives and property protected, a politics based on liberalism alone—without any supplement from biblical tradition—means that the persistence of independent national states will be, at best, a matter of indifference.[43] And if the independence and internal cohesion of nations are expected to exact a cost in lives or property, then even this indifference quickly disperses, leaving liberals with an inclination to do without the independent national state entirely.[44] Thus by the early twentieth century, Ludwig von Mises's *Liberalism in the Classical Tradition* openly advocated dispensing with national states in favor of a "world super-state."[45] Friedrich Hayek, the most important theoretician of liberalism of the last century, likewise argued that a consistent application of "the liberal point of view" leads to an international federal state without significant boundaries between nations—an aspiration that he strongly endorsed.[46]

Not long ago, such conclusions still sounded outlandish. But things have changed. In recent decades, liberal political and economic theories and conceptions of international law have succeeded in driving out more conservative and realistic accounts of the political order, becoming the virtually unquestioned framework for what an educated person needs to know about the political world. With a few exceptions, the most widely discussed debates among competing views in political theory, economics, and jurisprudence are now almost entirely internal to the Lockean paradigm, which is often taught and discussed as though there are no meaningful alternatives to it.[47] University-educated political and intellectual elites in America and Europe are for the most part now sequestered within this liberal frame, regardless of their party affiliation. One need only ask a thoughtful person trained in the fields of politics or economics or law to mount a defense of the institution of the national state, or of the family, or of public recognition of God's kingship, to immediately see how unfamiliar these things have become, and how foreign they are to the terms in which members of our elites are accustomed to conceptualizing the world. This isn't just a matter of disagreeing with the proposition that such things are vital to maintaining a civilized political order. It is rather a matter of being so immersed in the political framework of the liberal construction as to be unable even to imagine what a non-Lockean view of reality might look like.

Having been initiated into this liberal paradigm, educated men and women can now find employment within a vast array of projects that assume a liberal construction of the world is coming: the political program of European unification; the expansion of unfettered free trade and the free immigration of populations; the transitioning of business enterprises into "multinational" corporations that serve the global economy rather than any particular national interest; the subjugation of nations to an ever-expanding body of international law; the agitation for a universal regime of human rights through non-governmental organizations, UN bodies, and international courts; the homogenization of the world's universities by way of a system of international standards and peer review. All these things are pursued as a matter of course by university-trained Lockeans, hardly aware that there might be intelligent and decent persons whose estimation of the worth of such enterprises is very different from their own. It is simply assumed that one can either be "on the right side of history" or "on the wrong side of history," and that when you are working at building up the new liberal order, you are on the right side.[48]

But despite the great success these enterprises have had in altering the face of our world, and their genuine worth in some fields, the Lockean account remains what it was: a utopian view of human nature and motivations, and a radically insufficient basis for understanding political reality. Those factors in human political and social life that have no place in the liberal paradigm have not been eliminated, as I will argue at greater length in Part Two of this book. They have only been denied and suppressed. And like Marxists before them, liberals will discover that while denial is easy, suppression comes at an escalating cost.

V: Nationalism Discredited

UNTIL NOT VERY LONG ago, support for the independence and self-determination of nations was an indication of a progressive politics and a generous spirit. Not only did Americans celebrate their own independence on the Fourth of July each year with fireworks and music, parades, barbecues, and the ringing of church bells. As late as the middle of the twentieth century, the independence of other national states, from Greece, Italy, and Poland to Israel, India, and Ethiopia, was widely regarded as an expression of historical justice, and as auguring the advent of a better age.

But at the same time, a tidal shift was taking place in attitudes toward expressions of national and religious particularism. The two World Wars had brought a scarcely imaginable catastrophe on Europe, with the monstrous crimes committed by German forces during the Second World War serving as its crowning evil. And as the nations struggled to understand what had taken place, there were those—both Marxists and liberals—who were eager to explain that the cause of the catastrophe had been the order of national states itself. This argument made limited headway after the First World War, which was widely seen as having resulted from the imperial aspirations of the powers.[49] But after the Second World War, it finally found its mark. As photographs from the German death camps circulated, so too did the assertion that what had motivated Germany to set out to murder all of the world's Jews had been the Germans' "nationalism." By the 1960s, revulsion against Nazi destruction of the Jews, at times placed in the same category of evil as the racialist regimes in the American South and in South Africa, had succeeded in moving educated elites toward identifying national and religious particularism of any kind with Nazism and racism.

This line of thought was never altogether coherent. Despite the appearance of the word "national" in the name of the German National Socialist party, Hitler was no advocate of nationalism. He was a harsh critic of the Protestant order in general, but he paid particular attention to the institution of the national state, which he saw as an effete contrivance of the English and French, and vastly inferior to the Germans' historic imperial legacy. In place of the order of national states, he set out to establish a Third Reich that expressly drew its inspiration from the "First Reich"—that is, from the German Holy Roman Empire, with its thousand-year reign and universal aspirations (in the motto of Emperor Frederick III, *Austriae est imperare orbi universo,* "Austria is destined to rule all the world"). Hitler was hardly the first to give expression to this heritage, which the north-German emperor Wilhelm II was still drawing upon to inspire his troops when Hitler served in his army during World War I. As the kaiser wrote to his fighting men in 1915, "The triumph of Great Germany, destined one day to dominate all of Europe, is the sole object of the struggle in which we are engaged."[50] In almost the same tones, Hitler was frank in disseminating the view that Germany "must someday become lord of the earth."[51] Nazi Germany was, in fact, an imperial state in every sense, seeking to put an end to the principle of the national independence and the self-determination of peoples once and for all.[52]

Nor is there any way of interpreting Germany's effort to destroy the Jews as resulting from the Westphalian principle of national self-determination. The Nazi extermination of the Jews in Poland, Russia, and the rest of Europe and North Africa was not a national policy but a global one, exerting influence as far away as the Shanghai Jewish ghetto established by the Japanese at the Nazis' behest. It could not have been conceived or attempted outside the context of Hitler's effort to revive and perfect long-standing German aspirations to universal empire.

These things were perfectly clear during the war itself. In their radio broadcasts, the United States and Britain consistently emphasized that, as an alliance of independent nations, their aim was to restore the independence and self-determination of national states throughout Europe. And in the end, it was American, British, and Russian nationalism— even Stalin had abandoned Marxist claptrap about "world revolution" in favor of open appeals to Russian patriotism—that defeated Germany's bid for universal empire.

But none of this seemed significant to Western liberals, who moved swiftly after the war toward the view that national independence could no longer be accepted as the basis for the international order in light of German atrocities. Among the most ardent of the new anti-nationalists was the West German chancellor, Konrad Adenauer, who repeatedly called for the creation of a federal European union, arguing that only the elimination of the national state could prevent a repetition of the horrors of the war. As he wrote in his book *World Indivisible with Liberty and Justice for All*:

> The age of national states has come to an end. . . . We in Europe must break ourselves of the habit of thinking in terms of national states. . . . European agreements . . . are intended to make war among European nations impossible in the future. . . . If the idea of European community should survive for 50 years, there will never again be a European war.[53]

According to this way of thinking, the answer to the overwhelming evil of Nazi-era Germany was to dismantle the system of independent nation states that had given Germany the right to make decisions for itself, and to replace it with an overarching European union that would be capable of restraining Germany. Or in other words: Take away German self-determination, and you would bring prosperity and peace to Europe.

The proposal that one will be able to "restrain" Germany by eliminating the national states of Europe is repeated endlessly in Europe today. But it is closer to being a good joke than competent political analysis.[54] The German-speaking peoples of central Europe have themselves never been constituted as a national state. They have no historical experience of national unity and independence comparable to that of Britain, France, or the Netherlands. Moreover, these Western European nations had not feared the Germans because of their nationalism, but because of their universalism and imperialism—their aim of bringing peace to Europe by unifying it under a German emperor. It was this deeply entrenched German-universalist and imperialist tradition that had made it so easy for the preeminent German philosopher of Enlightenment, Immanuel Kant, to assert in his *Perpetual Peace* that the only rational form of government would be one in which the national states of Europe were dismantled in favor of a single government that would eventually be extended to the entire world. In repeating this theory, Kant was merely offering yet another version of the German-led Holy Roman Empire.[55]

Adenauer's repeated proposals to restrain Germany by eliminating the Westphalian system of national states did not, for this reason, envision Germans giving up on much that had been historically significant to them. The chancellor was in fact only reiterating a venerable German tradition as to what political arrangements in Europe should look like. Nations that had won their independence from the German emperors at such cost three or four centuries earlier, on the other hand, were being asked to make quite a considerable sacrifice for the sake of the promised peace and prosperity.

Both the British and the Americans supported the idea of unification on the European continent, thinking that their own national independence would not be affected. But they miscalculated. The Kantian argument for the moral superiority of international government cannot coexist in a single political order with the principle of national independence. Once that argument was unleashed again in postwar Europe, it quickly demolished the commitment to the Protestant construction previously held by much of the educated elite in Britain and even America. And this collapse only made sense. After all, why should anyone want to stand up for the idea of national independence, if national independence is what had brought about world war and the Holocaust?

Moreover, the willingness of the United States to post its armies in Europe for the better part of a century has meant that peace and security have come to the European nations without their having to invest in capabilities, whether military or conceptual, commensurate with the actual security needs of countries bordering on Russia and the Muslim world. This peculiar fact—that Americans continue to provide the financial and military resources needed to keep peace in Europe at relatively little cost to Germany or France—has been an underlying reason that Europeans are so smitten with the love of liberal empire. After all, why should anyone stand up for principles of national independence and self-determination if it is America that gives these countries their safety without their having to work to attain it, much as the oil gushing from the ground brings the Saudis wealth without their having to work for it?

Europeans have been reduced to the condition of a mere dependency, existing by virtue of American largesse. This keeps them in a condition of perpetual childhood, happily repeating Adenauer's claim that by dismantling the independent national state, they have found the key to peace on earth. But they have done nothing of the kind. Had there been no European Union, no political unification of France or the Netherlands with Germany, America's military presence and protection would in any case have guaranteed the peace in Europe. This is what empires do. They offer peace in exchange for the renunciation of a nation's independence—including its ability to think as an independent nation and to devise and implement mature policies fitted to the life of an independent nation.

The result is the political landscape we see around us. From Europe to America, the Protestant construction that gave the West its extraordinary strength and vitality has been discarded by urbane and educated people. Those calling to restore the institution of the national state are no longer recognized as proposing that we make firm the foundations of the political order upon which our freedoms have been built. Instead, any such advocacy is taken as a proposal to return to barbarism, to the bad old world that was supposed to have died in 1945.

VI: Liberalism as Imperialism

MY LIBERAL FRIENDS AND colleagues do not seem to understand that the advancing liberal construction is a form of imperialism. But to anyone not already immersed in the new order, the resemblance is easy to see. Much like the pharaohs and the Babylonian kings, the Roman emperors and the Roman Catholic Church until well into the modern period, as well as the Marxists of the last century, liberals, too, have their grand theory about how they are going to bring peace and economic prosperity to the world by pulling down all the borders and uniting mankind under their own universal rule. Infatuated with the clarity and intellectual rigor of this vision, they disdain the laborious process of consulting with the multitude of nations they believe should embrace their view of what is right. And like other imperialists, they are quick to express disgust, contempt, and anger when their vision of peace and prosperity meets with opposition from those who they are sure would benefit immensely by simply submitting.[56]

Liberal imperialism is not monolithic, of course. When President George H. W. Bush declared the arrival of a "new world order" after the demise of the Communist bloc, he had in mind a world in which America supplies the military might necessary to impose a "rule of law" emanating from the Security Council of the United Nations.[57] Subsequent American presidents rejected this scheme, preferring a world order based on unilateral American action in consultation with European allies and others. Europeans, on the other hand, have preferred to speak of "transnationalism," a view that sees the power of independent nations, America included, as being subordinated to the decisions of international judicial and administrative bodies based in Europe.[58] These disagreements over how the international liberal empire is to be governed are often described as if they are historically novel, but this is hardly so. For the most part, they are simply the reincarnation of threadworn medieval debates between the emperor and the pope over how the international Catholic empire should be governed—with the role of the emperor being reprised by those (mostly Americans) who insist that authority must be concentrated in Washington, the political and military center; and the role of the papacy being played by those (mostly European, but also many American academics) who see ultimate authority as residing with the highest interpreters of the universal law, namely, the judicial institutions of the United Nations and the European Union.

These arguments within the camp of liberal imperialism raise pressing questions for the coming liberal construction of the West. But for those of us who remain unconvinced of the desirability of maintaining such a liberal empire, the most salient fact is what the parties to these disagreements have in common. For all their bickering, proponents of the liberal construction are united in endorsing a single imperialist vision: They wish to see a world in which liberal principles are codified as universal law and imposed on the nations, if necessary by force. This, they agree, is what will bring us universal peace and prosperity. Ludwig von Mises speaks for all the different factions when he writes:

> The greatest ideological question that mankind has ever faced . . . is . . . whether we shall succeed in creating throughout the world a frame of mind . . . [of] nothing less than the unqualified, unconditional acceptance of liberalism. Liberal thinking must permeate all nations, liberal principles must pervade all political institutions, if the prerequisites of peace are to be created and the causes of war eliminated.[59]

Although Mises states the demand for an "unqualified, unconditional acceptance of liberalism" by every nation and every political institution in the world in stark terms, the aspiration he expresses represents what is by now an entirely conventional liberal standpoint. Dogmatic and utopian, it assumes that the final truths concerning mankind's fate have long since been discovered, and that all that remains is to find a way to impose them.

I do not mean to say, of course, that every liberal is dogmatic and utopian in this way. Especially in Britain and America, the views of many liberals are still tempered by other factors: by biblicism, by a nationalist recognition of the variety of human societies, by a humbling belief in God, by a historical empiricism and a moderate skepticism that in English-speaking countries used to be called "common sense." All these things are still palpable with certain Anglo-American liberals. But as the opponents of liberalism have been vanquished one by one, and universal liberal empire has seemed to come within reach, these mitigating factors have fallen by the wayside, leaving a dogmatic imperialism as the dominant voice within the liberal camp—a voice that has rapidly taken on the worst features of the medieval Catholic empire upon which it is unwittingly modeled, including a doctrine of infallibility, as well as a taste for the inquisition and the index.[60]

I would like to focus for a moment on this last point. One of the most striking features of public life in contemporary America and Europe is the way that the Western nations are now afflicted by public shaming campaigns and heresy hunts whose purpose is to stigmatize and render illegitimate one or another person or group of people, opinion or policy, that is perceived as having the ability to mount any kind of meaningful resistance to liberal doctrine. Much of what has been written about these campaigns has concentrated on the deterioration of free discourse in the universities, where official and unofficial censorship of the professorate's opinions—including their views about Islam, homosexuality, immigration, and a host of other subjects—has become commonplace. But the universities are hardly the principal locus of rage against views now deemed inappropriate. Much of the public sphere is now regularly visited by the same kinds of campaigns of vilification that were until recently associated with the universities. Indeed, as the scope of legitimate disagreement is progressively reduced, and the penalties of dissent grow more and more onerous, the Western democracies are rapidly becoming one big university campus.[61]

These increasingly insistent demands for conformity to a single universal standard in speech and religion are the predictable outcome of the transition away from the Protestant construction of the West, with its fundamental principle of national independence and self-determination. This principle, had, after all, mandated a diversity of constitutional and religious standpoints within the order of national states, which entailed a toleration of profoundly divergent views: Catholics had to tolerate the existence of Protestant regimes, monarchists had to tolerate republican regimes, and rulers concerned with tightly regulating their subjects' affairs had to tolerate regimes affording more extensive liberties—and in each case, the reverse was true as well. This formal grant of legitimacy to political and religious diversity among the nations then became the basis for the toleration of dissenting communities within the state as well. To be sure, not every individual felt comfortable living in every country. But there did exist the possibility of negotiating special provisions to accommodate dissenting communities, so long as they were willing to support the state and refrain from seeking a radical revision in national customs.

And if one did want to agitate for such revisions, there was the option of relocating to a neighboring state where one's views would be accepted or even embraced.[62]

Under a universal political order, by contrast, in which a single standard of right is held to be in force everywhere, tolerance for diverse political and religious standpoints must necessarily decline. Western elites, whose views are now being aggressively homogenized in conformity with the new liberal construction, are finding it increasingly difficult to recognize a need for the kind of toleration of divergent standpoints that the principle of national self-determination had once rendered axiomatic. Tolerance, like nationalism, is becoming a relic of a bygone age.

The calumnies and denunciation heaped upon the English public and its elected leadership in the wake of Britain's determination to seek independence from the European Union is an unmistakable warning to the West as a whole. From the point of view of the liberal construction, the unification of Europe is not one legitimate political option among others. It is the only legitimate opinion to which a decent person can subscribe. The moral illegitimacy of Britain's vote for independence was thus the unrelenting theme of political and media figures decrying the vote: It was alleged that only the aged supported exiting the European Union, thereby disenfranchising the young; or that only the uneducated had supported it, thereby diluting the say of those who really do know better; or that voters had meant only to cast a protest vote and not actually to leave Europe; and so forth. These angry pronouncements were then followed by the demand that the British public's preference be repealed— by a second referendum, or by act of Parliament, or by closed-door bargaining with the Europeans. Anything, so long as the one legitimate opinion should prevail.

The alarm and trepidation with which European and American elites responded to the prospect of an independent Britain revealed something that had long been obscured from view. That simple truth is that the emerging liberal construction is incapable of respecting, much less celebrating, the deviation of nations seeking to assert a right to their own unique laws, traditions, and policies. Any such dissent is held to be vulgar and ignorant, if not evidence of a fascistic mind-set.

Nor is Britain the only nation to have felt the sting of this whip. America is hardly immune: Its refusal to permit the International Criminal Court to try its soldiers, its unwillingness to sign international treaties designed to protect the environment, its war in Iraq—all were met with similar outrage both at home and abroad. Such outbursts have long targeted Israel, whether for bombing Iraq's nuclear facilities or for constructing housing complexes in eastern Jerusalem. Eastern European countries, too, have been excoriated for their unwillingness to accept immigrants from the Middle East. Moreover, similar campaigns of delegitimization, in both Europe and America, have been directed against the practice of Christianity and Judaism, religions on which the old biblical political order is based, and whose free exercise has usually been protected or at least tolerated by Western national governments. We have already seen attempts, especially in Europe, to ban such Jewish practices as circumcision and kosher slaughter in the name of liberal doctrines of universal rights, or to force liberal teachings on sexuality and the family upon Christians and Jews in the workplace and in schools. It requires no special insight to see that this is only the beginning, and that the teaching and practice of traditional forms of Judaism and Christianity will become ever more untenable as the liberal construction advances.

There is a sense today throughout the Western world that one's beliefs on controversial matters should no longer be discussed openly. We are now aware that we must think a second and third time before acting or speaking as though the Protestant political order were still in place. Genuine diversity in the constitutional or religious character of Western nations persists only at mounting cost to those who insist on their freedom.

VII: Nationalist Alternatives to Liberalism

MARGARET THATCHER'S OUSTER AS prime minister of Britain in 1990 marked the beginning of nearly three decades of liberal political consensus, a period during which prominent political and intellectual figures fell into the habit of speaking as though the triumph of a new liberal order was inevitable. In Europe, the German-led effort to subordinate the independent nations of the continent to the European Union proceeded apace. In the United States, the effort to establish an American "world order," with Europe effectively an American protectorate, was the order of the day. On both sides of the Atlantic, the unpleasant history of past European and American imperialism prevented most from speaking openly of empire. What was repeated endlessly by elected officials, diplomats, businessmen, and media personalities—as well as in a profusion of utopian political tracts, from Francis Fukuyama's *The End of History and the Last Man* (1992), to Thomas Friedman's *The Lexus and the Olive Tree* (1999), to Shimon Peres's *The New Middle East* (1995)— was that the "international community" was being brought under "global governance." The world would have a single regime of law and a single economic system, governed by Americans and Europeans in accordance with liberal political doctrines. And when a nation "broke the rules" of this new world order, as was the case in Serbia, Iraq, and Libya, the American military, with allied European contingents, was going to go in and re-establish these rules.[63]

A worldwide regime of peace and prosperity. A liberal empire. This was the consensus policy of all major political parties in both America and Europe for a generation.

But with the British vote for independence and a nationalist revival in the United States, the triumph of this liberal order has come to seem less inevitable. The Protestant construction, left to die by the political and intellectual elites of both the Republican and Democratic parties in America, and of both the Labour and Conservative parties in the UK, has proved it still has some life in it.

What do opponents of the liberal construction wish to see happen? The Protestant construction of the West was founded upon two fundamental principles. And so one can, in theory, be opposed to the new liberal order in very different ways—either by attempting to restore one of these principles or the other; or by striving to retain them both. Thus there are today three different anti-liberal camps, each of which is readily discerned in the politics of Western nations:

First, there exists what may be called a *neo-Catholic* opposition to the liberal construction. This is not a view espoused by all Catholics, nor is it only Catholics who are attracted to it. Rather, it is a view held by individuals who are inclined to embrace an updated version of medieval Catholic political theory. Such a theory is focused on maintaining one or another version of the biblical moral minimum (often identified with a theory of universal reason, rather than with Scripture) as a touchstone for the legitimacy of the state. At the same time, a neo-Catholic political theory is sympathetic to the advantages of an international regime—a kind of new Christendom, one might say—for the enforcement of human rights and individual liberties throughout the world. In practice, neo-Catholics have been politically outspoken in defending traditional religious views of marriage and the family, opposing the legalization of assisted suicide and abortion, and objecting to the removal of Jewish and Christian symbols (such as public displays of the Mosaic Ten Precepts) from government properties. But they have been ambivalent about the order of national states, tending to support the growth of a regime of coercive international law that will override the powers of national governments.

Second, there is a *neo-nationalist* (or *statist*) view, which follows the example of Rousseau and French revolutionary nationalism in jettisoning traditional conceptions of the nation, its constitution, and its religion, seeking instead to establish the individual's loyalty and service to the state as man's highest end. Such nationalism is known for its tendency toward absolutism and atheism, as well as for the chronic instability it has historically produced in France. Neo-nationalist movements may be regarded as conservative in their objections to the dismantling of independent national states by the European Union, to the transfer of the powers of elected governments to the United Nations and other international bodies, to unrestricted immigration, and to coercive international law. However, they are often distant from national religious tradition, unaware of the biblical sources of their own nationalism, and uninterested in the decisive role that biblical moral standards once played in restraining the excesses of individuals and of the state alike.

Neither of these positions strikes me as offering a plausible alternative to liberalism. Neo-Catholics will continue to fight rearguard culture wars against liberal elites on issues such as abortion or the definition of marriage. But at the same time, they will be found offering active or passive support to the liberal imperialism that is uprooting the ability of nations to maintain their independence on constitutional and religious matters of precisely this kind. Neo-nationalism, on the other hand, may prove effective in pulling certain nations out of the liberal order. But because of its fascination with the state and its distance from the religious and moral traditions of the nation, it can also lead to the establishment of authoritarian governments, thereby reinforcing the claim (promoted from their respective viewpoints by liberals and authoritarians alike) that the only alternative to liberalism is authoritarianism.

The third alternative to the liberal order is what may be termed a *conservative* (or *traditionalist*) standpoint, which seeks to establish and defend an international order of national states based on the two principles of the Protestant construction: national independence and the biblical moral minimum for legitimate government. I am here using the term "conservative" in a broad sense, to refer to any political movement whose aim is to preserve the foundations of the Protestant construction, recognizing it as the freest, and in many respects the most successful, international order that has ever existed. This may include different kinds of movements in different nations, based on the variety of constitutional and religious traditions (including those that do not possess a biblical heritage and are therefore rooted in a different traditional moral system). Of these, the most important has been the *Anglo-American conservative tradition,* descended from the thought of individuals such as

John Fortescue, John Selden, and Edmund Burke. This is a nationalist political tradition that embraces the principles of limited executive power, individual liberties, public religion based on the Bible, and a historical empiricism that has so often served to moderate political life in Britain and America in comparison with that of other countries. It is this Anglo-American conservative strand within the larger nationalist political inheritance that has proved most productive of sound government, and has worked so well to encourage the flourishing of the United States, Britain, and other English-speaking nations.[64] It is in this tradition, updated in keeping with the needs of our times, that I believe statesmen and political thinkers can find the most useful and salutary alternative to liberal empire.

———

ON THE SURFACE, BRITAIN and America sometimes give the impression of having become utterly unmoored from their biblical heritage. But these are still nations that were formed by the biblical message of freedom of the nation from empire, limitation of the power of kings, and fundamental precepts establishing the basis for a just and decent society.[65] Events have shown just how powerful the Protestant construction remains in both countries, even after decades of ceding ground to the new liberal order that had seemed on the verge of replacing it. These events offer an opportunity to rethink, from a more critical point of vantage than has been possible until now, the commitment to a universal liberalism that has been embraced by elites in Europe and America. They have also given us a chance to ask ourselves whether the biblical freedom bequeathed to us by our forefathers might not still be the better choice.

In the first part of this book I have offered a historical framework for understanding the confrontation unfolding between the forces of nationalism and empire that vie for the allegiance of Western nations in our time. I now turn to a general argument in favor of the independent national state as the best political ordering principle available to mankind.

Part Two

THE CASE
FOR THE
NATIONAL STATE

VIII: Two Types of Political Philosophy

GREEK POLITICAL PHILOSOPHY IS especially attentive to the question of the best regime or the best form of government, and modern liberal political thought maintains this concern with how government should be structured. This kind of inquiry assumes that human beings will organize themselves as a *state*—that is, a community sufficiently cohesive that it can be, and in fact is, ruled by a single standing government, independent of other governments. It then proceeds to ask what form the government of the state should have: Should the state be a monarchy, an aristocratic republic, or a democracy? Should the authority of the state be concentrated in one branch of government or dispersed among several? Should the state be constrained by a written constitution, and who should determine when it has been violated? Should the state guarantee basic rights and liberties to the individual, and if so, what are they?

These and similar questions assume the existence of a cohesive and independent state. But political philosophy can also ask other, more fundamental questions—questions that recognize that human beings have not always lived in internally unified and independent states, and that do not take the existence of the state as a given. I have in mind questions such as the following: What allows a community to be sufficiently cohesive to be ordered as a state? Is the state formed when independent individuals consent to living under government, or through the unification of previously existing cohesive communities? Is the state really the best institution for ordering human life, or are there other forms of political order, such as a clan or feudal order, that are better? And if the state is the best form of political order, should authority be in the hands of one universal state or dispersed among many competing states?

When these questions are taken into account, we see that political philosophy is naturally divided into two subjects, one more fundamental than the other. One subject is the *philosophy of government*, which seeks to determine the best form of government, given the existence of a state with a high degree of internal unity and independence. Prior to this is the *philosophy of political order*, which seeks to understand the causes of political order, and on the basis of this understanding, to determine what are the different forms of political order available to us and which of them is best.

Individuals who are confident of the cohesion and independence of the state in which they live are naturally attracted to the philosophy of government. After all, if the state is assumed to be permanent, what student of politics would not want to get to work determining the kind of government it should have?

But philosophy of government can be misleading and even pernicious if not preceded by a careful study of the causes of political order. An iron law governing the operation of human reason is this: Whatever is assumed without argument comes to be regarded as self-evident, whether it is true or false. This is no less the case in the philosophy of government. Since this discipline begins by assuming the existence of a cohesive and independent state, it trains the minds of those who study it to suppose that they see cohesive and independent states all around them, not only in theory, but in reality. When they look abroad to other regions of the world, they see cohesive and independent states where there are none, or believe that such states can easily be brought into being where no such possibility exists. And when they consider the state in which they live, they cannot recall that all states are perpetually on the verge of losing their cohesion and independence, and so they take the unity and independence of their own state entirely for granted. As a consequence, they tend to disdain the kinds of efforts that are needed to maintain the cohesion and independence of the state, happily advocating for policies that work directly to destroy its cohesion and dilute its independence, all the while believing that the state can sustain all this and yet remain sound as it was before.

Philosophy of government is useful in its proper, limited sphere. But to be competent, it must be built upon an understanding of the underlying causes of the formation, cohesion, and independence of the state, as well as of its destruction. This is the kind of political inquiry that we find in the first great works of the Western political tradition—namely, those that have been collected in the Hebrew Bible. It is here that we encounter a constant awareness of the possibility of human beings living outside the state, in an order of households and clans and tribes, and a mindfulness of the threat that is posed to such an order by the state. It is in the Bible, too, that we are exposed to the ambiguities that attend the founding of the state, and are taught to recognize the fragility of all such states, which are at every moment either rising or falling, moving toward either consolidation or dissolution. It is here that we are taught to think of how just government contributes to the consolidation of political order, whereas foolish policies lead to the dissolution of political order, paving the way to anarchy and conquest by others. It is here that we are first exposed to the question of whether human freedom is aided or hindered by the state, and whether the extension of the imperial state does not necessarily lead to mankind's enslavement.

What follows is a study in foundational political philosophy. Rather than assuming that reasonable men will necessarily form a cohesive and independent state, I will consider the underlying causes of political order and examine the ways in which these causes shape the alternatives that are open to us. On the basis of this examination, I will suggest that the best form of political order is an order of independent national states. In particular, I will argue that such an order is superior to the other principal alternatives that are known to us: the order of tribes and clans, which preceded the state; and imperial order.

IX: The Foundations of Political Order

SOME THINGS CAN BE attained by the individual acting alone. But most aims or ends require that we act in concert with others. However, our neighbors have aims and motives of their own, and they are often uninterested in the goal we have proposed, if not hostile to it. How, then, can we influence others so that they act to accomplish the goals that we see as necessary or desirable? This is the fundamental problem of the individual living in a community of others. The need to find answers to this question gives rise to *politics*, which is the discipline or craft of influencing others so that they act to accomplish the goals one sees as necessary or desirable.

One response to this fundamental problem is the establishment of standing bodies or collectives of individuals—the family, clan, tribe, or nation, a state or an army, a religious order or a business enterprise. These and other *institutions* are human collectives that maintain their existence through time, holding fast to certain fixed purposes and forms, such as a particular name by which they are known and accepted procedures by which they make decisions and act as a body. Each institution teaches, persuades, or coerces its members to act according to these fixed purposes and forms, abiding by accepted general rules and procedures, so that they can reliably act as a body, without each time having to be persuaded or coerced anew.

But what brings individuals, despite having their own unique aims and motives, to join together in an institution, reliably acting as a body together with its other members, in accordance with the fixed purposes and forms of the institution?

Three possibilities are well known: First, individuals will join if threatened with reprisal. Second, they will join if they are offered payment or other advantage. Finally, they will join if they see the interests and aims of the institution as their own. Of these, the second alternative produces the weakest institutions, for those who join up in some arduous struggle or effort in exchange only for a sum of money are constantly calculating whether the risks are worth the pay, and hoping that they will be able to defect to a different cause offering better pay and entailing fewer risks. Institutions are only somewhat more stable when individuals are recruited by intimidating them and their loved ones, since they cannot be relied upon once the threat is felt to recede, and are forever on the verge of mutiny so long as it does not.

For these and other reasons, strong institutions are established where the individuals involved identify the interests and the aims of the institution as their own. Think, for instance, of a soldier who takes up a rifle in the hope of establishing the independence of his people after a long history of persecution. Such individuals do not need to be coerced to fight, or to be well compensated for their services. The fact that they are fighting for the benefit of their people is enough for them to be willing to throw their lives into the balance for the sake of a collective such as a tribe or a nation, stirring up an ardor in their breasts that moves them to acts of bravery and self-sacrifice that no intimidation or promise of pay could elicit.

Many political theories assume that political events are motivated by the individual's concern for his own life and property. Yet anyone who has witnessed the behavior of individuals in wartime, or under conditions of nonviolent conflict as in an electoral campaign, understands that this assumption is wildly inaccurate. It is true that one is sometimes motivated by a concern for his own life or property. But human individuals are also capable of regarding the aims and interests of a collective or institution of which they are members as their own, and of acting upon these aims and interests even where such action will be detrimental to their lives and property. Indeed, political events are frequently determined by the actions of individuals whose motives are of just this kind.[1]

A political theory designed to understand human beings as they are in reality, and not to tell us stories about the adventures of some fantastic creature invented by philosophers, cannot avoid this capacity of the human individual to recognize the aims of the collective as his own. Astonishing and yet as common as the air we breathe, this ability is with us every day and every hour. It is basic to our empirical nature, and there can be no convincing account of how strong human institutions are built unless this capacity is at its center. Let us, therefore, consider this matter more closely.

We know that the human individual is by nature fiercely concerned to ensure the integrity of his or her own self. By the *self*, I mean, in the first instance, the individual's physical body, which is protected by a reflexive urge to fight or seek immediate escape when threatened or maligned. However, this urge to ensure the integrity of the self is by no means limited to the protection of the body. The very same ferocity that the individual displays in protecting his physical body is also evident in the actions he takes to defend his reputation when accused or insulted. And it appears, as well, in the urge to protect his land or other physical possessions that he regards as his own. Indeed, the very love that he evidently feels for his wife and children, and for his parents, and for brothers and sisters, and that moves him to protect them when they are in danger, is nothing other than another name for this same urge to protect the integrity of his self—for these loved ones have been embraced, insofar has his own consciousness is concerned, within the rubric of his own self, and are experienced as if they were a part of him.

This capacity to protect and defend others as if they were a part of one's own self is not limited to kinsmen. We see this same ferocity in the urge to defend a friend or a townsman, the member of one's platoon or street gang, or, more generally, any other human being who is, for whatever reason, regarded by the individual as a part of his self. And many other examples could be mentioned. What we see across the range of human activities and institutions, then, is that the self of the individual is by nature flexible in its extent, and is constantly being enlarged so that persons and things we might have supposed would be outside of him and alien to him are in fact regarded as if they were a part of himself.[2]

When an individual includes a certain other within the purview of his or her self, we call this attachment *loyalty*. When two individuals have each taken the other under the protection of their extended selves, the bond that is established is one of *mutual loyalty,* which allows these two individuals to regard themselves as a single entity. The existence of such bonds of mutual loyalty does not mean that they entirely cease to be independent persons. These bonds do not eliminate the competition, insult, jealousy, and quarrels that are always present between individuals who are loyal to one another. A husband and wife may quarrel frequently, and brothers or sisters may bicker and fight, by these means seeking to adjust the hierarchy of relations between them. While these conflicts are taking place, they are experienced as a struggle between independent persons. But as soon as either of them faces adversity, the other suffers this hardship as if it were his own. And in the face of this hardship, the disputes that had troubled them before are temporarily suspended or entirely forgotten. Moreover, once the hardship before them has been overcome, they experience a sense of relief and pleasure, of walking together in joy, each recognizing the happiness of the other as his own. These experiences, in which another individual is recognized as a part of one's self in adversity and in triumph, establish a strong distinction between an *inside* and an *outside*: an inside, comprising the two individuals, each of whom regards the other as part of a single identity; and an outside, from which a challenge arises against them, and in the face of which they experience a joint suffering and a joint success.[3]

Human institutions can and often do contribute to their cohesion by providing financial compensation to their members or by coercing them. But enduring and resilient institutions are those that are constructed principally out of bonds of mutual loyalty. The *family* is the strongest and most resilient of all small institutions known to human politics, precisely due to the existence of such ties of mutual loyalty between each member of the family and all of the others. These ties are partly biological and partly adoptive. A mother forever feels that the children she has carried are a part of herself. But adoptive family relations, such as those between a husband and wife, or between either of them and their in-laws, or between parents and an adopted child, are frequently no less powerful than those between parents and the children who are born to them. Particular bonds of family loyalty can thus be either birth ties or adoptive ties, but in either case their solidity and resilience are unmatched as a result of the daily shared experience of relying on family members for assistance and support, which establishes family members as a part of one another's extended self.

The family is the most familiar of small institutions, but there are many others. A small-scale military unit called a *squad* (or *section*) is, for instance, the basic formation out of which all armies are constructed. Modeled after the family, it consists of roughly ten men commanded by a junior officer or a sergeant. Here, too, the capacity of the unit to function under extreme duress depends on ties of mutual loyalty—ties that become especially strong in a unit that is small enough to ensure that each individual knows the others personally, and has extensive experience of relying on them for assistance and support during the hardships of training and combat.[4]

Small institutions like the family or the squad, consisting of individuals bound together by mutual loyalties developed over long years of shared hardship and triumph, are the bedrock of all political order. It is out of such small units that larger-scale political institutions of every kind are built. It is possible, for example, to bring together heads of families in an association of mutual loyalty to one another, in this way tying together the members of the various families in a *clan*. And indeed, all over the world, and in all ages, clans have been established to provide for collective defense, to establish procedures for justice between them, and to pursue common service to their gods. A child growing up in one of these families will not necessarily have a way of directly developing a bond of mutual loyalty with most other individual members of the clan, who may number in the hundreds or thousands and may be scattered over a considerable territory. But his parents, who have direct bonds of mutual loyalty to the other heads of families, experience the suffering and triumphs of the clan as if these were happening to themselves, and they give expression to these things. And so the child, who experiences the suffering and triumphs of his parents as if they were happening to him, is able to feel the suffering and the triumphs of the clan as his own as well. Thus even a very young child will feel the harm and shame when another member of his clan is harmed or shamed by members of a rival clan. In this way, the child's self is extended to embrace the entire clan and all its members, even those whom he has never met. And because of this extension, he will be willing to set aside even bitter disputes with other members of his clan when a threat from the outside is experienced as a challenge to all.[5]

When we speak of the *cohesion* of human collectives, it is this that we have in mind: the bonds of mutual loyalty that hold firmly in place an alliance of many individuals, each of whom shares in the suffering and triumphs of the others, including those they have never met.[6]

Cohesion of this kind is not limited to the scale of family and clan. Heads of clans can unite to form a *tribe* that may have tens of thousands of members. And heads of tribes can come together to form a *nation* whose members number in the millions.[7] Such a process of consolidation is familiar to us, for example, from the biblical History of Israel, which emphasizes the question of whether the Israelite tribes will come together to form a unified nation. And it is familiar from the history of the English, the Dutch, the Americans, and many other nations.[8] Like ties of loyalty to the clan, the bond of loyalty to one's tribe or nation grows out of loyalty to one's parents: The child experiences the suffering and triumphs of his tribe or nation as his own because he experiences the suffering and triumphs of his parents as his own, and the parents feel and give expression to the suffering and triumphs of the tribe or nation as these unfold. And again, this attachment means that the individual will set aside disputes with other members of his tribe or nation, coming together with them "as one mind"[9] in moments of danger or when great public projects are under way.[10]

Are there limits to the process of consolidation, by means of which clans unite as tribes, and tribes as nations, extending the loyalties of individuals outward? We know that nations can develop attachments to other nations, and that these can, with time, resemble the attachments of tribes to one another in the formation of the nation. There is such a thing, in other words, as a "family of nations," as the English-speaking nations often regard themselves, or as the Hindu peoples of India have at times. But what brings these families of nations together is, again, a mutual loyalty that is revived and strengthened by joint adversity in the present: The solidarity of English-speaking peoples becomes most prominent in their common struggle against the axis of Fascist powers, or against the Communist nations; and the mutual loyalty of the Hindus comes to the fore during their common struggle to free themselves from English and Muslim domination.[11] What we have never seen, however, is a genuine tendency toward a mutual loyalty among all human beings—which is something that could only form under conditions in which all mankind stood together before a joint adversity.[12]

The mutual loyalty of individuals to one another is the most powerful force operative in the political realm. Feelings of mutual loyalty pull individuals tightly together, forming them into families, clans, tribes, and nations, in much the way that the force of gravitation pulls molecules together, forming them into planets, star systems, galaxies, and systems of galaxies. Modern writers, who have been too much influenced by Darwinian science, tend to look for ways of explaining this as a process driven by biological kinship. But this has never been so. An isolated human individual, having survived a war or disease that has cut him off from his family and his clan, will invariably attach himself to a new family or a new clan, adding his strength to theirs and receiving their protection in return. In so doing, he establishes new bonds of mutual loyalty to replace those that had been lost, and this without any necessary tie of biological kinship. This constant regeneration of shattered bonds of mutual loyalty means that families can and do adopt individual members that were not born among them, and that clans adopt entire families that were not born among them. In the same way, nations adopt not only foreign individuals and families, but entire tribes that were once foreigners but are not considered foreigners any longer.[13]

Thus while all nations use the metaphor of brotherhood to invoke a family-like relationship of mutual loyalty among their members, actual biological kinship is never more than a raw material upon which a nation is built, if it is even that.[14] In the end, the decisive factor is the ties of mutual loyalty that have been established among members of a nation in the face of long years of joint hardship and success.

This constant regeneration of bonds of mutual loyalty, which we find in nearly every human being, means that there can be no society whose member individuals are without loyalty to anyone other than themselves. This is true even in modern society, in which the traditional order of tribes and clans has been weakened by the national state, and liberal philosophy has taught the individual to think constantly in terms of his own life and property.[15] Even here, collectives built from bonds of mutual loyalty are visible everywhere, and not only within the family: Local political chapters, churches and synagogues, schools, and other community organizations are still strongly reminiscent of the old clans. On a national scale, powerful religious, ethnic, sectoral, and professional associations play a role in the life of the nation that is still very much that of the tribe with its fierce mutual loyalties, each one striving with other tribes in shifting coalitions in the effort to turn the course of the nation in their favor. These do not, to be sure, possess the strength and resilience of the clans and tribes that preceded the state. The variety of such associations permits the individual much greater freedom in choosing or declining allegiance to them, and since they are not politically independent entities at war with one another, the mutual obligations among their members can be much less demanding. Nevertheless, their presence points to an undying tendency of individuals, even under the modern state, to ally themselves to collectives, not only at the level of the family, but also at the clan, tribal, or national level.[16] This is a tendency that becomes dramatically more pronounced when members of our "clan" or "tribe" are threatened, and it reasserts itself with all its old force when our tribe comes to see the national state as no longer able to protect it as before.*

The bonds of mutual loyalty that make families, clans, tribes, and nations stable and enduring institutions also ensure that human beings constantly experience what happens to the collectives to which they are loyal as things that are happening to themselves. As a consequence, far from being motivated only to secure their own life and property, human individuals are ceaselessly concerned to advance the health and prosperity of the family, clan, tribe, or nation to which they are loyal, frequently in a manner that puts their own life and property at risk.

What do I mean by the *health and prosperity* of the family, clan, tribe, or nation? Like nearly all the terms we use to

---

* Although this usage is somewhat unfamiliar with reference to society in the modern state, I will continue to use the term *clan* to refer to local institutions and organizations, and *tribe* to refer to larger-scale collectives that are strong enough to vie for national influence. I have chosen to use these terms rather than a more familiar one such as "community" because it lacks the connotation of a hierarchical ordering of collectives that is essential to empirical political theory. For the sake of simplicity, I have adopted a four-tier hierarchy: *family, clan, tribe,* and *nation.* But the choice of a four-tier system is somewhat arbitrary. In actual political societies, one can often find many more layers of hierarchy before reaching the top of the political structure.

describe human collectives, these are metaphors drawn from the life of the individual. Yet the characteristics of human collectives to which these terms draw our attention are no less real for being described using metaphors.

Consider first the family. The health and prosperity of the family, we can say, consists in three things: First, it requires physical and material flourishing. This means that children are born and grow strong, that the family gains in terms of the property at its disposal, and that its physical capabilities and productivity, such as the ability to produce or obtain food, advance from year to year. Second, the health of the family is recognized when it possesses a strong internal integrity—when its members are loyal to one another, celebrate one another's achievements, and defend one another in adversity, even at risk to themselves; when its members readily honor the differences in age or status among them, so that the family can take effective, unified action without coercion; and when the competition and tensions that inevitably arise among them are conducted in relative peace, so that they avoid doing long-term damage to the family as a whole. Third, the health of the family is recognized in the extent and quality of the cultural inheritance that is transmitted by the parents and grandparents to the children. This factor is often overlooked, but it is no less important to the health and prosperity of the family than either of the others. Both the physical capabilities and the internal integrity of the human family depend to a very great degree on the cultural inheritance that the older generations bequeath to the younger ones, and on the degree to which this inheritance is successfully handed down.[17]

These are the measures of the health and prosperity of the family, and every member of a given family has an intuitive understanding of what these things are, whether more or less developed and refined, just as he has an intuitive understanding of what contributes to his personal life and property. Moreover, the individual at all times experiences the strengthening or weakening of his family as something that is happening to himself. And because this is the case, he is constantly moved to take action to defend and build up the family in its material prosperity, in its internal integrity, and in its capacity to transmit an appropriate cultural inheritance to the children. Indeed, it is out of such motives that parents act for many, if not most, of their waking hours: They take employment that is not to their liking so as to be able to feed their family. They humble themselves to mend relations with an unhappy husband or wife so that there will be peace in the home. They devote long hours to the tutelage of the recalcitrant young, whose ability to recognize the value of what they are taught is often quite limited. And they do so not out of an altruistic impulse to help a stranger, but because strengthening the family is experienced as strengthening themselves.

The health and prosperity of every human collective is measured in much the same way as that of the family. We can measure the health of the tribe or nation, for example, by taking stock of its material prosperity, its internal integrity, and the strength and quality of the cultural inheritance that it passes on from one generation to the next. Similarly, the individual who is loyal to his tribe or nation cannot avoid sensing that it is growing stronger or weaker, and feeling that this strengthening or weakening is something that is happening to him, just as he feels this with respect to his family. And for this reason, when the tribe or nation is felt to be weakened, we will see individuals rise up to take this matter into their own hands, acting with all their heart and all their soul to strengthen the tribe or nation, just as they act to strengthen their family. They do so not out of altruism, but because strengthening the tribe or nation is experienced as strengthening themselves.

Human beings constantly desire and actively pursue the health and prosperity of the family, clan, tribe, or nation to which they are tied by bonds of mutual loyalty: We have an intense need to seek the material success of the collective. We work to strengthen its internal integrity by ensuring that its members are loyal to one another in adversity, honor their elders and leaders, and conduct the inevitable competitions among them peaceably. And we toil to hand down the cultural inheritance of the collective, its language and religion, its laws and traditions, its historical perspective, and the unique manner in which it understands the world, to a new generation. Remarkably, this last concern—for the transmission of the cultural inheritance of the collective to future generations—is often experienced as a need no less powerful than the desire to feed and clothe our children. Even in a family ravaged by poverty and near starvation, the efforts of the parents to transmit this inheritance to their children does not cease. One need only interfere with the language people speak, with the religion of their community, with the customary rights by which they conduct their affairs, or with the way they raise their children, to quickly inflame them and drive them to the brink of violence. Because these things impinge on the internal integrity and cultural inheritance of the family, clan, tribe, or nation, they are experienced with such bitterness, and give rise to such consuming anger.

No universal ideology—not Christianity or Islam, not liberalism or Marxism—has succeeded in eliminating this intense desire to protect and strengthen the collective, or even in diminishing it much. Nor should we wish to see this desire eliminated or diminished, any more than we want to see the desire of the individual to defend his own life and improve his material circumstances diminished. To be sure, this fierce concern for the material prosperity, internal integrity, and cultural inheritance of the collective makes every family, clan, tribe, and nation into a kind of fortress surrounded by high, invisible walls. But these walls are a necessary condition for all human diversity, innovation, and advancement, enabling each of these little fortresses to shelter its own special inheritance, its own treasured culture, in a garden in which it can flourish unmolested. Inside, what is original and different is given a space of its own where it can be tried and tested over the course of generations. Inside, the things that are said and done only in this family, clan, or tribe, and nowhere else, are given time to grow and mature, becoming solid and strong as they strike roots in the character of the collective's various members—until they are ready to make their way outward from the family to the clan, from the clan to the tribe and the nation, and thence to all the families of the earth. Every innovation that has brought about an improvement in understanding or industry, in law or morals or piety, has been the result of a development of this kind, beginning as the independent inheritance of a small human collective and then radiating outward. At the same time, these fortress walls of tribal language and culture can be seen as preventing novelties from spreading too quickly, giving time for what is misguided and destructive to be tried and found wanting, to run its course and die out, before all humanity is overtaken.

X: How Are States Really Born?

THERE IS A STORY that mothers tell their children about how babies are born. They tell them that when the time is right, a stork flies the newborn baby to the doorstep of its new home.

No parent believes there is any truth to this story. So why speak as if it were true? I suppose it is because the truth is, in the eyes of some parents, ugly and unpleasant. In telling their children this white lie, they hope to make the world seem more beautiful than it is, and in so doing protect their young ones from thoughts that may cause them distress and fear.

Similarly, there is a story that instructors in politics, law, and philosophy tell their students about how states are born. They tell them that while living in a state of perfect freedom and equality, each individual consents, together with countless others, to form a government and to submit to its dictates.[18] No university instructor or civics teacher believes this is true. So why speak as if it were?

Here, a plausible answer becomes more difficult. Like the story of the stork, it can be said that the tradition of introducing students to the theory of government by means of this fantastic story protects the minds of the students from some ugly and unpleasant truths. But there the similarity ends. For the story of the stork is only intended to keep children in their childhood innocence a little while longer, recognizing that at a certain point their parents will tell them the truth. Whereas the story of how the state is born is impressed upon young men and women time and again at every stage of their education—first in high school, then in college, and then again in law school or graduate school. Eventually, they become legislators and jurists and scholars of renown, and yet this fairy tale clings to their thoughts about political life, taking up the space where actual competence in the subject should have been. And we see every day how much damage is done in many important endeavors, both in domestic policy and foreign affairs, because actions are pursued by statesmen who continue to rely on this myth in their decision-making on behalf of the state. This point has been made vigorously by virtually every political theorist who has attempted to approach the subject empirically, including Selden, Hume, Smith, Ferguson, Burke, and Mill.[19] It is impossible to think intelligently about the principles of government without first freeing oneself from the fiction that states are formed by the consent of individuals, a view that only hides from us the way in which states are born, and goes on from there to confound our understanding of how they continue to exist through time, of what holds them together, and of what destroys them.

How does the state come into being? On the basis of what has been said, we can see that there never has been a "state of nature" of the kind imagined by Hobbes or Locke, in which individuals were loyal only to themselves. As long as human beings have lived on this earth, they have been loyal to the broader family, clan, and tribe that provided for their defense, for justice among them, and for rites of thanks before the gods, each according to its own unique customs. This *order of tribes and clans* is, in fact, the original political order of mankind. How are we to think about this form of political order?

In the first place, the order of tribes and clans is not the state. It is true that the clan and the tribe are concerned with defense, justice, and religion—the same matters that are of concern to states. But the original form of human political order is distinguished from the state in that it is, in the strict sense, *anarchical,* meaning that it functions without a permanent central government: There is no standing army or police force, no bureaucracy capable of raising taxes sufficient to maintain such a force, and therefore no one with the ability to issue decrees that can then be imposed by means of armed force. Each clan or tribe has its head or chief. But without an armed force dedicated to carrying out his will, such a clan or tribal head rarely possesses the power to coerce his fellows where they do not wish to follow him. What moves the clan or tribe to act as a unified body? First, the agreement of the clan or tribe that its leaders have decided a given matter correctly. Second, the loyalty of the clan or tribe to its leaders where such agreement is lacking. And finally, the pressure that those who agree with the decision and those who accept it out of loyalty together bring to bear on anyone who remains uncertain. Where these are insufficient, the clan or tribe does not act as a unified body.[20]

As is readily evident, the advantages of such an anarchical political order flow from the same source as its disadvantages. It is an order that is little concerned with taxation or with the impressment of men for large-scale construction projects or for war. This means that each family or clan possesses a freedom that is unknown after the establishment of the state, with each family, clan, and tribe participating in larger-scale collective purposes as it sees fit. On the other hand, defense is based on a fractious and irregularly trained militia, justice is attained only with great difficulty, and the customs of religion are maintained only voluntarily. When tribes and clans fall away from loyalty to their common customs and to one another, warfare among the tribes, injustice, and defeat at the hands of foreigners inevitably follow, with no one having the ability to set matters aright.[21]

The state is born out of the relative weakness of the old order of tribes and clans. It is a permanent revision of the political order, which introduces a standing central government over the tribes and clans. This includes the establishment of a professional armed force that is not disbanded in peacetime; a bureaucracy capable of raising taxes sufficient to maintain such a force; and a ruler or government with the authority to issue decrees that are then imposed, where necessary, by means of armed force. Such government concentrates an unprecedented degree of power in the hands of a small number of individuals—power that can be used to defend the tribes against external enemies, for adjudicating and suppressing disputes among them, and for instituting uniform religious rites on a national scale.

But how can such a state, which necessarily deprives the clans and tribes of their freedom and imposes such heavy burdens on them, come into being? We know of two ways:

First, there exists the possibility of establishing a *free state,* which is one in which the cooperation of the ruled is given to the government voluntarily. This can happen if the heads of a coalition of tribes, recognizing a common bond among them as well as a common need, come together to establish a national standing government. In such a case the tribal chieftains themselves participate in the selection of the ruler of the nation and sit in his councils when important decisions are to be made. The loyalty of the individual is thus given to the state out of loyalty to his parents, his tribe, and his nation, and he will endure suffering and sacrifice if the government calls upon him to do so for this reason. Moreover, this loyalty of the individual to the state may be forthcoming even if the particular persons serving in government at a given time, or the particular policies they determine to pursue, are not to his liking. His loyalty to the nation and the fierce desire to maintain its integrity moves the individual to continue to fight in the wars decided upon by the national government, and to obey its laws and to pay it taxes, all the while hoping that better leaders and policies will be forthcoming sooner or later.[22]

We have seen many such states established in history. The most famous case of such a unification of tribes is that of ancient Israel, which has served as the model of a national state.[23] The Athenian state, although it is usually referred to as a "city-state," was in fact created through the unification of a number of clans in just this way. We should therefore recognize it as a tribal state—the state of a particular Greek tribe. This is because, although Athens was cohesive enough to be ruled by a standing government, it also retained its independence from other Greek tribes, and this despite the evident existence of a broader Greek nation that remained divided into independent tribes.[24] Both the Israelite and the Athenian states were thus able to function on the whole as free states, their existence made possible due to the loyalty of their people to nation and tribe, respectively, which contributed the necessary cohesion to the state. And the same may be said of the founding of the kingdom of the English nation unified under Alfred, or of the coming together of the Netherlandish tribes as a national state under the Dutch Republic, or of the establishment of a unified state by the English colonies in America, the United States. All of these and other free states can be seen to have been born through the unification of mutually hostile tribes under a single national government in accordance with the decision of the leadership of these tribes to form a free state.

Second, the state can be established and maintained as a *despotic state*. By this I mean a state whose clans or tribes have not united voluntarily to maintain their freedom, but have, on the contrary, been subjugated by a conqueror against their will. In this case, the ruler of the state is not chosen by leaders of the tribe or nation to which the individual is tied in bonds of mutual loyalty. Rather, they are foreigners or usurpers to whom the loyalty of the tribes is not given at all. And because the tribe to which the individual is loyal gives him no reason to be loyal to the state, he will not voluntarily go to war or obey the law or pay taxes to the state. In the absence of such cohesion, what is needed is a force capable of compelling the individual to act as though he is loyal when in fact he is not. And the only form of government that can impose this semblance of cohesion where a genuine cohesion does not exist is a tyranny—a state that can suppress widespread dissent by force and terror, impress large portions of the population into military service or for other public works, and extract taxes that are used to bribe compliance from those who will take such bribes.

I have described two different ways in which the state can come into being, one by means of the free establishment of a government by a coalition of clans or tribes within a given nation, and the other by means of conquest. In practice, the state is often established through a combination of these, with some tribes and clans joining together voluntarily, and others being coerced. Notice, however, how distant these accounts, as well as an account that combines them, are from the founding of the state as described in the theories of Hobbes or Locke.

These philosophers assert that the agency for establishing the state is the consent of each individual, and that the motive for this consent is a calculation that the establishment of the state will best protect his life and property. In reality, however, there is no such consent and no such calculation. In the case of conquest, the consent of the common individual is utterly irrelevant. And even when a free state is formed through the unification of a nation's tribes, this takes place because bonds of mutual loyalty have been established among the heads of these tribes with the aim of establishing peace among them and securing their joint independence and way of life in the face of foreign menace. The common individual is not asked to consent to national unification and independence, which is decided upon in counsels to which he has little access, and as a rule he will adopt a posture of loyalty to the national state out of loyalty to his tribe, even if he regards the decisions of its leaders to have been questionable. It is thus the interests and aspirations of the tribe and the nation, as these are understood by the tribal leadership, that are decisive in the birth of a free state.

XI: Business and Family

THE ENDURING WEAKNESS OF political philosophy descended from Hobbes and Locke is due to this one great falsehood: It pretends that political life is governed largely or exclusively on the basis of the calculations of consenting individuals as to what will enhance their safety and protect and increase their property. This is another way of saying that liberal philosophy ignores mutual loyalty as a motive, suppressing the most powerful cause operative in political affairs.

The consequences of adopting this falsehood as the foundation for political philosophy can be appreciated by comparing two small institutions: the business enterprise and the family.[25]

No doubt there are institutions that are governed primarily on the basis of the individual's assessments as to what will enhance his physical welfare and protect and increase his property, and by his ongoing consent to the terms of an agreement with others for the joint attainment of these purposes. A business enterprise is such an institution. When a factory, store, or investment house is established, its purpose is to provide for the life and property of the individuals who consent to participate in the business. For those who are closer to poverty, this means earning wages that will provide them with a minimum of food, shelter, and clothing. For those who are financially better off, it means accumulating property that can be used for enlarging one's business enterprises and establishing new ventures, as well as for education, luxury, and charitable works.

It is true, of course, that business enterprises can at times inspire loyalty in their employees, and that they will often seek the benefits of such loyalty by insisting on the family-like character of the business. But this does nothing to alter the fundamental character of a business as a consensual pact whose purpose is to enhance the welfare and property of those participating in it. And in general, all who participate in it do so only so long as they continue to regard the business as personally profitable in this sense. This means that the bonds that tie the participants in the business to one another are by their nature quite weak: An employee, or even a partner in the firm, may be honored as a great asset to the corporation for years, and yet find himself removed without so much as a letter of thanks when the management of the business come to feel they might be more successful without him. In the same way, both partners and employees will frequently withdraw from a firm the moment a more lucrative opportunity presents itself.

Nor is the weakness of the bonds holding together a business expressed only in the ease with which its members withdraw or are expelled. Those who remain are affected by the changeable and temporary character of any human tie whose basis is in ongoing consent, and they limit how much of themselves they are willing to invest in the business accordingly. Thus it would be an unusual individual who would be willing to give up his life for the sake of the factory or store or investment house that employs him, and this is true of the owners of the business as well. Indeed, one would have to look hard to find a businessman, much less an employee, who would be willing even to incur persistent financial losses for the sake of a business if he calculates that he is unlikely to recoup the losses later on.

Compare this to the family. Like a business, the family is founded in an agreement—a marriage agreement—so that it, too, begins in an act of mutual consent. And like a business, the family also operates as an economic enterprise, seeking to provide for the physical welfare and property of its members. But the family is built to attain very different ends, and because of this it is able to establish bonds between human beings that are of an entirely different kind.

What are the purposes for which the family has been instituted? It may be true that married individuals enjoy better health and greater prosperity than persons remaining unmarried. But men and women do not marry, bring children into the world, and endure the many years of hardship and sacrifice involved in remaining married and bringing their children to maturity merely because of an assessment that doing so will contribute to their personal health and prosperity. The purpose of the family is rather something else entirely: Marriage and family are instituted in order to pass on to another generation an inheritance that has been bequeathed to us by our parents and by their ancestors. This inheritance includes life itself and perhaps some property, but it also includes a way of life, a religion and a language, skills and habits, and certain ideals and ways of understanding what is to be valued that are unique to each family, and that others do not possess. A man and a woman join together to combine what each has inherited from their parents and grandparents, knitting together an inheritance for their children that combines the best of what each has received—and therefore, if possible, to improve upon it. One way to understand this effort is to say that a family is established to repay a debt to one's parents and forefathers for the inheritance that has been received from them, a debt that can only be repaid by raising up new generations that will receive it and, if possible, improve upon it in turn.

These are not aims that can be attained in a few years, or in twenty. We tend to focus on the way in which parents influence the development of their children in their earlier years, and for good reason. Less noticed is that a significant part of what parents impart to their children cannot even be understood by them until they are twenty-five or thirty-five years of age; and that once our children have children of their own, their need, and often their desire, to gain the inheritance that is available to them from their parents only grows. Nor do parents have responsibilities only to their children. When our children's children come of age and are unable or unwilling to find what they need in the example and conversation of their parents, it frequently happens that they turn to their grandparents for answers. The truth is that the enterprise of cultivating the garden that is one's family never ceases until death or infirmity stays our hands.

Consider, now, the implications of this fact. The responsibilities undertaken in a business enterprise are, as I've said, based on ongoing consent, and can be periodically re-evaluated to determine whether the benefits gained still outweigh the costs. Every individual participating in the venture can, at any time, announce his intention to end the relationship, quickly conclude any outstanding responsibilities, and be done with the entire affair. By contrast, the responsibilities undertaken in bringing children into the world are permanent, remaining in force for the rest of our lives whether we consent to them or not. True, a husband and wife did usually agree, at one point, to bring a child into the world. But not long after this original act of consent, the difficulties involved in raising a child already bear little resemblance to anything the young lovers may have thought they were consenting to at the time. And the project of raising children only continues to throw up ever new surprises over the decades, including hardship and pain that were scarcely imagined when they first entered into it. Yet this original decision cannot be revisited, giving the parents a chance to renew their consent based on an updated assessment that weighs the benefits each child brings against the suffering endured. Just the opposite: The parents' consent or lack thereof is irrelevant to their continuing responsibilities, and it is nothing like consent that motivates them as they persist in their efforts to raise their children to health and inheritance.

What motivates them is their loyalty, which is the fact that the parents understand the child as a part of themselves—a part of themselves not only for twenty years, as certain philosophers suppose, but for the rest of their lives, forever.

Something similar can be said of the relationship between a husband and wife. It is true that they did consent to be married at a given moment. But the things they experience in their life together, including not only pleasure and joy, but also sorrow and hardship that neither ever dreamed of, are not the things that were imagined when they first wed. Nevertheless, they remain together, not because of a calculation undertaken every few months or years in which their original consent is renewed. Rather, they are sustained by mutual loyalty, which is the recognition of each that the other is a part of themselves—a part of themselves not only until their children reach adulthood, which is, after all, only the first part of the burden of a parent, but for the rest of their lives, forever.

Some will object that this distinction between a business and a family is overdrawn. There is, after all, such a thing as divorce and estrangement within the family, just as there is such a thing as loyalty to one's business partners. Such caveats are surely important when one is not speaking in theory, but considering particular conditions in which real-life human beings find themselves. That said, we cannot hope to understand the political realm if we fail to see that the business enterprise and the family are not merely very different institutions, but institutions reflecting an opposition between two ideal types: The business enterprise operates in that sphere of human life in which the individual's freedom, calculation, and consent are most beneficial. The family operates in that sphere in which loyalty, devotion, and constraint are most beneficial. Because business enterprises are able to bestow great material benefits on those who participate in them, as well as on the broader community, we tolerate an entrepreneurial ethic in which the individual is encouraged to act as if he is free from all constraint other than that to which he has consented. But the license and promiscuity that reign in the sphere of business are worse than worthless in the relations between parents and children, husbands and wives, brothers and sisters, grandparents and grandchildren. Within the domain of the family, to be reliable, to stand true in the face of adversity, to refuse the urge to start everything anew, is the main thing that is needed and the root of all other virtues. One would be a fool to conduct one's family life by the principles that benefit his business, subjecting his parents, wife, and children to periodic assessments and abandoning them when he calculates that they have ceased to profit him as much as others might. The very same attitudes and behaviors that bring the greatest prosperity in business are those that bring utter ruin to the family.

What, then, are we to say about clan, tribe, and nation? These collectives are of the same kind as the family, albeit on a greater scale—and indeed, in Hebrew, these larger collectives are referred to as "the families of the earth."[26] Like the family, their purpose is to pass on to another generation an inheritance that has been bequeathed to us by our parents and by their ancestors, an inheritance that includes life itself and property, but also a way of life, a religion and a language, skills and habits, and ideals and ways of understanding that are unique, and that others do not possess. And like the family, they arise and are maintained due to the strong bonds of mutual loyalty that have been established among their members. Moreover, when a tribe or a nation is constituted as a free state, enjoying the allegiance of the individual who willingly obeys its laws, pays its taxes, and serves in its armed forces, all this only happens thanks to the bonds of mutual loyalty that bind this individual to his family, tribe, and nation. For it is only from his family, tribe, and nation that he has inherited the custom of obeying the laws of the state, paying taxes to it, and serving in its armed forces—all of which would otherwise be alien and unthinkable to him. It is thus the strong bonds of mutual loyalty that are characteristic of the family, rather than the weak bonds of consent that are of the essence in a business enterprise, that serve as the foundation for a free state.

When a philosopher seeks to found the state on the individual's freedom, calculations of personal benefit, and consent, he asks us to see the state as a large business enterprise. He takes an ideal type that has been developed to describe behavior in the marketplace, and transfers it into the political sphere, supposing it will permit us to understand political behavior in the same way that it permitted us to understand economic behavior. But a free state is not a business enterprise. It is constituted, and continues to exist in time, not because of business-like calculations of personal benefit and ongoing consent among its members, but only due to the family-like bonds of mutual loyalty that persist among them. It is true that the financial affairs of the state are understood in terms drawn from economics, and that voluntary immigration and emigration reflect the choices of individuals as to whether to participate in the state. But these things do not make the free state into an institution akin to a business enterprise. A family, too, has financial affairs that must be understood in economic terms. A family, too, may adopt new members who were not born into it, or have members who have been estranged and no longer retain relations with it. However, these things do not affect the basic character of the family, which is constituted, and continues to exist in time, only due to the bonds of mutual loyalty that persist among its members. The free state, which is likewise constituted and able to endure only due to the bonds of mutual loyalty among its members, is in this respect a collective of the same kind as the family, albeit on a greater scale.

XII: Empire and Anarchy

IN MOST TIMES AND places, human beings have lived under an anarchical political order, by which is meant that they have lived in a loose hierarchy of families, clans, and tribes without a standing government or ruler. With the rise of large-scale agriculture, however, the great accumulation of wealth made it possible, for the first time, to establish a standing government capable of imposing its will by means of professional armed forces. It became possible, in other words, to replace the order of tribes and clans with a new kind of political order, that of the state. The transition was not immediate. The first states were "city-states," in which a number of clans united under a tribal government established around an urban center. In these city-states, the strength of the competing clans was still felt in all things. But once these cities had the means to support a ruler in command of a standing armed force, they quickly began to dream of strengthening themselves by annexing their neighbors. Beginning with only a few thousand professional soldiers, Sargon the Great was able, in the twenty-fourth century BCE, to conquer the city-states of Sumer and Akkad one by one until he ruled all of Mesopotamia and could declare himself "king of the universe."[27] In this universal aspiration, he was followed by countless other builders of imperial states, who sought to bring peace and prosperity to the entire earth by bringing it under their unified rule.[28]

Should every state, then, seek to rule the universe? Or is there a reasonable boundary that can be set for the state other than that which is dictated by defeat on the battlefield in a never-ending contest among contending empires?

In answering this question, it is useful to think of the possible forms of political order as appearing along a continuum defined by the extent of the collective to which the individual is presumed to be loyal. At one extreme, we can say, is the ideal of *empire,* a state that is in principle boundless, so that the individual under such a state is expected to be loyal to a collective that may include, if not today then tomorrow, any other human being on earth. At the other extreme is *anarchy,* in which there is no centralized state and the loyalty of the individual is given to a small bounded collective—a family or clan, a village, manor, or gang—consisting of individuals who are familiar to him from personal experience.

Notice that the difference between these forms of order is not only one of scale. It is also substantive: Imperial and anarchic orders are based on a presumption of loyalty that is directed toward very different things. An anarchic or feudal order is built upon relations of mutual loyalty among familiar individuals.[29] The head of my clan or the lord of my manor is not an abstract entity, but an actual person to whom my allegiance is given in gratitude for personal acts of generosity or aid. I am aware of his needs, hardships, and triumphs, and can play some real part, whether small or large, in assisting him. He is aware of my needs and hardships, and the moments in which he interferes to assist me in some matter are of great significance to me. And if the difficult day comes when the head of my clan or the lord of my manor withdraws his allegiance from his own tribal chieftain or lord, my loyalty to this individual, who has done so much for me and for the others in my community, will remain unshaken. Under empire, on the other hand, my allegiance is, above all else, to the empire itself, and to all mankind, which it is supposed to represent. The empire, too, is ruled by an individual human being—an emperor, king, or president—to whom I have sworn my allegiance. But this ruler is no familiar individual, as under anarchy. The emperor knows nothing of me as an individual, nor can I make myself known to him, or of concern to him. I do not receive personal assistance from him, nor do I assist him in his troubles in a way that can be known to him. The emperor is so remote as to be, for me, nothing more than an abstraction. Just as I am, to him, nothing more than an abstraction. And just as mankind, over which he has extended his rule, is for me only an abstraction.

In anarchy, then, my loyalty is given to an individual who is familiar to me; whereas in empire it is to a great abstraction that I owe allegiance.[30] It is this distinction that allows us to understand why, in an imperial order, anarchy is regarded as the greatest imaginable evil. For it is the premise of the imperial state that the great masses of humanity depend for their peace and prosperity on the universal mind of an emperor, who brings great abstractions to bear on the world, and on the universal peace and prosperity that he is able, in this way, to provide. By placing loyalty to the familiar individual who is one's chief or lord above loyalty to the empire as a whole, one in effect renounces his obligation to the universal order, and to all the masses of unfamiliar humanity who are said to benefit from this universal order. In this way, he becomes an enemy not only of the empire, but of humanity as well. Similarly, we can see why those who are committed to an anarchic order regard the encroachment of agents of the imperial state with such horror. In demanding that allegiance to the empire be placed above loyalty to the familiar individual who has afforded them protection and cared for their needs, these agents of empire demand nothing less than the sundering and betrayal of the concrete personal attachments that have stood as the foundation of society.

From these observations we understand that empire and anarchy are not merely competing methods of ordering political power. Each is a normative ordering principle, drawing its legitimacy from the manner in which it is rooted in the moral order. This conforms with our experience as well, in which the defenders of empire and anarchy present their views not only in terms of the practical advantages that each kind of order is supposed to provide, but in terms of the moral legitimacy and sanction that should be attributed to each. We can think of these normative ordering principles in the following way:

In an anarchical order, one's loyalties and political life itself are rooted in the moral principle of gratitude to familiar individuals from whom assistance has been received. The individual lives under the protection of the family or clan—protection that includes material sustenance, recourse in cases of injustice at the hands of others, defense against outsiders, an education in the skills and traditions of one's people and rituals for appealing to the gods. Out of gratitude to, and respect for, those who have provided him with these things, the individual contributes service, as assessed by the heads of the family or clan.

In this way, the individual has everything he needs, and his obligations to those who have established him in life and provided for him are fully met.

Although the moral basis for such a politics is compelling and evident, the difficulties involved in maintaining an anarchical or feudal order are well known. In the first place, the clans and tribes living in an anarchical society are constantly on the verge of warfare between them—so that war, which we tend to imagine as taking place on the periphery of society, is brought into the very center of life for people everywhere. Similarly, while anarchical societies can and do develop elaborate traditions for settling the competing claims of individuals and collectives, such justice is often difficult to enforce without resorting to the threat of war, so that justice itself is hostage to the power relations among clans and tribes. Moreover, the role of the familiar individual in ruling the clan is not an unalloyed good: The personal nature of localized rule means that the quality of one's personal relations with a chief or lord affect every aspect of one's life. As a consequence, even the most fateful matters may be decided on the basis of prejudice, based on an old insult or some other irrelevant matter, without the possibility of an appeal. Finally, the freedom afforded to each clan and tribe in an anarchical order means that coordinated defensive action is difficult, and cannot be sustained over time in the face of the disciplined military action of an encroaching state possessing a professional armed force under a unified command.

In an imperial order, on the other hand, all political life is rooted in the moral principle of the unity of unfamiliar humanity, which is the principle that each individual has obligations to the common welfare of mankind. The conquest of the anarchical realm of clans and tribes, which the imperial state always regards as a realm of savagery, a "realm of war," creates a realm of peace and prosperity. Through conquest of lands governed under the order of clans and tribes, the imperial state drives warfare out of these territories and exiles it to a distant border, establishing in its place a universal law that is impartial among men. And by means of this peace and this universal law, the imperial state opens up a vast sphere to agriculture, industry, and trade, bringing economic prosperity to all. It is this peace and prosperity that gives moral sanction to the laws and wars of the imperial state, which are said to benefit all mankind.[31]

As in an anarchical order, we find that the moral basis for the imperial state is, at least initially, compelling. Yet, here, too, there are difficulties. First among these is the fact that wherever the principle of the unity of unfamiliar humanity is imbedded in the heart of the state, it necessarily gives birth to conquest, to the subjugation of distant peoples, and to the destruction of their way of life so that the "realm of peace," as the empire understands it, can be extended. This is true even where the imperial state appears, at a given moment, to be benevolent in its relations with outsiders, because the principle of the unity of humanity does not permit any consistent comity toward outsiders. In the normal course of political affairs, every neighboring clan or tribe must sooner or later come into conflict with the empire over some bit of land, resource, or policy. But the imperial mind, which regards every resource as rightfully belonging to all mankind, and which sees the imperial state as responsible for the welfare of mankind, cannot accept any outcome to such conflicts other than the "pacification" of the dissenting clan or tribe and the annexation of the disputed land or resource. Each such conquest involves depriving another clan or tribe of its freedom, which it tends to give up only at a horrific cost in human life. And since the empire possesses no internal principle that can prevent this monstrous habit of conquest and devastation from reasserting itself each time it is provoked, the recurrence of this pattern is limited only by the measure of force that the imperial state can bring to bear on its surroundings.

No less troubling, moreover, are the burdens imposed by the imperial state for the maintenance of its armies and fortifications, its palaces, temples, and bureaucracy. The imposition of taxation and impressment, both for public works and for military service, is a heavy load for the individual to carry, where they are not in fact a calamity. Indeed, from the perspective of tribes and clans accustomed to a life of freedom and self-determination, the entire imperial order has the character of enslavement.

In addition, the regime of peace and prosperity imposed by the empire has a very particular quality to it. The empire, which claims to give law to all mankind, necessarily concerns itself with abstract categories of human need and obligation, categories that are, in its eyes, "universal." But these categories are always detached from the circumstances and interests, traditions and aspirations of the particular clan or tribe to which they are now to be applied. This means that from the perspective of the particular clan or tribe, imperial law will often appear to be ill-conceived, unjust, and perverse. Yet the very premise of the empire, which is its concern for the needs of humanity, leaves the unique clan or tribe with no standing to protest, for its assertion of its own interests and aspirations must inevitably strike the imperial order as narrow-minded and contrary to the evident good of mankind as a whole. Thus the principle of the unity of humanity, so noble in theory, rapidly divides mankind into two camps: those who are regarded as favoring the good of mankind, in that they adopt the empire's categories for determining what is beneficial and right; and those who are regarded as opposing the good of mankind, in that they insist on thinking in terms of the customary categories of the tribe, which the empire invariably condemns as primitive and barbaric.

This clash between imperial law and the traditions and ideals of the tribe draws our attention to what is perhaps the central dilemma facing the imperial state, which is how the aspiration to unify humanity can be reconciled with empirical human nature. Empire, as has been said, requires that the individual establish and express a loyalty to a collective that may, in principle, include every other human being on earth. But why should the individual develop bonds of mutual loyalty extending so far? We have seen that loyalty finds its most characteristic expression in the effort to defend the members of a particular collective against threats from outside: A husband and wife quarrel until they are faced with adversity, but then they rise to meet the challenge before them as a unity. In the same way, the tribes that make up a nation compete against each other until danger unites them in their common defense.[32] What, then, is supposed to establish the loyalty of the individual to every other human being on earth? In the absence of a common threat to provide a genuine basis for unified action, the call to unite all mankind appears worse than vacuous. It amounts to an invitation to ignore the very real dangers that a given tribe or nation may face at the hands of others in the name of a common cause that is, in its eyes, no more than a pious fiction.[33]

Human beings do of course engage in acts of sympathy and kindness toward strangers, without reference to nation or tribe. But these motives, much as we may approve of them, tend to be short-lived and cannot compete with the ties of mutual loyalty that are the foundation for political order.[34] And the reality is that we are rarely moved to action by a bond of loyalty to all other human beings. Nevertheless, the imperial state has to be built on some bond of mutual loyalty, or its soldiers will not be willing to fight and die for it. We have seen that neither the prospect of compensation nor threats of violence, which every empire uses in one degree or another, can be relied upon to hold fast in the long term. What, then, is the bond of loyalty that holds together the empire?

The truth is that, since the dawn of recorded history, the government and armed forces of the imperial state have been built upon the ties of mutual loyalty that bind together the members of a single nation—that of the ruling nation around which the imperial state is constructed.[35] This was true of the Persians, Greeks, and Romans, not less than the Spanish, French, and English, each of whom established a vast empire in which a given nation ruled over many others. In each case, the ruling nation forms a tightly bound core of individuals who will defend one another at all cost against the peoples whom they have conquered, and whom they consider to pose a permanent threat.[36] Around this core, the empire may then add other allied nationalities—as the Persians added the Medes to their core forces, and as the English added the Scots, Irish, and Welsh—as well as smaller numbers of individuals drawn from many other nationalities. All of these are valuable in expanding the supply of trustworthy manpower, while at the same time imparting to the imperial effort an air of universality that helps bolster its claims to represent the unity of all mankind. Yet this expansion does not change the fact that the empire is ultimately held together by the mutual loyalties of members of a ruling nation, its language and customs, and its unique way of understanding the world, which the other nations are invited or coerced into joining. Thus while empires like to identify their cause with the ultimate good of all humanity, this cause is almost always closely associated with the domination of one nation at the expense of all others.[37]

Anarchy and empire are each based on normative principles of immense plausibility and power: the loyalty to familiar individuals that characterizes the anarchic order; and the unity of mankind that is the aspiration of imperial order. We cannot say that either of these principles is mistaken. Each has a certain place in a balanced moral system. Nevertheless, when either one is permitted to exceed its proper place and embraced as the primary ordering principle of the political world, it quickly engenders not the freedom of peoples, but their enslavement: Just as empire tends toward the enslavement of peoples to the customs and ideals of a ruling nation, so too does anarchy tend toward their enslavement to an endless strife among local strongmen.

XIII: National Freedom as an Ordering Principle

EMPIRE AND ANARCHY ARE the horns of a dilemma that has dogged mankind's steps since antiquity. The earliest political images of the Bible—the story of the tower of Babylon, for example, in which the leadership of that city sought to unite humanity under one language in a single community of purpose; and that of Noah's ark, a tiny, familiar community cast out of a violent and anarchic mankind—give a sense of how deeply these two evils impressed themselves on the thought of our forefathers.[38] And indeed, the problem of empire and anarchy is central to the political teaching of Hebrew Scripture. What the prophets of Israel proposed in response to this dilemma was a third type of political order: the distinctive Israelite institution of the national state, which seeks to transcend the dilemma of empire and anarchy by retaining what is most vital in each, while discarding what makes each of them most dangerous.[39]

Let us consider this alternative political order. I have said that under empire the loyalty of the individual is supposed to be directed toward humanity as a whole; whereas in an anarchical order, it is devoted to the politically independent family or clan. Here, what is proposed is an order in which loyalty is turned toward an institution that sits precisely at the conceptual midpoint between these others: the national state.

By a *nation,* I mean a number of tribes with a shared heritage, usually including a common language or religious traditions, and a past history of joining together against common enemies—characteristics that permit tribes so united to understand themselves as a community distinct from other such communities that are their neighbors.[40] By a *national state,* I mean a nation whose disparate tribes have come together under a single standing government, independent of all other governments.

These definitions mean, in the first place, that a nation is a form of community, a human collective recognizing itself as distinct from other human collectives. Such a community can exist independently of the state, and does not have to include every individual living within the state.[41] Second, these definitions means that the unity thus created is always a composite—because the tribes united in this way continue to exist after national independence.[42]

What does it mean to say that the national state sits at the conceptual midpoint between empire and anarchy? In the first place, a national state rules over many families and clans, whereas an empire rules over many nations. The national state is midway between the family or clan and the imperial state in terms of scale.

In addition, however, the national state is also qualitatively different from anarchical and imperial political order. The nation is distinguished from the family or clan in that it is not a community of individuals who are known personally to one another. No one, no matter how much he may invest in the effort, can be personally acquainted with even a small fraction of the individuals who comprise a nation. The nation, in other words, is not comprised of familiar individuals, but is an impersonal abstraction, in the same sense that humanity is an abstraction. Yet at the same time, the nation is also distinguished from all of humanity in that it possesses a quite distinctive character, having its own language, laws, and religious traditions, its own past history of failure and achievement. This means that each nation is different from all other nations, and that to the individual who is a member of a certain nation, it is known as a concrete and familiar being, much like a person, family, or clan. When the tribes of a nation unite to establish a national state, they bring to this state the familiar and distinctive character of the nation, its language, laws, and religious traditions, its past history of anguish and triumph. And the individual, who shoulders the burdens imposed by the national state, does so out of loyalty to the concrete and familiar nation of which he is a part.

In this, the national state is distinct from the imperial state, to which the individual usually has no such ties of loyalty (unless, of course, he is a member of the ruling nation, or allied to the ruling nation, that sees the empire as its own).

I would like now to consider what type of ordering principle arises once we have conceived of a political allegiance that rises above the familiar individual of the anarchic order, but stops only half as high as the celestial dome of unfamiliar humanity. Here, at the inflection point between anarchy and empire, we find a new ordering principle rooted in the moral order: the principle of *national freedom.* This principle offers a nation with the cohesiveness and strength to maintain independence and self-government, and to withstand the siren songs of empire and anarchy, an opportunity to live according to its own interests and aspirations. More generally, this principle supports the establishment of a world in which there are many such national states, each pursuing its own unique purposes and developing its own vision of human life, every one "under its own vine or its own fig tree."[43]

The principle of national freedom can thus be regarded as taking what is vital and constructive in each of the two principles with which it competes: From the principle of empire, it takes the idea of an allegiance that is directed toward the abstraction of the state rather than to familiar men, the practical effect of which is the creation of a large space of domestic peace; and the possibility of an impartial judicial system that is no longer tied to the politics of familiar collectives. From the principle of anarchy, it retains the ideal of a ruler devoted to the unique needs and interests, traditions and aspirations of a particular community that is different from all others. This finds expression in the aim of government over a single nation—an aim that devalues foreign conquest, and for the first time permits a conception of the freedom of nations other than one's own as a potential good in itself.

Is it really possible to speak of the freedom of a nation? To be sure, Israel is said to have rejoiced in its escape from the bondage of Egypt at the Red Sea, and it is this kind of freedom of the nation from empire that is celebrated every year on independence days in Czechia, Greece, India, Ireland, Israel, Poland, Serbia, South Korea, Switzerland, the United States, and many other countries.[44] Today, however, because nearly all political thought focuses on the freedom of the individual, the very idea of national freedom has come to seem doubtful. Is not freedom something that belongs only to an individual, a human being who experiences both choice and constraint, and rejoices when he is "free to choose"?[45]

It is true that *freedom* describes an aspect of the actions and experience of the human individual, just as interests and aspirations, triumph and tragedy, desire, fear, and pain are features of the life and mental landscape of the individual. But these and similar terms are also used to describe human collectives. When a mother with a number of children is wounded in an accident or falls ill, for example, we say that the family is in pain. It is possible, if one insists, to imagine the mother, her husband, and each of her children as distinct individuals, each experiencing his or her own personal pain as a result of this traumatic event. But this is not what the members of a family experience in such circumstances. They are accustomed to thinking of the family as a collective, as a unity, each one regarding the other members of the family as a part of his own self. And this is the way they experience the family's pain now: Each feels the pain not only of the mother, but of the father, brothers, and sisters as well, and each knows that the others are suffering for him in this way too. All this is experienced as a single pain, a single grief and burden. And we, their friends and neighbors, when we visit them, experience the suffering of the entire family in this way, as a single pain, a single grief and burden. A family is not, in other words, only a collection of individuals. It is also an entity possessing certain properties that belong to it as a collective, as a whole. One of these is that a family, because each of its members experiences what happens to the others as something happening to himself, can be recognized by any observer as sharing certain experiences. It is this experience of a single, shared pain that is meant when we say that the family is in pain, that the family has been convulsed, that the family has suffered a terrible blow and will need time to recover.[46]

Just as a family can feel pain, so too can it experience triumph and tragedy, desire and fear, interests and aspirations. A family that plows with oxen can have a shared interest in purchasing a tractor. It can share a triumph as a daughter who feared that she could not have children gives birth. It can share an aspiration to one day make the trip to the Holy Land, and can share a recognition that the time has come to undertake the journey. None of this takes anything away from the individual, who is free to resist the inclination to feel as his family does in particular instances. Indeed, a person may choose to cut himself off from his family entirely. But in times of great duress, even these exiled souls have a way of returning to their brothers, discovering that they still share feelings with them, and a wish to share actions.

All of these things can be said of larger human collectives such as the clan, the tribe, and the nation. We are familiar, for instance, with the way in which a nation can suffer pain, for we have all experienced it. We have experienced it when a president or prime minister is assassinated, when the members of our nation are cut down in our streets or held hostage in a foreign land, or when our soldiers or policemen are defeated in battle. An individual who is bound to his nation by ties of loyalty experiences these things as if they were happening to his own self. And as in the family, it is hardly relevant to say that each of these millions of individuals experiences his own pain as an individual. On the contrary, each one experiences at once the pain of the others. A heavy sense of hurt and humiliation fills the public spaces and clings to everything taking place throughout the land, so that even very young children, who do not understand what has happened, feel pained and ashamed. It is the nation that has been harmed. It is the nation that has been shamed.[47]

And as a nation can be in pain, it can also suffer the experience of slavery. When a people finds that its property is confiscated and its sons and daughters forced to serve others for the sake of ends they do not desire; when they are prevented from speaking their own language, or from fulfilling their religious obligations; when their children are taken from them or forcibly deprived of instruction in the traditional manner; when they are murdered, imprisoned, and tortured for resisting—when these things happen, a nation experiences enslavement. Indeed, even if there is one who is for some reason spared the direct effects of the persecution that the nation is suffering, he too will share the feeling of enslavement, as if these things were happening to his own self.

If a nation can experience slavery, then surely it can experience freedom. The members of a nation can share an experience of being released from oppression, the joy of liberation.

And they can go on to share an experience of power, of building themselves up and determining their course according to their own aspirations, without being forced to bow to any other nation or empire. Recall that the purpose of the discipline of politics is to bring about circumstances in which the many act to accomplish goals seen as necessary or desirable. When the individual feels the collective is able to move toward the aims he sees as necessary or desirable, he feels a great liberation from constraint. He feels, in other words, the freedom of the collective: the freedom of the family, clan, tribe, or nation to which he is bound by ties of mutual loyalty.[48]

In taking part in the freedom of the collective, I experience something that is quite distinct from the strictly individual freedom of saying whatever I please or going wherever I want. It is tempting, for this reason, to say that individual freedom is one thing and collective freedom another, and that political freedom consists in having some of both. But the reality is not so simple. Because the individual is always bound by ties of mutual loyalty to his family, tribe, or nation, it is a mistake to suppose that he can have political freedom when the family, tribe, or nation is not free.

Consider, for example, the problem of the released slave. We tend to believe that to have the joy of release from bondage and a life of self-determination, a slave needs only to purchase his freedom from his master, or to escape in secret. However, this is not necessarily true. If one's wife and children are enslaved, then attaining one's personal freedom brings no such release. As has been said, the individual constantly seeks the health and prosperity of the collective to which he is tied by bonds of mutual loyalty. Attached to his family in this way, the released slave continues to experience their anguish every day as something that is happening to his own self. He feels neither the joy of liberation nor the power to determine his own course according to his own will. And is it not insulting and foolish to tell such a person that he can now "determine his own course," when at every moment he remains helpless to assist his wife and children who remain enslaved? It is true that he may freely choose among the alternatives that are left to him. Yet he will recognize, as we too must recognize, that the courses of action he truly desires are unavailable to him. They have been stolen from him by the constraints imposed by others, and he will not taste freedom until his family is free as well.

The same is true of the individual who flees his country, while the tribe or nation in which he was raised continues to suffer persecution at the hands of a despotic regime. Such an individual can no more "determine his own course" under these conditions than can a man whose wife and children are being held hostage. Knowing that his people are tormented and in danger, living out his life in exile, he is like the freed slave, with all the courses of action that he might truly desire stolen from him. He looks forward to tasting real freedom only when they are freed and he can return home.

An example from the recent history of my own nation may be instructive. During the Second World War, most of the Jews in Europe were murdered by the German government and its collaborators. At the time, there were millions of Jews in America and Britain, and in British protectorates such as Palestine, where my grandparents lived. These Jews were well aware that their brothers in Europe were being massacred, and a cry arose among Jews who wished to rescue them. One of them was my grandfather Meir, who wrote a letter to the authorities demanding to be armed and sent to Europe, and he was surely not alone. But his letter received no reply. The Americans and British were concerned with their own interests, which did not align with rescue efforts. The British worked diligently to prevent Jews from reaching safety in Palestine, intercepting refugees and deporting them to internment camps overseas. The United States, too, declined to bomb the railway tracks carrying Jews to the extermination camps. The machinery of extermination thus operated throughout the war without significant American or British resistance to it. The millions of Jews living dispersed among these great nations enjoyed generous personal freedoms, yet as their fellow Jews were slaughtered with none to save them, they understood, as we too must understand, that all the courses of action that they truly desired were in fact unavailable to them. Despite the formal individual liberties that had been granted to them, they did not have national freedom, and so they were not free. National freedom came only with the establishment of a Jewish national state in Israel, which my grandfather lived to see.

In this case, as in others, the freedom of the individual is seen to depend on the freedom of his family, clan, tribe, and nation—that is, on the freedom and self-determination of the collective to which he is loyal, and whose pain and degradation he experiences as his own. If the collective is so partitioned, persecuted, threatened, and abused that there is no hope of its attaining its aims and aspirations, then the collective is not free, and the individual is not free either.

XIV: The Virtues of the National State

THE ECONOMIC SYSTEM OF free enterprise is based on the recognition that the individual desires to improve his own life and material circumstances, and it is ordered so as to give the most beneficial and least damaging expression to this urge. It seeks, in other words, to be realistic about the true characteristics of human nature and to achieve the best that can be attained in light of these characteristics. In the same way, the political order of national states is based on the recognition that the individual constantly desires and actively pursues the health and prosperity of the family, clan, tribe, or nation to which he is tied by bonds of mutual loyalty, and it is ordered to give the most beneficial and least damaging expression to this urge.

In this chapter, I describe five ways in which the order of independent national states is recognized as being superior to the anarchic and imperial forms of political order with which it competes, once the human desire for collective freedom is taken into account and allowed to find its fullest and most salutary expression.

1. Violence Is Banished to the Periphery. Under an anarchical political order, the desire for collective self-determination is given expression through the independence of every clan and tribe from all others. In such circumstances, the loyalty of the individual to the clan or tribe requires that he go to war for the sake of these collectives, whether in pursuit of their interests or in order to obtain justice when nonviolent mediation has failed. Indeed, neither their interests nor justice tends to be attainable without the constant threat of violence, and all of life is painted with its colors.[49]

When the loyalty of the individual is shifted upward to the national state, the focus of his desire for collective freedom and self-determination shifts upward as well. This does not mean that he renounces his loyalty to his clan or tribe. But where the unification of the tribes under a national state is successful, the longing for the freedom and self-determination of the clan or tribe is restrained by an intense desire to achieve the internal integrity of his nation. The desire for the internal integrity of the nation works, in other words, to suppress warfare as an instrument in pursuit of clan and tribal interests, so that it is expelled from this arena and deployed only in defense of the large national sphere of domestic order and peace. Similarly, the administration of justice, which had been a matter to be resolved, when necessary, by violence among clans and tribes, is relocated within a system of law, policing, and courts that is answerable to the national government, and so independent of the influences of particular family, clan, or tribal affiliation.[50]

In this way, the national state suppresses warfare as a means of resolving conflict over an extended territory, and war is banished to the periphery of human experience. To be sure, those who serve the state in government or as soldiers continue to devote themselves to the struggles among national states and their wars. But now violence impinges on the life of the individual much more rarely, and almost always at a distance from his home, where his family can often live quietly even as war takes place elsewhere. The creation of this sphere of peace, in which family and economic life can proceed largely unspoiled by violence, is the first innovation of the national state, upon which its many other innovations are built.

2. Disdain for Imperial Conquest. A national state is an institution on a limited scale. This means that the rulers of the national state inherit a political tradition that recognizes the boundaries of the nation and its defensive needs as placing natural limits upon its extension, and so tend to disdain the idea of conquering foreign nations. This is as opposed to the imperial state, which hands down a political tradition that recognizes no such boundaries, and whose rulers are forever finding reasons to conquer additional peoples. As has been said, each of these views is rooted in the moral order—with imperialists insisting that it is only right to extend the realm of peace and economic prosperity that their rule will bring mankind; and nationalists emphasizing that what is right is the freedom of nations and their self-determination. Each of these positions has a certain plausibility. But the disdain for wars of indefinite expansion, which is both a cause and a consequence of the political ideal of the national state, is so great a benefit that it may, in itself, be sufficient to decide the argument between these views.

Although an aversion to conquering foreign nations is often presented as a kindness to others, it is important to recognize that it is, before anything else, the expression of a certain view of the interests of one's own nation. It is often mistakenly supposed that all nations tend to regard themselves, as the Romans did, as gaining in strength when they force additional nations to submit to their rule, expanding the size of the economy from which they can collect taxes and therefore the size of the armies that they can field. But there is an alternative tradition descended from ancient Israel, which regards such imperial states as intrinsically weak, and disdains their indefinite extension as something that harms the nation that seeks it, rather than benefiting it. This is well expressed by Herder when he writes of the intrinsic fragility of imperial states, and of the durability, by contrast, of the national state:

> The most natural state is, therefore, *one* nation, an extended family with one national character. This it retains for ages and develops most naturally if the leaders come from the people. . . . Nothing, therefore, is more manifestly contrary to the purposes of political government than the unnatural enlargement of states, the wild mixing of various races and nationalities under one scepter. A human scepter is far too weak and slender for such incongruous parts to be engrafted upon it. Such states are but patched up contraptions, fragile machines, . . . and their component parts are connected by mechanical contrivances instead of bonds of sentiment. . . . It would only be the curse of fate that would condemn to immortality these forced unions, these lifeless monstrosities. But history shows sufficiently that the instruments of human pride are formed of clay, and like all clay, they will dissolve or crumble to pieces.[51]

In this passage, Herder describes the imperial state as nothing other than a "curse" to all involved. According to this point of view, human government is inherently limited in what it can attain, and can be strong and effective only when it relies on the "bonds of sentiment" that unite a single nation in a national state whose leaders are drawn from the people. The "unnatural enlargement of states," which forces many nations together under a single rule, is not based on such bonds of sentiment. It only increases the burdens and difficulties piled on the state as "incongruous parts" that are not bound together by mutual loyalty are added to it, until eventually it survives only as a "patched up contraption" groaning under the weight of these troubles.

Underlying such an approach is the recognition that the health of a nation is measured not only in terms of its military and economic strength, but also along other dimensions that are no less significant. What Herder describes as a "national character[, which] it retains for ages and develops," refers to what I have called the internal integrity and cultural inheritance of the nation. And it is these things that tend to be lost as the imperial state expands. This is because conquered nations bring their own aspirations, troubles, and interests into the state. And this growing diversity makes the state more difficult to govern, weakening the mutual loyalties that had held it together, dissipating its attention and resources in the effort to suppress internal conflicts and violence that had previously been unknown to it, and forcing the rulers to adopt oppressive means of maintaining the peace. As this happens, the rulers become absorbed in intrigues and negotiations among distant parties in distant lands. This appeals to their vanity, as it allows them to see themselves as "men of the world." But in reality, their understanding of the foreign nations they seek to pacify is nearly always limited to externals, to hollowed-out caricatures, so that they tend to do as much harm as good by applying the shallow, supposedly "universal" categories at their disposal to circumstances at the ends of the earth.[52] In the meantime, when anyone approaches them with a matter that concerns the health and prosperity of their own nation, they have only scant attention to devote to it, and secretly resent this intrusion of "domestic affairs" when greater things are pressing. In this way, the minds of the rulers turn away, and they become almost as unaware of the concerns of their own people as they are of the interests of the foreign nations they seek to govern.

All of this is regarded with horror by peoples with strong national-state traditions, which tend to scorn the idea that their country's leaders should lose themselves in efforts for the preservation and government of an empire of foreign nations, rather than strengthening the tribes of their own nation in their own land. From such a perspective, the rulers of the nation are appointed from among its members because of the ties of mutual loyalty that bind them to their own people, enabling them to experience the nation's needs as their own. Where this allegiance is honored, the eyes of the rulers remain fixed on increasing the health and prosperity of their own nation, not only expanding its economic and military might, but also maintaining and strengthening the internal integrity of the nation, and seeing to the consolidation and transmission of its cultural inheritance. Remaining loyal to their own people, they will experience these things as if they themselves were steadily growing in strength, and will be fearful of dissipating it in imperialist expansion. Indeed, alongside defeat on the battlefield, this aversion to wasting the strength of the nation governing foreign lands is the greatest factor that stands against the inclination of rulers to aggrandize themselves through ever-further conquest. It is therefore bonds of mutual loyalty, together with national-state traditions that emphasize and re-emphasize the importance of this allegiance of the rulers to their own people, that sharply limit the political horizon of the national state, establishing a state that prefers to allow the other nations to govern themselves, rather than attempting to annex them all, one after another.

This is not to suggest that the national state tends, by its nature, toward peace. The dangers the national state faces from foreign enemies can be quite real, and the rulers of the national state must judge whether to use force in responding to these dangers, seeking to alter conditions along its borders or outside its borders, or attempting change the borders themselves. We have seen many such wars between nations: those between the English and the Irish, Serbs and Croats, India and Pakistan, Israel and the Arab states, and so forth. In such conflicts, the leaders of national states may be sometimes justified and sometimes misguided. No one can deny that pompous over-confidence and bigotry have often characterized public discourse when it comes to war with one's neighbors, or that national leaders often resort to unnecessary warfare in order to gain some territorial, political, or economic advantage.

But even if the national state does not necessarily tend toward peace, there is another claim to be made on its behalf, which is hardly less significant: Because the national state inherits a political tradition that disdains the conquest of foreign nations, wars between national states tend to be relatively limited in their aims, in the resources invested in them, and in the scale of the destruction and misery they cause. This has frequently been emphasized with respect to the national states of Western Europe after the Westphalia treaties, which for centuries continued to fight limited wars among themselves with an eye to gaining political or economic advantage, but refrained from engaging in unlimited warfare with the purpose of eliminating other national states entirely.[53]

Europe has, of course, known general wars of virtually un-limited devastation in the past four hundred years. The wars that now haunt Europe—and with it the world—were not, how-ever, wars among national states seeking to gain advantage over their rivals. Rather, they were ideological wars, fought in the name of some universal doctrine that was supposed to bring salvation to all of humanity. For the sake of this universal doc-trine, armies were sent out into the world to swallow one na-tion after another, with the aim of overturning the established order of life in every nation conquered. This was the case in the Thirty Years' War, which was fought in order to assert a German-Catholic Empire over Europe. It was true, as well, of the Napoleonic Wars, which sought to overturn the old political order and establish a French-Liberal Empire across an entire continent and beyond it. And it was no less true of the Second World War, in which a German-Nazi Empire aimed at establish-ing a new order according to its own perverse universal theory of how mankind's salvation was to be brought about.[54]

In contrast with these ideological upheavals, the First World War is often invoked as a paradigmatic war among national states. Countless volumes have been written about the causes of this catastrophe, and it is doubtful whether an unequivocal conclusion will ever be drawn. This having been said, I find the most common explanations for the war, which are taught to every high schooler throughout the West today, to be en-tirely unconvincing. To be sure, the collision between Serbian nationalism and the Austrian Empire was the most immediate cause of the conflict. But nothing in the Serbs' desire to lib-erate certain territories controlled by Austria-Hungary could have motivated or sustained a war that mobilized the fullest re-sources of all of the most powerful empires on earth for more than four years, killing perhaps twenty million human beings and physically destroying a continent. Nor is any of the rest of the discussion—about the rigidity of the European alliance system, the interlocking promises of mutual aid in case of conflict, the rapidity with which mobilization timetables had to be implemented—convincing as an explanation. At most, these things describe the way the war began. They do not come close to explaining why the war was prosecuted for so many years and at such cost, rather than being settled by an armistice as soon as the scope of the casualties began to become evident.

To understand what sustained the First World War and made it the horror that it became, I believe there is no choice but to look to the imperialism that had come to dominate the policies of Britain, France, Russia, and Germany. As was emphasized by many observers at the time, there is no way to separate the war from the frenzied expansion of overseas empires, which between 1871 and 1914 had led to the conquest and annexation of roughly one-quarter of the earth's land surface, largely in Africa, Asia, and the Pacific, by Europeans and the Japanese. The astonishingly aggressive expansion of the British and French empires in particular had led many—especially in Germany—to conclude that the era of the European national-state system had in effect come to an end. What was emerging instead was a struggle among a small number of "world states," each one a universal empire seeking to mold the world according to its own character. This seems to have been Kaiser Wilhelm II's view, and he and his ministers apparently believed they could compete with the British world state, already in a position of overwhelming global dominance, only by eliminating France as a significant power on the continent and unifying much of central and eastern Europe under German "leadership." It was the necessity of bringing about such a permanent change in the character of European politics that stood behind the German Empire's determination to face a *weltkrieg*—a world war—just as imperialist war aims like the annexation of the entire Middle East loomed large in British and French decision-making.

The First World War was to a great extent the fruit of the European national states' infatuation with imperialism. So long as the competition for overseas empires remained a contest among traditional Western-European national states such as Britain, France, and the Netherlands, it had been possible to maintain the national-state system within Europe as a mark of relations among "civilized" nations (whereas the "uncivilized" peoples in Africa and Asia were not seen as deserving independent national states of their own). But the newly established German Empire had not committed itself to the ideal of the national state. Nor could its leaders see much reason to focus their resources on attempting to expand in Africa when a vast empire could be built more easily and to greater advantage on the European continent.[55] The cause of the First World War was, in other words, the determination of Germany to revive imperialism on the continent, thus ending the European order of national states forever—and the equal determination of Britain to prevent this. The causes of the First World War are, in this regard, remarkably similar to the causes of the Second World War. Both were fought principally over the question of whether Germany would unite Europe under a German emperor. Both were imperial wars reflecting universal aspirations. And the destruction they wreaked was commensurate with this aim.[56]

In general, then, the aspirations of national states tend to produce petty wars whose purpose is adjustments in the hierarchy of power among them, or to achieve an alteration in the boundaries among them. Whereas the universal aspirations of imperial states tend to produce vast, ideological wars, which seek to set the world aright once and for all, and bring devastation on a commensurate scale. Among peoples with strong national-state traditions, the ties of mutual loyalty that bind the members of the nation have this effect: They limit the extent of the wars conducted by national states by constantly returning the attention of the rulers to the hardships being endured by their own nation, and to what they can do to strengthen the material prosperity, internal integrity, and cultural inheritance of this nation within its own borders. This encourages, in the nationalist statesman, a salutary disgust for the use of the armed forces at his command to suppress foreign nations, and for squandering his term of office on the management of crises in foreign lands that have been caused or exacerbated by the presence of these forces.

In this regard, it is instructive to consider the fate of American imperialism after the first brief enthusiasm for it in the 1890s.[57] Under President William McKinley, the United States resolved to become a world empire with a mission to bring its cultural inheritance of Christianity and capitalism to the uncivilized reaches of the globe. In the name of this great vision, the United States conquered the Philippines, Cuba, Puerto Rico, and other island possessions of the Spanish Empire, only to meet with tenacious military resistance. Americans, who had regarded themselves as liberators, found themselves mired in a series of wars of colonial repression.[58] The powerful disdain for foreign empires that had originally given birth to the United States reasserted itself, and the American leadership, from Teddy Roosevelt to Woodrow Wilson, quickly lost interest in overseas expansion. Both the Philippines and Cuba were soon promised independence. Having experimented with the idea of a great, ideologically fuelled world empire, Americans returned to their national-state tradition—a preference that remained in place until after the Second World War.[59]

But what of the European national states? Even Protestant national states such as England and the Netherlands originally backed away from imperialism only in terms of their aspirations in continental Europe. The might of Catholic Spain had been built on wealth from its vast overseas empire, and these new Protestant powers, as well as the French, sought empires of their own in order to compete financially and militarily. This duality of the independent European powers—nationalist at home, but imperialist insofar as the conquest of the peoples of Asia, America, and Africa were concerned—presents a picture that is in many respects appalling.[60] In the end, aggressive British, French, and Dutch overseas expansion served as a provocation and a model for imperialist ideologies in Germany, Italy, and Japan—ideologies that regarded the entire European national-state system with contempt. In the two World Wars that followed and their aftermath, it was primarily American statesmen who recognized the imperialist roots of the catastrophe, and eventually obtained widespread acceptance for the principle of a nationalist political order.[61]

3. Collective Freedom. Human beings constantly desire and actively seek the health and prosperity of the family, clan, tribe, or nation to which they are tied by bonds of mutual loyalty. Under an order of independent national states, mankind attains the greatest degree of freedom to pursue such collective health and prosperity. Let us understand why this is so.

The order of tribes and clans is one in which the freedom and self-determination of the collective are given great prominence. Here, concern for the material prosperity of the collective, its internal integrity, and cultural inheritance is all-embracing. Nevertheless, it is impossible to say that human beings enjoy the greatest possible degree of collective freedom and self-determination under such an order. For these clans and tribes, although enjoying the benefits of independence, live everywhere at war, to an extent unknown to those of us who have grown up living under the state. And because their efforts are constantly turned toward survival and war against one another, they tend to live in dire poverty, lacking the resources for advancement in the arts and industry, and the attention needed to advance the cultural inheritance they have received from their forefathers. Thus rather than being free to do as they please, each clan or tribe finds that it is in fact enslaved to a life of war and disorder that it cannot escape, even if it might wish otherwise.

Compare these circumstances with the prospects for collective self-determination under a national state. In such a state, a permanent peace has been concluded among a number of competing tribes that share a common language or religion and an earlier history of banding together for the sake of common efforts. Under the protection of the national state, each tribe renounces a measure of its own self-determination, giving up the option of violent responses to the provocations of the other tribes, and exposing itself to the interference of the state. Yet each tribe also gains great advantages in terms of its collective freedom. In part, these advantages stem from the fact that a greater material prosperity is now possible with war having been driven out to the borders of the state. And under these new conditions, each tribe can expand its own abilities in agriculture, in the arts and industry, in learning, and in the practice and development of its religion, each in accordance with its own cultural inheritance.

However, there is also something much more profound that is ushered in by such a national peace. The individual had always been able to see the larger constellation of tribes of which his tribe was a member—the nation—as a unified entity during periods when an alliance was struck to meet outside threats. At those times, he had felt that what happens to the nation is what happens to himself. With the forging of a national state, this condition becomes permanent in his soul. He thinks not only of the great improvement in his tribe's ability to defend itself against external enemies, and of its expanded freedom to pursue material prosperity and the upbuilding of its cultural inheritance under the protection of the national state. He also thinks in terms of the nation as a whole, and of the incalculable improvement in the nation's internal integrity. And he thinks of the nation's enhanced ability to pursue material prosperity, and of its ability to develop its cultural inheritance—the joint cultural inheritance of the tribes that was the basis for establishing the national state in the first place. He now sees the things that happen to the nation as a whole as things that are happening to himself, not only during rare periods of tribal alliance, but always. And while he remains concerned about his own tribe, so long as it is not singled out and threatened by the others, it will be the independent life of the nation that is uppermost in mind. This means that the individual, like the rest of his tribe, will experience a far greater collective freedom and self-determination than he had known before.

The advocates of an imperial or universal state assert that these advantages, which the clans and tribes gain in terms of their collective self-determination in the national state, can be provided as well or better under an imperial state. After all, they say, if tribes can come together in a bond of mutual loyalty to form a national state, why should nations not form a similar bond of mutual loyalty and make of themselves an empire?

But the analogy between the founding of an imperial state and that of a free national state is a false one. The transition from an order of tribes and clans to the national state offers a great improvement in the possibilities for the collective self-determination of the tribes. This is because the great obstacle to the self-determination of clans and tribes when they are armed and politically independent is the incessant harm they do to one another through their relentless warfare. The national state takes advantage of the basis for a genuine mutual loyalty that already exists among these warring tribes—a common language or religion, in addition to a past history of defending one another as allies in the face of common enemies— to establish a unified national government, thus greatly relieving the constant proximity to war, while creating a vast new arena for the expression of a joint self-determination for these tribes.

No such dramatic improvement occurs in the transition from the national state to empire. The national state, if it is internally cohesive and strong, has already driven the violence of war to its borders. Thus while the imperial state may well remove war even further from the territory of the nation, such a change is not, in practice, experienced as being a great improvement in conditions. On the contrary, it means that the

soldiers of the nation, rather than defending their own borders, find themselves far from home and engaged in defending
the territory of foreigners. In exchange for this doubtful benefit, the nation is to come together under a single government
with other nations with which it does not share a language or
religion, and does not share a history of having defended one
another as allies in broader wars, so that the basis for a genuine mutual loyalty is entirely absent. Being yoked together with
alien nations with their own very different cultural inheritance
and their own needs and interests, the nation experiences only
a great loss of collective self-determination. It certainly experiences nothing like the freedom that was felt throughout the
country with the unification of the tribes under an independent national state.

It is now frequently asserted that a nation need not feel
alienated from an empire under which it has been subsumed
together with numerous foreign nations. Why, it is asked,
should a nation not have feelings of loyalty for the imperial
state that provides it with material benefits, and offers it an opportunity to join in the noble cause of unifying mankind? And
it is certainly true that some peoples may benefit greatly from
the favor of the imperial state, even as it reaches out to conquer additional nations. But the same arbitrary imperial power
that at one time confers favor on a subject nation can as easily
revoke this favor. This has, of course, been the historical experience of nations time and again, and in practice, it is senseless
to hope that an imperial state will have a permanent interest
in the welfare of any particular subject nation. The empire has
many other concerns and many other nations vying for its fa-
vors. Circumstances change, and an empire that was steered
in a certain direction comes under the influence of different

officials, with other priorities and other views. In the end, the wheel always turns, and a nation that was once favored awakes and finds itself enslaved. Of course, it was always enslaved, being the subject nation of an imperial state. But in good times, the fact of one's enslavement is easily forgotten.

An imperial state cannot be a free state. It is always a despotic state. It may be a benevolent despotism or a vicious one, depending on the circumstances and the character of its officials at a given moment; and it may be benevolent toward one subject nation while being vicious to another, each in its turn. But in any case, the imperial state does not offer freedom to the nation. Only the national state, governed by individuals drawn from the tribes of the nation itself, can be a free state—because only rulers who are bound to this nation by ties of mutual loyalty, and who experience the things that happen to the nation as things that are happening to themselves, will devote themselves to the freedom and self-determination of this nation on a permanent basis.

It follows that an order of national states will be the order that offers the greatest possibility of collective self-determination to the nations. This conclusion may be stated in terms of the well-known thesis that freedom exists only where multiple, independent centers of power are maintained. This observation is familiar in the economic sphere, where a system dominated by a single corporation or a cartel invariably means others will not have the freedom to compete, regardless of what formal rights they may possess. And it is true in the domestic politics of the nation, in which tribal freedoms and individual liberties are both nearly impossible to maintain if the ruler's power is not restrained by the presence of other centers of power. The same phenomenon is evident at the level of the order of nations as well: A nation can exercise its freedom and self-determination only in a system that is not dominated by a single center of power, the imperial state, whose ability to dictate the law will invariably be brought to bear in due course. Of course, the order of national states, in which multiple centers of power compete, does not in itself guarantee that a given national state will have the resources to withstand outside pressures that may drive it toward policies contrary to the interests of its people. But where there are multiple centers of power, the attempt to resist such pressure can, in principle, find support from other centers of power that may be able to offer assistance. Thus it was by appealing to England and France that the Dutch were ultimately able to secure their self-determination despite pressure from Spain. In the same way, the Americans, having failed to gain independence from Britain, succeeded thanks to infantry and naval forces from France.

This point is well summarized by Vattel, who observed that the entire reason for the principle of the "balance of power" in international affairs, which insists on a constant vigilance lest any one nation gain too much power, is precisely in order to preserve the possibility of national freedom throughout the system of states. As he writes:

> This is what gave birth to that famous idea of the political equilibrium, or the balance of power. By this is meant a disposition of things such that no power is in a state of predominating absolutely, and of making law for the others. . . . [It is best] to have recourse to the method just mentioned, of forming confederacies to stand up to the

most powerful, and to prevent it from giving law. This is what the sovereigns of Europe do today.[62]

Notice that Vattel does not regard the balance of power among nations as being maintained for the sake of peace or stability, as is often said. Rather, the purpose of the balance of power is to ensure that no nation grows so strong that it is in a position of "making law" for the others. Its purpose is, in other words, to preserve the freedom of nations to make law for themselves—which is to say, to preserve their independence and self-determination.

The good of collective self-determination, which our forefathers knew under the order of tribes and clans, thus finds its greatest possible expression in the institution of the national state. A nation that is able to establish peace among its diverse tribes, and resists the urge to expend its resources in attempts to conquer the other nations and impose its own order on them, is one that has set the stage for a life of national freedom—the liberty that is shared by a people that are mutually loyal to one another, and are able to direct their energies to building themselves up in light of their own unique inheritance, without being forced to bow to any other nation or empire. In this way, the human desire for collective freedom and self-determination is preserved and cultivated, and channeled so that it may gain in strength and in the benefits it bestows, while as much as possible reducing the harms that arise by it.[63]

Nor is it the case that only those who are born members of the nation, originally sharing its language, religion, and history, can take part in the collective freedom that is made possible by the national state. The independent national state can and frequently does adopt new tribes and clans that are willing to establish bonds of mutual loyalty to the nation and to bring their unique capabilities to its efforts. Thus the English adopted the Scots, Welsh, and Northern Irish into a broader British nation. The Hindu majority have adopted the Sikhs into the Indian nation, and in Israel, the Jewish majority have likewise adopted the Druze, Bedouin, and other communities that serve together with them in the military.[64] The same is true everywhere in the world, where smaller clans and tribes choose to establish ties of permanent mutual loyalty with a larger nation that is willing to honor their unique traditions and provide for these a place to grow. In this way, these adopted tribes can take part in the nation's freedom, experiencing it as their own, much as the members of the nation's other tribes do.

The cultivation of one's own nation is abhorrent to the imperialist, who regards it as narrow-minded and parochial. But a devotion to the improvement of conditions for one's own people and the upbuilding of one's own inheritance is far superior to a life absorbed in the suppression of foreign rebellions. The self-imposed boundaries of the national state, seemingly narrow and parochial, in fact hold the key to the freedom of the nation, liberating it from the shackles of empire. Thus freed, the national state permits the energies of the national leadership to be directed toward creating a thing of real worth: a unique land and people with a character and truth that is their own.

4. Competitive Political Order. It was the mark of Napoleon's imperialism that he could countenance no states that were not modeled after his own revolutionary regime, in effect establishing one legal system for all of Europe. Even as ancient an institution as the Venetian city-state, whose constitutional traditions had survived for more than a thousand years, was to him no more than an abomination that had to be destroyed.[65] This same conviction that one has grasped the ultimate political truth and that all must now accept it likewise characterized Lenin's thought and Soviet imperialism during its entire seventy-year course. And it appears again in our own time in the doctrines of European Union, which finds no satisfaction in the rule of one nation, but seeks constantly to impose an ever-greater uniformity on all nations in accordance with the political truths its bureaucrats regard as universally evident.

All three of these European imperial states saw themselves as applying, each in its own way, the Enlightenment doctrine of a universal reason, which dictates a single evident political truth for all mankind. The principle of national freedom is premised on an entirely different, and indeed opposite, view of mankind's capacity for knowledge. It is premised on the supposition that political truth is not immediately evident to all, whether through the exercise of reason or by any other means. As John Selden emphasized, human reason is capable of arriving at virtually any conclusion, and has never in history been able to arrive at a single political truth that all can agree upon. Thus the importance of national freedom, which permits each nation to develop its own unique purposes, traditions, and institutions that may be tested through painstaking trial and error over centuries. This conception of the need for a diversity of nations, each pursuing the truth according to its own understanding, is not intended to deny that there are principles of government and morals that are best. What is denied is that these principles are known to anyone who will but exercise reason to try and get to them. The great English philosopher and statesman insisted on the legitimacy of diverse national traditions because of his empiricism: It is only through the many national experiments that we can learn, over historical time, what is in fact best.

The choice between an imperialist and a nationalist politics thus corresponds to a choice between two theories of knowledge: In Western history, at least, imperialism has tended to be associated with a *rationalist* theory of knowledge. Having an unbounded trust in human reason, such a theory is bold in its assertion that the great universal truths are already at hand, and that this knowledge needs now only to be brought to bear on humanity. Nationalism, on the other hand, has tended to be based on an *empirical* standpoint, exercising a moderate skepticism with regard to the products of human reason, and mindful of the calamities that men have brought upon us in the political realm time and again by their over-confidence in their own reason. And being skeptical, it recognizes the wisdom of permitting many attempts to attain the truth, each different from the others. In this way, some experiments will be successful, while others will fail. And those that succeed will do so in different ways, so that the unique experience of each nation will teach us different things that we had not understood before.[66] We may say, in other words, that a nationalist politics invites a great debate among the nations, and a world of experiments and learning. Whereas an imperialist politics declares that this debate is too dangerous or too troublesome, and that the time has come to end it.[67]

A similar argument between rationalist and empiricist theories of knowledge is familiar from economics. The socialist has always believed that the necessary knowledge is at hand, so there is no need for competition in the marketplace. The economy needs only to be directed by a rational planner who will dictate the transactions that are to proceed for everyone's benefit. The capitalist, on the other hand, has understood this proposal to be nothing but a conceit, a product of human arrogance and folly—because in reality there is no human being, and no group of human beings, that possesses the necessary powers of reason and the necessary knowledge to correctly dictate how an entire economy should proceed for everyone's benefit. Instead, the capitalist argues, from a skeptical and empirical point of view, that we should permit many independent economic actors and allow them freely to compete in developing and providing economic products and services. It is understood that because each of these competing business enterprises pursues a different set of aims, and is organized in a manner that is different from the others, some will succeed and some will fail. But those that succeed will do so in ways that no rational planner could have predicted in advance, and their discoveries will then be available for the imitation and refinement of others. In this way, the economy as a whole flourishes from this competition.

The political order is in this respect much like the economic order. The reality is that no human being, and no group of human beings, possesses the necessary powers of reason and the necessary knowledge to dictate the political constitution that is appropriate for all mankind. Anyone tending to a skeptical and empirical point of view will thus recognize the advantages of a nationalist order, which permits many independent national states and allows them freely to compete. Each national state pursues a different set of aims, and is organized in a manner that is different from the others. And yet despite this diversity, the rulers of these independent national states, in constant competition with other members of the order of similar states, are also forever glancing sideways at their competitors to see what is bringing them success, imitating that which they regard as wise and useful and beautiful in the institutions of other nations in order to improve their own. In this way, the rulers of each nation, while concerned principally for the strength and standing of their own nation among its competitors, nevertheless end up sharing with all humanity from their own unique store of experiment and experience.

This competition among independent states explains the fact that those periods of history that we find most admirable in terms of the kinds of individuals they produced, and their fruitfulness in terms of works of science, religion, and art, were periods in which the political order was one of small, independent states in competition with one another, whether national states or tribal city-states. One thinks of ancient Greece and Israel, as well as of the Italian states of the Renaissance and the national states after the Protestant construction of Europe, especially the Netherlands, England, France, and the German states of central Europe. This has been noticed by a long line of empiricist philosophers, among them John Stuart Mill, who attributes Europe's progress to the "plurality of paths" that its political order has allowed:

> What has made the European family of nations an improving, instead of a stationary, portion of mankind? Not of any superior excellence in them—which, when it exists, exists as the effect, not the cause—but their remarkable diversity of culture. Individuals, classes, nations, have been extremely unlike one another. They have struck out a great variety of paths, each leading to something valuable.

And although at every period they have been intolerant
of one another, and each would have thought it an ex-
cellent thing if all the rest could have been compelled to
travel his road, . . . each has in time endured to receive the
good which the others have offered. Europe is . . . wholly
indebted to this plurality of paths.[68]

We cannot pass over the fact that so very great a proportion
of the heritage of mankind has been the product of systems of
independent states, whereas the contribution of imperial states
has been, in comparison, strikingly sparse. An era of competition in an order of independent national states or city-states
seems to offer the greatest opportunities to individuals of ability who can bring advantage to the national state or city-state.
The imperial state naturally promotes an altogether different
environment, ultimately offering a man of ability but one opportunity: to mold himself to the desires of the one great political power that is the empire. And this kind of opportunity, it
seems, comes to little when compared with the flourishing that
is possible under an order of independent national or tribal
states, each jealous of its own health and prosperity, its own
strength and reputation.[69]

This argument for a competitive political order should, as
I have suggested, be appealing to economists, who claim, after
all, to have developed an empirical science, and who should for
this reason welcome the world of experiments that the many
independent nations, each with its own policies, can offer. And
yet we constantly hear economists (and many who have been
schooled in economics) speaking out against the order of independent national states, on the supposition that economic
efficiency would be greatest in a single world market in which

all national boundaries have been removed. As Hayek puts it, a world without national boundaries would be one in which all conflicts of interest would be between "groups of constantly varying composition," rather than between national states with a consistent internal solidarity, and therefore with local policies that remain stubbornly fixed through time.[70] Thus the economist, who prides himself on his empiricism when it comes to the structure of the domestic economy—where he hopes for competition among independent firms so as to permit progress through free innovation—suddenly becomes a rationalist when it comes to thinking about the world economy. When it comes to the world economy, he feels safe in assuming, like every rationalist, that the rules necessary for the flourishing of human economies are already in hand, that a central governing body or bodies can therefore decide the policy appropriate to all mankind, and that from such centralized planning, all will prosper!

It was just such rationalist theories that Margaret Thatcher resisted in Europe, arguing that the attempt to give a central economic body policymaking authority across all nations would have the effect of putting an end to "the diversity and competition between states," which is a "condition for successful free enterprise." As she writes:

> The aim was said to be a "level playing field." The phrase has a reassuring ring to it, but it actually encapsulates a fundamental error about trade. Free trade allows firms in differing nations to compete. But because a "level playing field" stops that part of competition that comes from differing regulative systems, it actually reduces the gains from trade. . . . If harmonization is taken beyond techni-

cal standards and the like, and is also applied to labor laws, social security and taxation, it is profoundly economically destructive. This is because competition between different countries to provide the most conducive international conditions for enterprise is a powerful engine for economic advance.[71]

According to Thatcher's view, a genuinely empiricist approach to economics will favor variation in the economies of different nations. This will be true in economics as it is in every other sphere: The competition among independent national economies will offer the greatest field for experimentation, leading, by means of trial and error, to advances in legal and regulatory structure, in taxation, and in the kinds of trade agreements that are concluded between nations—advances that would not be made in the context of a single economic system imposed on all. Such innovation will be made by independent national states competing with one another, and will be imitated and spread across the globe where they are shown unequivocally to have benefited the nations that first adopted them.

Voluntary coordination among nations has always been desirable where there are evident common interests. Thatcher here mentions cooperation among countries in setting technical standards so as to permit firms to compete across borders, and she could as easily have mentioned collaboration in matters of security, the environment, health, disaster relief, and more. Such cooperation can benefit every nation, so long as it remains strictly within the framework of agreements among fully independent nations, and does not place them under the decision-making authority of international bodies.[72]

5. Individual Liberties. The independent national state is the best institution known to mankind for establishing collective freedom and self-determination. But collective freedom is not identical with the freedom of the individual. Americans expressed their national freedom and self-determination while tolerating slavery and odious race laws for much of their history. The French have a long history of expressing their national freedom through the suppression of languages and religious practices they find offensive. And countless other examples may be adduced in which national independence has not led to the protection of individual freedoms.[73] With this in mind, it has been suggested that individual rights and liberties might more easily be protected in an imperial or universal state, in which a multiplicity of nations, languages, and religious traditions could be accorded a kind of equality—one that cannot exist in a national state, where the language and religious traditions of a single nation are given primacy.[74]

But there is little historical evidence to support the supposition that the imperial state is better suited to protect individual freedom. On the contrary, the imperial states known to us have all been autocratic regimes of one kind or another. Meanwhile, the development of the tradition of individual rights and liberties arose only in national states, and some political theorists have suggested that the national state is the only environment in which free institutions can be made stable. Mill, writing in *Considerations on Representative Government* (1861), speaks for the prevailing nineteenth-century view in arguing that it is "a necessary condition of free institutions that the boundaries of government should coincide in the main with those of nationalities."[75] Nothing that has taken place in the subsequent century and a half has given us reason to believe that his assessment is mistaken. Why should this be?

The tradition of individual rights and freedoms is rooted in the constitution of Moses, and has been developed most diligently and successfully in the laws of England and America. In these countries, the rights and freedoms of the individual have never existed by themselves, but have been part of a more extensive structure of what may be called *free institutions*. These provide that: (i) the laws of the nation are prior to the will of the king (or president) and independent of it; (ii) the powers of the king (or president) are limited by the representatives of the nation, whose advice and consent he must obtain to tax the nation, alter its laws, or appoint officers over them; (iii) the rights of the individual are to be infringed upon by the state only by due process of the laws; (iv) the laws are ordered so as to protect, among others things, the right of the individual to life, marriage, and property, as well as freedom of speech, movement, association, and religion; and (v) public elections are held to designate officials in some branches of government.[76]

In examining these characteristics of free institutions, we see that the freedoms of the individual guaranteed in England and America are not something that the individual simply has "by nature," but are, on the contrary, the result of an intricate machinery developed through many centuries of trial and error. These principles establish extensive rights and freedoms for each individual by balancing the powers of the ruler against those of the various tribes or factions of the nation assembled in the parliament; and by balancing the powers of both the ruler and the strongest tribes or factions against those of independent judges and juries that are tasked with determining the application of the laws to the individual. The functioning of this entire machinery depends, as is immediately obvious, on the willingness of the ruler, and of the strongest tribes or factions in the nation, to permit their powers to be limited in this way. That is, they must agree to a weakening of their own powers, and accept outcomes that are undesirable without seeking restitution through violence.

Under what conditions would the ruler, generally the head of the most powerful tribe or faction in the nation, as well as the heads of the other powerful tribes or factions, agree to be weakened in this way? This is possible only under the conditions that obtain in a national state: conditions in which the heads of the respective tribes or factions are tied to one another by bonds of mutual loyalty; and in which the tribes or factions that they lead are likewise loyal to one another. Where such bonds of mutual loyalty exist, the individual freedoms protected by such a cumbersome machinery of government, and the consequent benefits to the material prosperity and internal integrity of the nation, are experienced as benefits that have been gained by one and all. Where they exist, even the activities of a political faction that one abhors, or of a church one disapproves, or of a newspaper one sees as filled with irresponsible incitement, can be experienced as advancing the cause of the nation because they are expressions of free institutions that are the strength and glory of their nation. We have seen how just such ties of mutual loyalty, arising within the context of the English, Dutch, and American national states, are powerful enough to permit extensive individual rights and liberties to arise. And we have seen these conditions imitated in other national states around the world, often with an impressive degree of success.

But what of an imperial state? Can it not achieve a similar machinery of government, so that it, too, provides for extensive individual rights and freedoms throughout its empire? I have already said that every imperial or universal state must be a despotic state. An argument of this kind was suggested by Mill, himself no stranger to the operation of empires. Observing Austria-Hungary of his day, he saw that the respective nationalities have no way of attaining a mutual loyalty to one another in an imperial state. Sharing neither language nor religion, they cannot recognize themselves as a genuine unity, but rather as competitors, each threatened by the others. There is no such thing as a common political leader, but rather each nation has leaders of its own. Similarly, there are no common publications, and so no common sphere in which a shared knowledge is established, but each nation has its own publications and its own view as to what passes for knowledge of events. Indeed, all that holds these rival nations together is the force of Austrian arms, which is used to suppress the rebellions of each nation in turn.[77] To this analysis I would add that every empire is ultimately held together by the cohesiveness of an actual nation whose members really are tied to one another by bonds of mutual loyalty. In the Austrian empire, this was the German nation, which was able, with the greater or lesser assistance of the Magyars, to rule by force so long as it did not grant extensive freedoms to its other subject nations.

An imperial state such as the Austrian empire is not held together by bonds of mutual loyalty among its various nations. This means that when the imperial state experiences triumph or failure, its subject nations do not experience this as something that has happened to them. Rather, they experience it as something that is happening to someone else: to the ruling nation, and to the helpers it recruits from other nations, who are regarded as having turned their backs on their own

people. Under such conditions, every grant of individual liberties—freedom of speech, for example—is a grant to the various subject nations, who use this new right to press ever more
forcefully for the dissolution of the imperial state. This was the
case for the Austrian empire when, in its last stages, it experimented with free institutions and in so doing hastened its own
demise. And we have seen this, too, in modern multinational
states such as the Soviet Union and Yugoslavia. These states
were held together for generations only by the severest oppression, and immediately disintegrated into their respective nationalities as soon as attempts were made to allow individual
rights and freedoms at the end of the last century.

If we are interested, then, in the establishment of free institutions such as those that have developed within the Anglo-
American political tradition, our first concern must be for the
cohesiveness of the nation. This mutual loyalty, which is derived
from genuine commonalities of language or religion, and from
a past history of uniting in wartime, is the firm foundation on
which everything else depends. Where this bond is, over long
years and through bitter experience, made firm, we will find
that individuals are willing to sacrifice their own momentary
political advantage, or that of their clan or tribe, for the collective good of the nation. This willingness to forsake momentary
advantage may then pave the way for the development of free
national institutions, including traditions of individual rights
and freedoms, much as it paves the way for self-sacrifice in the
defense of the nation against external enemies.

XV: The Myth of the Federal Solution

IMPERIALISM AND NATIONALISM represent irreconcilable positions in political thought. We can endorse the view that the entire earth should be subjected to a single regime whose authority will embrace all nations; or we can seek a world of independent national states as the best form of political order. We cannot embrace both of these views at the same time.

Many writers have struggled to evade this dichotomy, seeking an intermediate or compromise position between these theoretical standpoints. Most commonly, they have proposed that the solution to the dilemma of having to choose between the imperial state and an order of national states is a world federal government, or a similar international regime that would hold the nations accountable for their actions under international law.[78] Immanuel Kant's regime of "perpetual peace," for example, was to be attained through such a world federation.[79] Woodrow Wilson's "sovereignty of mankind" similarly proposed to grant independence and self-determination to the nations, while at the same time establishing an international regime to decide disputes among them and, where necessary, impose its rulings by coercion.[80] Friedrich Hayek, the most important theoretician of liberalism in the last century, likewise argued that the independence of nations causes war, and that peace and prosperity can be achieved only by means of an international federal state.[81]

Such proposals for an international federation are thought to be an improvement over the imperial state, since the international federal government would be restricted to the adjudication of disputes among otherwise independent and self-determining national states. Under the universal federal state, it is said, each nation will remain independent in nearly all things: It will be free to determine its own constitution and laws, follow its own language and religion, conduct its economy, and educate its children according to its own understanding. In short, it will be free to pursue its own course. Only the recourse to violence across borders will be proscribed, and conflicts will be resolved through the institutions of the federal government that rules over the states.

This argument is, however, based on a misunderstanding of what kind of political order is required to establish an international federation of states. In fact, the international federal government that has so often been proposed is indistinguishable from an imperial state in any significant respect. The idea of an international federation simply is the idea of empire. It should be deplored and rejected, along with all other imperialist schemes.

Before I explain myself, I should emphasize that I, too, am concerned for the attainment of peace among nations. The prophets of Israel planted the ideal of peace among nations at the birth of our political tradition, so that we may always recognize that whenever a dispute can be resolved peaceably, the recourse to bloodshed must be considered an unspeakable evil.[82] Nevertheless, the world described by the prophets is one in which nations will bring their disputes to Jerusalem to be adjudicated freely. It is not an international federal state with the ability to compel adjudication and impose its decisions by force. These are, in fact, two entirely different aims for the future of humanity, reflecting an aspiration to attain two entirely different forms of political order:

A. *Voluntary adjudication.* Nations in conflict choose whether to submit a dispute for adjudication, and the choice of whether to comply with the decision of the judge or adjudicating body remains in the hands of these independent nations.

B. *Compulsory adjudication.* Nations are compelled to submit a dispute for adjudication by the officials of the international federal state, and compliance with the decision is likewise enforced by the agents of the international federal state.

The conditions described in these two scenarios reflect two different forms of political order with which we are already familiar: Under scenario A, voluntary adjudication of disputes takes place within an order of independent national states. When we refer to the independence of these states, we mean precisely that there is no international authority that can compel them to submit a dispute for adjudication, and none that can force them to abide by the terms of the decision if they choose not to do so. Whereas under scenario B, compulsory adjudication takes place precisely because of the existence of an international authority that is able to settle disputes among nations whether they wish it or not. And exactly this is a defining characteristic of an imperial political order. Although the entities that are in conflict may be called "states," they are not independent and self-determining entities. They have no choice as to whether a given matter will be removed from their hands to be determined by the international federal government, for the power to make such a determination rests with that international body. Likewise, they have no choice as to who will decide the matter or when, for this decision too rests with the international government. Nor do they have any choice as to whether to abide by the decision that is made by the international government, for it will be imposed upon them by force if necessary—again according to a decision that is entirely in the hands of the international federal government.

The choice between these two scenarios is thus, inevitably, a choice between an order of independent national states and an imperial order. The fact that philosophers and statesmen may prefer, for the sake of appearances, to refer to alternative B as a "federation of independent nations" rather than as an imperial state does not affect the substance of what is being proposed. The decisions as to how member nations will conduct their own affairs are to be made at the level of the imperial state.

As has been said, advocates of an international federation claim that the national state will retain its freedom in everything other than matters of war and peace. They say that the federation will be conducted in accordance with a written charter—a binding document that will enumerate those matters in which the international federation may intervene, leaving the rest of the powers of government in the hands of the states as a matter of legal right.

However, the supposition that an international federal government can somehow be constrained so that it will interfere only in certain prescribed matters is false, as can be seen both by considering the principle itself and by examining the historical practice of federal institutions.

With respect to principle, let us suppose that a state files a complaint (or a lawsuit) with the international federal government concerning the policies or practices of a neighboring state. The complaint may be with respect to the establishment of military bases on its borders or the rapid expansion of its neighbor's armed forces and arms industries. Or it may be about the neighboring state's suppression of certain national minorities or religious sects, which have asked repeatedly for outside relief. Or the plaintiff state may see itself as being harmed by the economic practices of its neighbor, or by the encouragement of illegal immigration across its border, or by the rise of drug cartels or terrorist organizations on the other side of the border. Or by the over-utilization or destruction of a joint water supply or other shared resources. Or by interference in its elections or its internal politics. Or by espionage or assassinations or public disturbances that it regards as having been instigated by its neighbor. Or by what it sees as hostile propaganda in its neighbor's media and schools. In other words, virtually any significant action or policy by one state can become a genuine motive for military action—and if not that, then at least a concocted pretext for military action. And now, after months or years of failed attempts to resolve the matter by way of agreements, bribes, and threats, the leadership of the plaintiff state, on the verge of deciding to resolve the matter by force, turn to the institutions of the international federation with the aim of having a solution imposed so that war may be prevented.

Who, then, will determine whether the complaint (or suit) is considered by the officials of the international federation? Who will determine whether the complaint justifies interference by the international federation in accordance with its charter? And if the federation interferes in the dispute, who will determine which side is right? Who will determine what remedies are needed to end the dispute? And if one or both of the parties refuse to accept the federation's decisions, who will impose these remedies through coercion or military action?

The obvious answer is that all of these things will be decided by the international federal authorities. Because if these decisions are not in the hands of the federal authorities, then we have returned to scenario A: Each national state will itself determine whether it participates in the federation's examination of the matter; and each will decide, as well, whether to comply with the federation's decisions once these have been made. In this case, this is no international federation, but simply an association for the voluntary arbitration of disputes among independent national states. But if it is the officials of the international federal government who answer the questions for themselves, and if they possess sufficient coercive authority to impose a solution, then we are observing a proceeding for the peaceful resolution of a dispute within an imperial state in accordance with scenario B.

But now notice what this means. The supposition that the international federation will interfere "only" in matters of war and peace has already been shown to be nonsensical. Any intervention to prevent a war or to end one will require a resolution of grievances—and these, as we have seen, can include any action or policy undertaken by a neighboring state if it is seen as sufficiently provocative or irritating. The mandate of the international federation to interfere in matters of war and peace is thus as broad as each state's list of grievances against its neighbors, both real and fabricated. The attempted resolution of these grievances through federal interference, to the extent that it is taken seriously, inevitably means curtailing the independence of the accused nation—and perhaps also of the plaintiff nation—in areas such as its military and security policies; its economic, immigration, and environmental policies; its religious and cultural policies; and ultimately its constitution and laws. In all these matters, the only barrier to federal usurpation of the rights of independent states under an international federal regime is the self-restraint of the officials of the international federation themselves. Nothing in our experience of human government suggests that these federal officials will be capable of such restraint. On the contrary, once charged with so weighty a task as that of "bringing peace" to the region in question, they will believe that they have no choice but to interfere vigorously in the hope of reshaping the warring nations until they match the international federation's expectations of what a compliant member nation should look like.

This analysis should not be interpreted as an objection to federalism itself, which can be a useful instrument of government. Every nation has within it various tribes, each with its unique customs, including, possibly, its own language, laws, and religion. A well-governed national state will often permit each tribe a measure of freedom to chart its own course, devolving or delegating to it authority in various areas, so long as it is not felt to pose a threat to the internal integrity of the national state as a whole. Under favorable circumstances, such a policy permits the tribes to feel that they have a greater degree of collective freedom and self-determination, while the nation as a whole benefits from the innovations that arise out of diversity and competition among them. Federalism is, in other words, what remains of the order of tribes and clans once they have ceased to live as independent entities with a right to wage war on one another. Because it maintains, in a weakened form, the original structure of human political organization, federalism preserves some of the benefits of this structure, and hewing to it in moderation will often be advantageous for the national state. This is no less true of an imperial state, which will like-wise find that it is advantageous to permit its subject nations to retain a measure of authority in certain spheres, and for this reason will often institute a federal structure of one kind or another—as the Persians awarded the Jews military and legal autonomy in Jerusalem, and as the British awarded the American colonies autonomy within the framework of their empire.

But a delegation of authority under a federal system never amounts to a grant of independence to the tribes or nations that are ruled under this system. It is not independence because the government that sits at the top of the federal structure remains responsible for determining the appropriate degree of delegated authority at all times. And where this federal government comes to regard the degree of authority that has been delegated to be too extensive, it finds the appropriate rationale for circumscribing it, if not today then tomorrow.

This has been demonstrated time and again in the United States, perhaps the most celebrated experiment in federal government. As is well known, the thirteen American colonies originally asserted their independence from Britain as a coalition of independent states. This is to say that, as in ancient Israel or in the Greek city-state system, independence originally remained with each tribe. The wisest among the Americans, seeing that they shared a common language, laws, religion, and history, sought to prevent conditions of constant warfare among the former colonies by uniting them under a single national state. The Constitution proposed in 1787, which permitted this unification and the creation of an American national state, was federal in character, reserving broad powers to the thirteen states.[83] But once the national government had been formed, it inevitably regarded itself as responsible for the material flourishing, internal integrity, and cultural inheritance of the nation as a whole, and its actions were in keeping with this responsibility. As president, Thomas Jefferson, for example, did everything in his power to overthrow the Protestant constitutional and religious order in Massachusetts and Connecticut, which he regarded as a threat to the cultural inheritance of the entire nation.[84] Abraham Lincoln went further, waging war against the secession of the Southern states and the appalling right they asserted to own and enslave human beings.[85] Successive federal governments fought the practice of Mormon polygamy in Utah until finally destroying it. Later, the federal government intervened in the internal affairs of recalcitrant states to overturn race laws against blacks, and to enforce uniform national moral standards with respect to matters such as Bible education and prayer in public schools, abortion, and homosexual unions. And many other examples could easily be named.

Throughout the history of American federalism, the national government has thus used the powers at its disposal to force the states to conform their constitutional and religious traditions to the range of behaviors it has considered acceptable. In this way, the original promise of a broad self-determination at the level of the states has been gradually revoked.[86] I do not mention this in order to object to it—I regard the racial oppression of the blacks in the American South as especially disgraceful, and so am sympathetic to the steps that were taken to uproot it. Nevertheless, it is important to recognize what the American national government's progressive revocation of rights and freedoms that had been reserved to the states in a written Constitution and Bill of Rights teaches us about the nature of federal government in general. There is no reason to believe that any federal scheme of government can be more enduring or successful than the American one. Yet we learn from the American case that the self-determination of the federated tribes or subdivisions (such as the Congregationalist states of New England, the slave-holding Southern states, or Mormon Utah) will not be permitted by the officials of a national government after such self-determination has been recognized to be a threat to the material prosperity, integrity, or cultural inheritance of the nation as a whole. No matter how generously a federal system is constructed, and no matter how unequivocally constitutional documents may set aside certain rights on behalf of its federated tribes, it is the officials of the national government who, in the end, determine the extent to which rights and powers are delegated to the federated tribes or subdivisions—and these will be reduced and abrogated, by coercion if necessary, in keeping with the views that pervade the national government as to the good of the nation.

The American case was in many respects quite favorable to maintaining a generous distribution of powers under a federal structure: The states united under American federalism shared the English language and common-law inheritance, the Protestant religion, and a joint history of struggle against adversity and eventual triumph, making it relatively easy for them to regard themselves as one nation tied by bonds of mutual loyalty. In comparison, the international federation proposed by philosophers and statesmen is a far more difficult enterprise. It supposes that a federal regime may be established to unite nations that have no shared language, laws, or religion, and no genuine history of joining together to fight a common enemy. The differences among these federated nations would thus be radically more pronounced than those that divided the American states. And when these differences give rise, as they inevitably must, to political confrontation, the government of this federation of nations will be faced with two alternatives: Either it will have the resources and the resolve needed to impose its will on the recalcitrant nations subservient to it, in which case it will be an imperial state in every sense. Or it will lack the resources and the resolve to impose its will, in which case it will fly apart into its constituent nations once more, just as the American federation would have disintegrated if its leadership had not been willing to coerce recalcitrant states.

This is what we see happening in the most prominent current experiment with international federation, the European Union. Established by the 1992 Treaty of Maastricht, the EU joins together dozens of formerly independent nations under the principle of "subsidiarity"—a medieval Catholic term now increasingly used in place of the American word *federalism,* with its strong biblical connotations.[87] The treaty explains the intentions of its framers as follows:

> In areas which do not fall within its exclusive competence, the Community shall take action, in accordance with the principle of subsidiarity, only if and in so far as the objectives of the proposed action cannot be sufficiently achieved by the Member states and can therefore, by reason of the scale or effects of the proposed action, be better achieved by the Community.[88]

Here, the Maastricht Treaty states explicitly what was left ambiguous in the American Constitution: The European government will make decisions for its subsidiary national states, both in those areas reserved to it by the treaty, and, in addition, in other areas in which "the objectives of the proposed action . . . [can] be better achieved by the Community." Since the decision as to which objectives can be better achieved by the federal European government is in the hands of the officials of this government itself, there is no barrier to the constant reduction of the authority of the member national states other than the self-restraint of these same officials. This restraint has not, however, been forthcoming, and the EU bureaucracy, backed by federal European courts, has consistently extended its powers over member nations in areas such as economic policy, labor and employment policy, public health, communications, education, transportation, the environment, and urban planning. The European principle of subsidiarity is thus nothing other than a euphemism for empire: The subsidiary nations of Europe are only independent insofar as the European government decides that they will be independent.[89]

The obviously imperial character of the European federal government has been consistently obscured, however, by claims that the European Union has discovered a new "transnational" form of political order, to which the traditional categories used to describe political institutions can no longer be applied. Partisans of the EU frequently deny, for example, that the loss of political independence suffered by the member national states of Europe has resulted in the establishment of a federal government, as one might suppose. Instead, Europe is said to have devised a new form of "pooled sovereignty," under which there is no government, only a joint "governance." And of course, if there is no European federal government, then it is impossible to say that this federal government has established an imperial political order.

But all of this is make-believe. The European Union does, despite the propaganda, have a powerful central government whose directives are legally binding on European nations and on their individual members. This government consists of a large lawmaking bureaucracy whose directives are imposed on Europe's subsidiary nations through their law-enforcement agencies and judicial systems, which are subject to European federal courts. Various appointed and elected bodies have the power to ratify these laws or to decline to do so, although ultimate authority remains with the judicial hierarchy.[90] It is true that none of this reminds us of the institutions of a free government. But it is certainly a kind of government: It is the kind of bureaucratic autocracy that imperial states have historically used to govern their subsidiary nations. Transnationalism and pooled sovereignty are not, in other words, a brilliant new discovery in political theory. They are simply a return to Europe's imperial past.

The European Union does differ from the historical imperial states that are its predecessors in one important way, however: It lacks a strong executive—an emperor—capable of conducting foreign affairs and waging war. That the EU lacks such an executive is largely due to its ongoing status as a protectorate of the United States, which has been responsible for maintaining the peace and security of Europe since the Second World War through the agency of the North Atlantic Treaty Organization (NATO). The American president is, in other words, the commander-in-chief of Europe's armed forces—a fact that was emphasized once again in the recent NATO wars against Serbia. This is to say that the president, in effect, plays the role of the emperor in today's Europe. More than anything else, this arrangement is a consequence of the fact that neither Americans nor Europeans are especially enthusiastic about the alternative, which is German rearmament and a German emperor. The European nations are, as everyone understands, dominated by Germany. The European Union is a German imperial state in all but name. However, as long as Germany seeks to avoid building up its military and taking responsibility for the security of the continent, the EU will apparently remain an American protectorate—a protectorate that is also an empire in its own right. Should the United States ever withdraw its protection, all the talk of Europeans pioneering a new form of political order will quickly evaporate. At that time, a strong European executive will be appointed by Germany and empowered to maintain the security of the continent. Then the reconstitution of the medieval German empire in Europe will be complete, and the English-inspired experiment with an order of independent national states in Europe will have reached its end.

The truth, then, is that there is no "federal solution" that can allow us to evade the choice between an imperial order and an order of independent nations. An international federal government is nothing other than an imperial government—and this is so whether one prefers to look to American or European precedents. Any international federation will be ruled by officials with views of their own as to the appropriate limits that are to be placed on the self-determination of subject nations. No founding documents, no matter how well crafted, can stand over time as an effective barrier against the views of these officials. For it is they who have the authority to interpret these documents and thus to determine the course of affairs. They will interpret, ignore, or alter any documents in light of their own understanding of what is required for the health and prosperity of the imperial state—which they will inevitably, and in accordance with long-standing tradition, identify with the health and prosperity of mankind as a whole.

XVI: The Myth of the Neutral State

THE MEMBERS OF EVERY nation are geographically dispersed and mixed with other national populations. Moreover, history and topography place constraints on what territories the national state can hold and defend. These things mean that in practice, the national state never governs all members of the nation; and it always governs some populations that belong to other nations, whether greater or smaller. The entire Polish people does not live in Poland, nor are there only Poles living within that country's borders, and the same can be said of the Irish in Ireland, the Hindus in India, the Turks in Turkey.

Given these inevitable circumstances, it has often been asked why the order of independent states should consist of national states—that is, of states that express the self-determination of a given nation. Would the political order not be more just and peaceable if it were built around what is often called a *neutral state* (or a *civic state*), which would be without particularistic commitments to any of the different nations, languages, or religions within its borders? Such a state, it is said, would concern itself only with the common defense of the population, keeping the peace, and ensuring the rights and freedoms of the individual. The individual members of the respective nations or tribes could still freely pursue their collective efforts at self-determination, strengthening their own languages and religious traditions to the extent that they so choose. The apparatus of the state, however, would maintain a strict neutrality with respect to all such efforts. Proponents point to the United States, France, and Britain

as examples, claiming that these states have been so successful precisely because they are constituted as neutral states in
this sense.[91]

But the truth is that the neutral state is a myth. It is invoked time and again by those who imagine that the state can
exist in the absence of national or tribal cohesion—when in
reality it is only national or tribal cohesion that permits an independent state to be established and maintained without un-
ceasing political repression. The picture of the neutral state
is utopian in the same way that socialist descriptions of the
economy are utopian: The socialist wishes to have the prosperity that is possible under a market economy, but he wishes
to have it without the profit motive that makes this prosperity
possible in reality. In the same way, advocates of the neutral
state wish for the vigorous physical defense of the population,
obedience before the laws, and guarantees of individual freedoms that are possible in the national state, but they wish to
have these things without the mutual bonds of national or
tribal loyalty that make them possible in reality. This has been
said many times, so I will limit myself to adding only a few observations of my own.[92]

The ideal of the neutral or civic state involves a separation
of nation and state, very much along the lines envisioned by
Jefferson in his call for a "separation of church and state."[93]
The precise meaning of this proposed separation is that the individual is not expected to obey the laws of the state, pay taxes,
and serve in the armed forces out of a loyalty to his own tribe
or nation, which is what attaches the individual to the state
and moves him to do all of these things in a national state. The
central question for such an ideal is then this: If it is not loyalty
to the tribe or nation that moves the individual to shoulder

such onerous burdens, what will be the source of his motivation to make such sacrifices in the neutral state? Recognizing that some such motivation is needed, advocates of the neutral state propose that individuals should be loyal to the constitutional documents of the state, and to the various symbols that the officials of the state have invented to represent these constitutional documents in the minds of the population. Such a "constitutional patriotism" is commonly associated with its best-known advocate, the German philosopher Jürgen Habermas. But similar proposals are now heard in America as well, where a love of the founding documents (or the "American creed" that they supposedly contain) is now frequently invoked as a substitute for an attachment to the American nation itself.[94]

Is this possible? Can there be a state in which laws are obeyed, taxes levied, and soldiers conscripted for war by virtue of a widespread loyalty to the written constitution of the state?

We do know of instances of what seems to be such loyalty to a written document. Throughout history, Muslims have placed themselves at risk to protect their own founding document, the Koran, from being harmed or denigrated. Hindus have a similar veneration for the Vedas, and Jews for the *tora*, the scroll of books of Moses which is in effect their constitution. In the historical Christian world as well, many were once motivated to make sacrifices to protect certain sacred texts and images from damage or desecration. These and similar examples strengthen the sense that a motivating reverence for a constitutional document is within the realm of possibility. From experience, it does appear that if one were to press the public respect for the constitution in the direction of a genuinely religious awe, a political tradition of such a motivating reverence for the constitutional documents of the state could in this way be developed.[95]

What is impossible, however, is that such a sacralization of the constitutional documents of the state should take place without the framework of family, tribal, and national traditions in which the individual learns to revere and hold sacred certain things and not others. As a child, I was constantly exposed to the veneration of the *tora* in the synagogue. I sensed this veneration in the way the adults stepped forward to kiss the scroll when it was brought out to be read three times each week, and in the way the scroll was lifted high over our heads so that all could glimpse the hand-copied writing on the parchment. Moreover, I knew that if the *tora* were ever dropped to the floor, the congregation would fast for a month in penance, and gasped, along with the rest of the congregation, if I saw the scroll totter as it was raised. In these and many other ways, I experienced the reverence of the clan—for the congregation has long been, among Jews and Christians, the equivalent of the clan—as my own. This is to say that reverence for the *tora* and loyalty to it is learned by children as an inseparable aspect of their loyalty to their family and clan, who themselves display their veneration for the *tora* as an inseparable aspect of their loyalty to the Jewish nation. Christians, Muslims, and Hindus maintain an awe for their sacred texts and objects that is strikingly similar, and they cultivate it in each generation of children in analogous ways.

The sacred comes into existence only in the customs of the family, clan, tribe, and nation. There are certainly individuals and families that attach themselves to these sacred things in adulthood, but for most human beings an awareness of sacredness arises together with the bonds of mutual loyalty we form in our childhood and youth. This means that far from being able to replace loyalty to the tribe and nation, the constitutional documents of the neutral state will be revered and will become objects of loyalty precisely to the extent that the tribe or nation to which we are loyal transmits the sacredness of these documents to each new generation of children. The written documents would thus be the cultural inheritance of certain tribes or of a certain nation, and, once again, the loyalty of the individual to his tribe or nation—rather than a distinct and independent loyalty to the documents themselves—would be the source for any actions he is willing to undertake in defense of the neutral state. The same would apply to any other supposedly neutral offices, symbols, or rituals of the state that might be devised by its officers. The reverence for all such documents and symbols would be an artifact of a particular tribal or national tradition, and so not neutral at all. And this is precisely how they would be seen by those minority nations and tribes that are not tied by bonds of mutual loyalty to the national majority in the state, and do not regard what happens to the national majority as if it were happening to themselves. Far from being regarded with reverence as symbols of the neutral state, these documents and symbols would be seen by alienated national and tribal minorities as the quasi-religion of a different nation or tribe, and as hypocrisy to the extent that neutrality is claimed for them.

There are no neutral states. What holds a free state together is the mutual loyalty of the members of the majority nation or tribe, and their loyalty to the state—this in addition to the alliances, whether ad hoc or long-term strategic alignments, that this majority nation or tribe makes with others in order to stabilize and solidify the state. Every free state is, in other words, a national or tribal state.[96] Similarly, in despotic regimes, we find that the government is almost always controlled by a single tribe or clan or family that, together with certain allies, holds the great majority in check through fear and bribery.

How, then, is the myth of a neutral state, in which the state has been separated from the nation, able to persist? This myth depends, above all else, on the claim, mentioned above, that successful Western states such as the United States, Britain, or France are examples of neutral or civic states, and that these states have been successfully separated from any attachment to the nations or tribes that constitute them. There is, however, no basis for such a claim. The United States is held together by the bonds of mutual loyalty that unite the American nation, an English-speaking nation whose constitutional and religious traditions were originally rooted in the Bible, Protestantism, republicanism, and the common law of England.[97] The passage of centuries, and the incorporation of a large Catholic community and other smaller communities, means, in effect, that new tribes have been adopted into this same American nation. But this has not in any way changed the fact that Americans remain a single, highly distinctive nation.[98] No territory has yet been admitted into the American Union as a state before a clear majority of English-speaking settlers was established in it. The dominance of Native American or Spanish-speaking peoples, or speakers of Polynesian languages in Hawaii, has always been averted.[99] The continued presence of the native peoples of the land—such as a politically autonomous Navajo nation, which numbers in the hundreds of thousands and educates its children in the language and traditions of their people to this day—bears witness to the fact that the American nation, despite its overwhelming dominance in the United States, is still a nation like all others.[100] The same can be said of the French nation, which has over centuries maintained its cohesion by means of aggressive, and at times horrific, campaigns to uproot Occitan and other languages that were perceived as undermining the unity of the French nationality; and of the English nation, which was forged through centuries of wars to drive back the Celtic peoples on its periphery.[101]

The supposedly neutral or civic nature of states such as the United States, Britain, and France is thus illusory. The strength and stability of these free states is entirely the result of the overwhelming dominance of the American, English, and French nations over any and all competing nations or tribes within their borders—a dominance that was achieved in all three cases through the destruction of any significant competitors over centuries. It is the internal cohesion of these nations that makes the national states in question possible, and the cultural inheritance of these nations that establishes the character of each of their respective states. If there is anything to be learned from these states, it is that the overwhelming dominance of a single nationality within a given state allows for the growth of free institutions, including individual rights and liberties, that an internally divided state—that is, a *non-national state*—cannot, in general, either develop or maintain.[102]

One of the most striking features of the political order established with the retreat of the European empires in the last century is how many of the newly independent states that have been created in the Middle East, Africa, and elsewhere are non-national states in exactly this sense. That is, the English, French, and Dutch, in departing many conquered lands, did not generally elect to follow the pattern of their own successful model, drawing state borders that reflected national and tribal boundaries. Perhaps this was because these former imperial rulers did not wish to be bothered with redrawing arbitrary colonial borders, or engaging in large-scale population transfers so as to attain a reasonable fit between state borders and national populations. Or perhaps it was because, on the contrary, they actually preferred to establish states with arbitrary rather than national or tribal boundaries, recognizing full well that this would make these territories nearly impossible to govern, and thus easier to manipulate and control from afar. But whatever the reasons, it is remarkable that most of the new states established by imperial powers were brought into being as non-national states.

Thus, for example, the state of Iraq attained its independence from imperial Britain in 1932 as a consequence of boundaries drawn in negotiation with France. There had never in history been an "Iraqi" nation prior to this, but the British, ignoring national and religious boundaries, nonetheless asserted that such a nation could be created by forcing together Kurdish, Assyrian, Sunni Arab, and Shia Arab tribes, among others—peoples sharing neither language nor religion, nor a prior history of united action. They were called a nation and given a written constitution, a flag, and the right to send ambassadors the world over, as well as various other symbols of a national state. All these things were done with the aim of establishing that this new state of Iraq was in fact a national state in the same way that England or France or America is a national state. However, there was no truth in any of this. In reality, Sunni Arabs were the dominant tribal group, holding the state together through the ruthless oppression of the much larger population of Shiite Arabs. The large Kurdish population never accepted Arab rule. The poison gassing in 1988 of Kurds in Halabja by the Sunnis in Iraq is only the best-known example of the unspeakable brutality that the Sunni Arab regime felt it needed to exercise in order to maintain the integrity of the state. The American attempt to save the country by forcibly reconstituting it as a Western democracy, complete with a new written constitution guaranteeing individual liberties in 2005, quickly ended in failure and a terrible civil war.

A similar fate has befallen Syria, which was established as an independent state by the French in 1946. There had never in history been a "Syrian" nation prior to this, the name itself having been invented by the Greeks to describe this geographic region. Yet contrary to the evident facts, the Alawite, Druze, Kurd, Assyrian Christian, and Sunni Arab tribes in this arbitrarily drawn territory were declared a nation. The result has been that this mass of violently opposed groups lived through two decades of chronic instability and state oppression until the Alawites, a non-Muslim nationality or tribe with a religion and historic identity of its own, were finally able to seize power. Establishing a minority alignment together with Christians and Druze, they imposed a reign of terror on the majority Sunni Arab population, up to and including the famous destruction of the Sunni city of Hama by the Alawites. In the present decade, the Alawites have continued to prevent the establishment of a Sunni Arab regime at a cost of half a million deaths and the displacement of perhaps half the population of the country.

Compare these states to their close neighbor, Israel, which was founded at almost the same time. Israel was established in 1948 as a national state for the Jewish people after the withdrawal of the British from the country. Its purpose, as reflected in its Declaration of Independence and numerous laws of the state, was to permit the self-determination of the Jews as a

nation. As such, it absorbed millions of destitute Jewish refugees from Arab lands, Iran, central Europe, the Soviet Union,
and elsewhere. These Jewish immigrants have been offered
freedom from persecution, economic opportunity, and public
schools where their children can be introduced to the heritage of their people by learning Hebrew, Jewish history, and the
Bible. Israel has, in other words, conducted itself as the national state of a particular people. Yet at the same time, Israel
has also developed free institutions, which permit its minority
national and tribal groups to conduct their religious practices
as they see fit, and to educate their children in their own languages and cultural inheritance. Indeed, Israel is the only state
in the Middle East today in which Christians, Druze, and others
can openly practice their religions without fear for their lives.

What gives Israel the ability to flourish as a free state, even
offering extensive protections to national and tribal minority
groups, while states such as Syria and Iraq have at no point attained stability except through the most bloodthirsty state terror? There is a single principle that distinguishes these states
from one another: Israel has from the moment of its founding been constituted as a national state. This means, first, that
there is, both within the country and outside its borders, an
actual Jewish nation. The various Jewish tribes have in common
the Jewish religion and law, the Hebrew language, and a history
of unifying in the face of adversity extending back thousands
of years. In addition, these tribes united voluntarily to establish
the Jewish national state for the purposes of advancing their
collective self-determination. In Israel, this Jewish nation has
been the overwhelming majority of the population since the
founding of the state. The symbols and character of the state
have been derived from the national and religious traditions of

the Jews, reflecting the collective self-determination of which this independent state is an expression.[103]

Much of what has been written about nationalism in recent decades asserts that a state constituted as a national state will be less cohesive, and therefore both less stable and more oppressive, than a neutral or civic state. According to this argument, a national state entails special privileges for members of the majority nation in the state, thereby inciting resentment, resistance, and violence on the part of minority nationalities. The majority is then forced to respond with oppression in order to maintain its special status. In this way, there begins a "cycle of violence" that cannot be broken.

Experience, however, teaches the opposite. The overwhelming dominance of a single, cohesive nationality, bound together by indissoluble bonds of mutual loyalty, is in fact the only basis for domestic peace within a free state. By this I do not mean that the entire population must be drawn from a single nationality, for no such thing exists anywhere on earth. Moreover, there is no evidence that such a complete homogeneity is necessary for the cohesion, stability, and success of the state. Rather, what is needed for the establishment of a stable and free state is a majority nation whose cultural dominance is plain and unquestioned, and against which resistance appears to be futile. Such a majority nation is strong enough not to fear challenges from national minorities, and so is able to grant them rights and liberties without damaging the internal integrity of the state. Similarly, the national minorities that stand against such a national majority are themselves largely reluctant to engage in confrontations that they know they cannot win. For the most part, they therefore assimilate themselves into the system of expectations established by the constitutional and religious culture of the majority nation, learning its language and resorting to violence only on rare occasions. This has been the case in the most successful national states such as Britain, America, France, and other countries in Europe, in addition to national states such as Australia, Japan, Korea, Thailand, Turkey, India, and Israel. In each case, the overwhelming dominance of a single majority nation has produced states that are dramatically more stable, prosperous, and tolerant than neighboring states that have not been constituted as national states.[104]

Where the state is not constituted as a national state, precisely the opposite happens: The various nations or tribes that have been forcibly thrown together, having no common language or religion and no history of collaboration against common enemies, cannot form bonds of mutual loyalty, and so cannot become a nation. They battle for power until one national or tribal group does eventually seize control of the government. But because the population remains internally divided along national and tribal lines, this seizure of power does nothing to alter the fundamental unsoundness of the state. What prevents utter ruin are the bonds of mutual loyalty that unite the national or tribal group that has seized the government, and the iron hand of its leadership, which keeps all others afraid. In this way, the non-national state inevitably tilts toward a despotic regime, and finally, once the despotism of the state can no longer be held in place, dissolution. Not only Syria and Iraq, but states such as the Soviet Union, Yugoslavia, Czechoslovakia, Lebanon, Yemen, Sudan, Nigeria, and Congo, all of which were multinational entities claiming some kind of neutrality among the various nations under their aegis, exploded into civil war or simply collapsed.[105]

XVII: A Right to National Independence?

I HAVE PROPOSED THAT the best political order is one of independent national states. My view resembles that of Mill, who saw the independence of national states as an evident good and urged that such states should be established where this is feasible.[106] Such a position does not, however, require that we take the additional step of endorsing a universal right to national independence and self-determination, applicable to all peoples, as suggested by Woodrow Wilson.[107] And in fact, it seems that there can be no such right. I will here explain why this is so, and what it means for the making of foreign policy and the advancement of the order of national states.[108]

Much of present-day political discourse is concerned with the assertion of various natural and universal rights that are said to belong to individuals and collectives. In these discussions, there is often too easy a transition from the recognition that something is a good to the assertion that all individuals or nations have a "right" to this good. In reality, not everything that is good can be delivered to every individual or nation: The availability of one good to the individual forestalls the possibility of his attaining another; or else it deprives other individuals of various goods; or else its availability today results in a much more severe deterioration of conditions tomorrow; and so forth. This means that which goods can be made available is a practical matter that cannot be determined without trial and error in actual societies. True rights, those that incur obligations on others to take action, are for this reason incalculable without reference to the constraints of real-world contexts. For example, we can say that a good political regime will be one in which individuals do not suffer from hunger, and in which they are protected from the ravages of war. However, acknowledging these things as aspects of the political good is not equivalent to recognizing a right to them. An obligation to prevent every instance of hunger can exist, potentially, only in a society possessing the economic and logistical resources to carry out such a mission; just as a right not to be called to war can only exist, potentially, in a society whose armed forces are strong enough, and whose neighbors are peaceable enough, to permit such a guarantee to be made good. And the same can be said of many other universal rights that have been asserted over the last two centuries without considering whether the resources exist to make them available. It is difficult to understand how the mere naming of a good, where the resources to deliver it do not exist, can be said to entail a right, which is an obligation that is to be borne by others.

This is the case with respect to the proposed universal right to national independence. The best political order that is known to us is an order of independent national states. This is not to say, however, that every nation has a right to be independent. In suggesting that national aspirations would be respected, and that no people would be governed any longer against its will, Wilson was suggesting a certain view of what is good or best. But he was also asserting a right of peoples not to be governed against their will, and therefore an obligation, to be borne by others, to guarantee this outcome. The assertion of such a right and such an obligation assumes a world in which it is possible to make clear-cut determinations as to what constitutes a nation deserving independence, and in which there are resources sufficient to the task of securing an independent national state wherever a plausible claim to one is advanced. But the world of nations is not so clear-cut. Nor are there remotely sufficient resources available for granting such a universal right in every case where a plausible claim can be made.

Consider first the matter of determining what constitutes a nation. There are in the world today thousands of stateless peoples.[109] In India alone, 1,700 entirely distinct languages are spoken; another 1,500 are spoken in Africa, 700 in Indonesia, and a great many more throughout the world. Each of these languages is spoken by a distinct nation or tribe with a cultural inheritance of its own that could, under certain circumstances, make it a candidate for independence. Yet even the vast number of peoples that is suggested by a glance at the linguistic charts does not give us the full picture of the problem. The fact is that there is no way to place a downward boundary on what may be reasonably called a nation. Every nation can be reduced to its tribes, and each tribe to its clans—each with its own dialect, its own unique religious and cultural inheritance, and its own history. And every one of these will also, under certain circumstances, demand its own right to independence and self-determination. Of course, the condition in which every tribe and clan asserts its independence, insisting on a right to govern itself, conduct its own foreign policy, and wage war, is precisely what we recognize as an order of tribes and clans.[110]

By definition, an order of national states—understood as distinct from a tribal or feudal order—involves the aggregation and mutual cohesion of many such tribes and clans, which have given up their supposed right to govern themselves, conduct foreign policy, and wage war, in order to form larger, independent national states whose tribes are internally at peace. The principle of collective self-determination, if transformed into a universal right of independence for every tribe or clan that asserts it, is just the opposite of such an order of national states: It promises the dissolution of each existing national state in favor of ever-smaller national, tribal, and clan states, weakening the principle of national independence and eventually negating it by returning us to an anarchical order of tribes and clans. In other words, in trying to grant national independence to all, one in the end grants national independence to none. Like the foolish king who discovers he can pay his debts by ceaselessly minting currency, statesmen of the last century discovered they could reap good feeling by ceaselessly minting independent states. But independence, like currency, quickly depreciates in value when circulated in too great a quantity and is soon enough found to be worthless.

In addition to this tendency of the principle of collective self-determination to pulverize existing states, there is also the problem of limited resources. To maintain its independence, a national state must have not only internal cohesion but also military and economic strength and a defensible territory, so that it is not annexed by hostile foreign powers at the first opportunity, or overrun by criminal or terrorist organizations. Where these conditions are lacking, there will be no independent national state. A nation or tribe that does not have these things can only hope to live in peace by seeking an alliance with a powerful neighbor, which is to say, as a protectorate. This is perhaps not what everyone would wish for. But a federated or protectorate state with some measure of delegated authority is, for most peoples on earth, the greatest degree of collective self-determination that can be attained.

It is useful in this context to think about the right of national self-determination asserted by the Confederate States of America ("the South") during the Civil War. Those who believe that the Americans were exercising a universal right of all peoples to independence when they separated from Britain in 1776 will be hard-pressed to explain why the Confederacy did not have the same right in 1861. The Southern states are certainly most easily described as tribes of an American nation, with their own distinctive public culture but no separate language or religion. But much the same could have been said of the American English who revolted against British rule. What makes American independence seem to have been a plausible endeavor is not so much the relatively mild forms of abuse that Americans suffered at the hands of the British government, as the topographic fact that an ocean divided them. The Southern states were not on the other side of an ocean, and Lincoln correctly understood that the emergence of an independent slave-holding nation to the south would have ensured that the United States would suffer centuries of hostile competition from this quarter. He needed only to look at the biblical account of the fratricidal wars between the kingdoms of Israel and Judah, which in the end weakened both of them and paved the way for their destruction, to see the future before him. And this future, together with the evil of allowing slavery to endure in America forever, did indeed justify denying national self-determination to the Confederacy. The reasons for distinguishing the case of American independence from that of Confederate independence are thus not to be found in the way we define what a "nation" is, or in the way we formulate a proposed universal right to national self-determination. The cases are distinguished only in the balance of moral and prudential considerations for supporting or opposing independence in a particular case.

The same is true for all other cases. After World War I, the Versailles policy of dismantling Austria-Hungary into a number of national states was, following the collapse of Russia, an open invitation to German expansion to the south and east. Wilson himself had had the foresight to suspect Germany of seeking for herself "a place of mastery" among the peoples of the world, and yet the postwar settlement was aimed not at assuring that this could not happen, but rather at pursuing the principle of the national self-determination of all peoples, whether strong or weak. This policy dramatically strengthened Germany's eastward position, paving the way for Hitler's devastation, twenty years later, of each of these countries in turn.[111] Similarly, Eisenhower's support for Arab nationalism and self-determination in the Middle East helped to demolish the remains of the British Empire, thereby destroying one of America's most faithful and reliable allies in the struggle against Soviet Communism. At the same time, this support for Arab national self-determination in Egypt gave rise to the aggressive dictatorship of Gamal Abdel Nasser—who repaid America's kindness by taking Egypt into the Soviet imperial orbit.[112] These examples are not intended as arguments against Czech or Egyptian independence. But they do shed light on the way in which the principle of national independence, if applied without reference to other factors, can bring about its own negation and the oppression of peoples as readily as it can bring about their freedom.

Two additional examples reflect the way in which the principle of national self-determination is balanced against considerations of prudence in international affairs. As is well known, many British and American statesmen long opposed establishing a Jewish state in the Middle East, arguing that the disadvantages of alienating Arab and Muslim interests outweighed the Jews' moral claim to national self-determination. This balance of considerations shifted, however, in the eyes of many, after the Holocaust demonstrated with maximum clarity the moral case for Jewish national self-determination; and after the Jews' military victories on the battlefield, which suggested that they might in fact be able to establish a viable state if they received foreign support. In the Kurdish case as well, national independence is opposed by some out of a concern not to alienate Turkey, and this despite that country's long history of murder and oppression of the Kurds. Here, too, the Kurds' battlefield successes, and their demonstrated ability to contribute to the American war against radical Islamic movements, have strengthened the case for a Kurdish state, which had remained unpersuasive to most governments so long as it rested on the moral case for Kurdish national self-determination alone.

It is evident, then, that there is no universal right to national independence and self-determination. Whether a people should be supported in a bid for independence is a determination that must be made in consideration of a number of factors, including the needs of the people in question; the degree of its internal cohesion and the military and economic resources it can bring to bear; its capacity, if constituted as an independent national or tribal state, to benefit the interests and well-being of other nations; and the threat that this people, once independent, may pose to others. Such a balance of considerations suggests a theory of foreign affairs that is very different from Wilson's "idealism," which assumes that the principal concern of international order is the establishment and enforcement of a universal legal framework for guiding political affairs in accordance with the universal rights of nations. In the absence of an imperial state capable of granting rights to nations and wielding the military might necessary to enforce these rights, all such talk of the universal rights of nations is vacuous, tending to cloud the judgment of statesmen as to what can be achieved, and, moreover, as to what it is right that they should try to achieve.

However, the inappropriateness of legalistic reasoning to the conduct of foreign affairs does not mean that we should strive to conduct the politics of nations exclusively on the basis of calculations of national self-interest, as has at times been proposed by the school of *raison d'état* (or "realists"). This is not only because we find it repugnant to entirely renounce moral concerns, without which every murderer on his route to power would deserve our assistance in direct proportion to the number of the slain. It is also the case that the principle of national self-interest, when it is established as the only motive for foreign policy, is not able in all cases to provide unequivocal determinations as to the best policy of the state. There are, to be sure, instances in which it is obvious what course is dictated by the need of a nation to ally itself with the strongest parties that can serve as a counterweight to its enemies. But in many cases, a statesman simply cannot know which of two or more potential policies will have this effect. This can be because it is uncertain which party is the strongest, or because it is uncertain whether the strongest party can be relied upon to uphold its end of an alliance, or because it is uncertain whether the various harms that will result from further strengthening this party will not in the end outweigh the benefits to oneself or to other allies. Moreover, statesmen may make investments in weaker parties that they estimate will grow stronger with time, or in weaker parties where the appearance of a just policy will prove beneficial with the domestic public or in some other arena. These and similar factors mean that much of the time, calculations of national self-interest yield ambiguous answers to questions of policy. This inherent ambiguity in political affairs opens up a not insubstantial space for moral considerations to tilt the decision-making balance one way or the other, without in any respect betraying the statesman's responsibility to pursue the interests of the nation.

For these reasons, political figures who understand the irrelevance of Wilsonian idealism to world affairs may nonetheless be concerned with the upbuilding of the order of independent national states. The statesman, recognizing that this is the best form of political order, does not then set out, like some Napoleon, to overturn whatever exists so that he may impose this ideal everywhere on earth. Nor does he regard it as having the ability to dictate the appropriate policy in every case. Nevertheless, the order of independent national states will be for him a picture of the good that is kept firmly in view, entering into his deliberations and decisions in a balanced and moderate fashion, without ever drawing him into dogmatic folly. This means that where the independence of a particular people is not within the realm of possibility in his generation, he will not devote resources to pressing for this cause. And where applying the principle of national self-determination would harm his own nation, or do much damage to an important ally, or establish an unstable or hostile or pernicious regime, he will set himself against it. At the same time, he will continue to regard the freedom of nations as a good to be taken into account, and on rare occasion will also vigorously pursue the establishment of a new national state, or the dissolution of a failing non-national state. And he will take pleasure in this opportunity to place the weight of his influence in the balance, in favor of a nation whose evident need and capacities are such as to encourage the belief that their independence will be a blessing to themselves and to others.

The order of independent national states is not a blueprint for a new world that can be built upon the smoking ruins of the old in a generation or two of righteous activism. It is rather a distant aim, a guiding star or a compass that imparts a greater direction and purpose to the practice of foreign affairs. Each statesman, justly focused on the interests and aspirations of his own nation, can perhaps contribute only in limited ways to the slow, great movement of this order as it arises over centuries.

XVIII: Some Principles of the Order of National States

THE ORDER OF INDEPENDENT national states is maintained by adhering to certain practical principles. However, once the order of national states is recognized as the best political order, these cease to be regarded merely as practical principles and come to be seen as natural obligations, or as the natural laws of nations. In fact, what is today often misleadingly called "international law" has its source in just this—that the practical rules for maintaining the order of national states come to be viewed as a natural morality, as many writers have argued since the seventeenth century.[113] It will be useful to mention a few of these principles here.

In the first place, the order of national states is one that grants *political independence to nations that are cohesive and strong enough to secure it*. This means that if a nation can, over time, muster sufficient military and economic strength to prevent its own conquest by foreign powers, then other national states will recognize it as an independent nation within the order of national states. By the same token, where the component tribes of the nation do not possess sufficient unity to prevent internal disintegration and chronic violence, or where they cannot muster sufficient military and economic strength to defend against foreign powers, they cannot be considered an independent nation within the order of national states.

It is often said that in an order of national states, a nation cohesive and strong enough to secure its political independence has a "right to sovereignty" within its borders. Both of these terms are now problematic due to their association with rationalist and absolutist political theory.[114] What is meant by this is in fact two different principles, the second and third principles of the order of national states:

The second principle is that of *non-interference in the internal affairs of other national states*. This is what, in a free state, permits the nation to pursue its interests and aspirations according to its own understanding. Without this principle, powerful nations would take control of the affairs of smaller nations, and the order of national states would collapse into an imperial order.

The third principle is that of a *government monopoly of organized coercive force within the state*. According to this principle, the government of each national state has a right and an obligation to maintain and wield the only organized coercive power within its territory. Without this principle, the various tribes and clans would assert their own will and law in place of the unity of the national state, and the order of national states would collapse into an anarchical order.

These two principles are fundamental to the order of national states, and it cannot exist unless they are widely observed. Nevertheless, it is a mistake to regard them as conferring absolute rights that are applicable in every case. The principle of non-interference, for instance, is understood as an anti-imperialist principle. Yet too stringent an insistence on this principle can easily bring about the destruction of national states and the rise of an imperial order. We know, for example, what horrors were bred behind the fortifications of certain independent states: that of Napoleon in France, of Hitler in Germany, of Stalin in Russia, and so forth. The crimes these men committed against their own peoples were only a prelude to the attempt to destroy all the neighboring national states and to annex their populations to a universal empire. Faced with such aggressive imperialist actors, national states have no choice but to interfere, whether by political or military means, to slow or prevent their rise. The right to such interference derives from the nature of the order of independent national states itself, for without vigilant efforts to maintain this order, these states will fall one by one, and the freedom of nations will be lost from the world.

A similar limitation arises with respect to the government monopoly of organized force within the state. By virtue of the exclusivity of the powers it claims, the national state deprives the tribes and clans within its boundaries of the ability to arm themselves and wage war, which is to say that it limits their ability to defend their people and pursue their own collective self-determination.[115] In doing so, the national state also takes upon itself an obligation to protect all the tribes and clans within its borders. This obligation likewise derives from the nature of the order of national states, and from the requirements of a national government under such an order.

To see this, consider as follows. We know that a tribe or clan that is not protected by the state will organize to protect its members. A national state that fails to protect all the tribes and clans on its territory thus invites, and will quickly receive, the re-establishment of an anarchical order of tribes and clans within its borders. This begins in the districts and towns where these unprotected tribes are strongest, and then spreads until it threatens the existence of the state itself. Anarchical conditions also present an attractive field for organized crime, which offers protection in return for a profit; and they are no less attractive to imperialist opponents of the national state such as Marxist and Islamic terrorist organizations, which find in anarchy an ideal grounds for recruiting adherents to their cause. In the face of such threats, tribes and clans that have not yet succumbed to criminal or terrorist intimidation will often seek protection from foreign national or imperial states. In this way, anarchical conditions within almost any given state serve to incite imperial concerns and aspirations in other states. Thus anarchical conditions after the disintegration of Yugoslavia prompted an American intervention that in the end led to the bombing of Serbian cities and the permanent deployment of foreign forces in Bosnia and Kosovo—an anarchical order inspiring an imperialist response. Similarly, anarchic conditions in Syria and Iraq have inflamed American, Russian, Turkish, and Iranian imperial ambitions.

Under an imperial order, a single imperial state regards itself as justified in dictating a law to all nations and in enforcing this law according to its own understanding. The worth of the order of national states derives from the fact that no nation, or coalition of nations, is considered justified in determining the law for all the others. The ability of the nation to maintain and cultivate its own unique constitution and religious traditions is the heart of national freedom, and it is this which becomes possible under the order of national states. However, this freedom of nations, even once it is won, is difficult to maintain. The political order is not fixed, and so its stability can only be relative. Nations rise and fall. Their populations grow and decline relative to one another, and the same is true for their military and economic power, and of the degree of their internal cohesion. These things mean that each national state is in perpetual peril of losing its freedom to another nation or combination of nations. The danger invariably materializes in the same way: A given nation, having grown much stronger in relation to others, comes to believe that this increase is due to the superiority of its religion or constitution above all others, and so considers itself justified in imposing its rule on all the other nations. Needless to say, this imperialist nation regards empire not merely as its due. It also considers the superiority of its religion or constitution as itself a reason that all nations will benefit from being conquered and having its law dictated to them.

The presence of this constant peril suggests the fourth principle, which is the *maintenance of multiple centers of power*. This is, in other words, the familiar doctrine according to which the respective national states strive to maintain a "balance of power" among them, acting to prevent any one nation, or fixed combination of nations, from becoming strong enough so that its constitution or religion can be dictated and enforced as law upon the others. It is often said that this imperative of maintaining multiple centers of power in the national-state system is a contrivance whose purpose is stability or even peace. However, this explanation has always been doubtful, given that an imperial order, which suppresses all dissent, may be as good or better at providing stability and peace than an order of independent national states. Rather, the purpose of this principle is to ensure the freedom of nations. For no nation can long maintain its political freedom and self-determination in an order dominated by a single imperial state, which, regarding its own constitution or religion as superior, inevitably intervenes in the affairs of other nations in order to eradicate whatever is inconvenient or obnoxious to it. It was for the sake of their national freedom, then, that the nations of Europe established alliances that could contain the imperial aspirations of, first, the Germans, and then the French, and finally the Russians under Communism.

I have said that national populations grow and decline relative to one another. This is true numerically, in terms of their military and economic strength, and in terms of the degree of their internal cohesion. These alterations, which eventually work changes in the relations between each nation and its neighbors, mean that national borders cannot be frozen in perpetuity.[116] A redrawing of antiquated state borders to conform to real national or tribal boundaries must be an available instrument of diplomacy if national states are to maintain their internal cohesion and their external capacity for self-defense, both of which are required to uphold the national-state system as a whole. In the extreme case, the establishment of new national states and the dissolution of failed non-national states must be undertaken as well, although these steps should in general be reserved for cases of dire necessity, such as the decay

of Syria, Iraq, Bosnia, and the Congo, where the drawing of
new national boundaries offers the only genuine prospect for
achieving a degree of national freedom and peace.

However, such establishment of new national states and
redrawing of borders must be guided by the fifth principle
of the order of national states, *parsimony in the establishment
of independent states.* A parsimonious policy should be distinguished from one of progressively dividing existing states into
ever-smaller independent entities, so that the number of independent states grows ever larger and never smaller. Such a
mindless policy is evident in the establishment of Kosovo as a
second Albanian state under international protection. A parsimonious policy would have permitted a resolution that would
either annex Kosovo to Albania or leave it as a historic and
integral part of Serbia. In such matters, the eyes of the statesman must be turned at least as much to the annexation of
territories to existing national states, thereby increasing their
viability, as they are to the decomposition and fragmentation
of existing national states. In this regard, it is important to
notice that the "reunification" of Germany in 1990 was in fact
an annexation of East Germany to West Germany, a redrawing
of borders to enable the greater national self-determination
of the German nation. What was deemed desirable in the German case can and should be considered as an option in other
regions as well.

This principle of parsimony is also relevant where the establishment of a new state would threaten the viability of one
or more existing national states. Since the first principle of the
order of national states is the viability of independent nations,
nothing is gained by placing one national state in jeopardy by
establishing a new state on its borders that renders it greatly

more difficult to maintain, whether militarily, economically, or as a cohesive cultural unity.[117]

In an order of national states, the problem of unprotected minority populations is an aspect of the problem of anarchy. Every minority nation or tribe has interests and aspirations that are at least slightly removed from those of the majority national or tribal group in the state, and often more so. But where such a minority nation or tribe does not enjoy the protection of the national state, or where it suffers abuse at the hands of the state, it necessarily becomes a fertile ground for disaffection, for the attenuation of bonds of loyalty to the state, and therefore for the establishment of a sphere of anarchy within the state. *Protection of minority nations and tribes by the national government* is thus a necessary sixth principle in an order of national states. Although this principle has moral force on other grounds as well, I am here concerned with it as an obligation deriving from the nature of the national-state system itself. It is a principle without which the order of national states cannot persist, for wherever the obligations arising from it are not met, anarchy and empire follow. This is the case despite the fact that this principle obviously places limits on the collective self-determination of the majority nation or tribe in every state.

The protection and accommodation of minority nations and tribes cannot express itself in the same way in every national state. There are national and tribal minorities whose disaffection is to a substantial degree the result of abuse and neglect, in which case the national state is itself guilty of creating a sphere of anarchy within its own borders, and consequently of undermining the order of national states as a whole. At the same time, there are national and tribal minorities whose disaffection is aggressively cultivated by other national states or by imperial powers, which stoke fear and anger among them for their own purposes. And of course, both may be true. In some cases, the problem of disaffection must therefore be dealt with by greater attention to the needs of the people in question, which may involve a greater measure of political or religious autonomy than had been considered tolerable; while in others, there is no choice but for the national state to apply more rigorous measures to deprive imperialist and anarchic elements of their aspirations by force. And it may be that both approaches have to be applied at once.

Finally, I will add a seventh principle, which is the *non-transference of the powers of government to universal institutions*. This is a matter that has become especially pressing over the last century, in which statesmen have repeatedly sought the establishment of international institutions whose purpose is to relieve national states of their capacity for independent judgment and action in the name of universal peace and prosperity. As I have suggested, international institutions, if they have the ability to coerce their member states, are nothing other than the institutions of an imperial political order. And one cannot transfer authority to these institutions without the order of national states collapsing into an imperial order.

It may be asked whether this principle does not contradict the ideal of national independence and self-determination. After all, if a given nation is so dissatisfied with political independence that it wishes to be ruled under an imperial or universal state—which is to say that it would prefer to be ruled by others—then to renounce its national freedom would seem to be its right, its last grand act of national self-determination.

I see this matter as being more complicated. If the Dutch, for instance, wish to become a federated or protectorate state of Germany, regarding such an action as the best course open to them, then we may have no choice but to accept it, much as we may regret seeing a national state with such a splendid cultural inheritance pass from the world. Such a step can be justified under the principle of parsimony, and could, in theory, be regarded as an adjustment of the borders of a German national state.[118] But it is another thing entirely to transfer the powers of the state to a German-dominated European Union, which is in effect a universal state, having no natural boundaries and governing in the name of universal doctrines whose reach will be limited only by the power that this empire can bring to bear. When a national state transfers powers of government to such an imperial state, it not only renounces its own national freedom, as would also be true in the case of the Netherlands becoming a state within a federal Germany. It also participates directly in the destruction of the order of independent national states—by transferring power to an unlimited international state, and to the imperial order that the leadership of that state seeks to establish. Such an imperial order cannot and will not tolerate the existence of independent national states. As it grows stronger, it will work to delegitimize and undermine the independence of all remaining national states, declaring them to be a holdover from a savage and primitive age. To the extent that the imperial order is able to muster the powers necessary, it will strive to coerce the remaining national states and ultimately to reduce them to a state of subjugation, all the while declaring that it is taking these steps for the sake of peace and prosperity for all mankind. This is true not only of the European Union, but also of all other schemes for the establishment of a coercive international order—including attempts to establish the Security Council of the United Nations as having the authority to make binding determinations for all nations in matters of war and peace; or the World Trade Organization as an authoritative body regulating the economies of nations as a condition of their participation in international trade; or the UN Human Rights Council and various European courts as the highest moral authorities in matters concerning the dignity and welfare of individuals throughout the world.[119]

If we cherish the freedoms we have come to enjoy under an order of independent national states, we have no choice but to insist on the complete independence of the national state from international institutions that seek to wield coercive authority over their member nations. Of course, the national state must be concerned for the improvement of conditions in other countries, both out of a regard for its own self-interest and for moral reasons. But these concerns are properly expressed through bilateral and multilateral negotiations among independent national states, and not by erecting coercive international bodies. We should not let a hairbreadth of our freedom be given over to foreign bodies under any name whatsoever, or to foreign systems of law that are not determined by our own nation. What today seems but a small concession invariably becomes a large one tomorrow. And when a nation wakes up from its sleep and discovers that it has been slowly, inexorably conquered, at that time no options will remain to it other than to acquiesce in eternal enslavement or to go to war.

It requires much artfulness and dedication on the part of the statesman to maintain and strengthen a viable order of independent national states. In this, the institution of the national state resembles other institutions required for free government, such as the division of the powers of government and the maintenance of a regime of individual property rights.

Such institutions cannot be maintained except by the utmost vigilance and a constant concern for their preservation and improvement. Of course, where the reasons for which an institution was originally established are no longer familiar, such vigilance and concern become ever more difficult. In our generation, when the virtues of the order of independent national states are not taught and only dimly remembered, then calls for a return to the simplicity and grandeur and supposed moral goodness of universal empire will grow more insistent and more pressing. Yet so long as our freedom remains important to us, there is no other way to ensure it. We must engage in the difficult work of maintaining and strengthening the independent national states that our forefathers built and bequeathed to us as a precious inheritance.

Part Three

ANTI-NATIONALISM
AND HATE

XIX: Is Hatred an Argument
Against Nationalism?

THE MOST COMMON ACCUSATION against nationalism is that it gives rise to hatred. Nationalists tend to be most concerned for the welfare of their own nation and wish to see it succeed in its competition with others. This concern for one's own is said to express itself in a hatred of others and in violence against them. The imperialist, on the other hand, claims to be concerned with all of humanity equally. Caring for mankind as a whole, the imperialist says he has overcome the hatred that characterizes the personality of the nationalist.

It is true, of course, that there are nationalists who hate their opponents and rivals. The competition among tribes and nations inevitably leads to the accumulation of stories of past injustice, whether real or imagined, and these do color the present and fuel ongoing resentment, prejudice, and violence.

But does this hatred on the part of certain nationalists amount to an argument against nationalism—that is, against a political order based on independent national states? For the hatred of certain nationalists to be a compelling argument against nationalism, it would have to be shown that the aspiration to establish a universal political order does not incite and fuel hatred in the same way. After all, if an imperialist politics is as prone to inciting unrelenting hatred as a nationalist politics, then the claim that we should avoid nationalism for the hatred it produces is not much better than propaganda. It is a piece of rhetoric that may be useful in drumming up contempt for the national state and those who are loyal to it. But it does not possess the virtue of being true.

Adding to the confusion surrounding this issue is the tendency of many contemporary liberals to attribute hatred and violence not only to nationalism but also to religion. Yet the principal religions that are mentioned when religious hatred is invoked are Christianity and Islam. And both of these have been, for much of their history, universalist movements seeking to establish the rule of a single empire in the world. In this respect, they resembled Communism or Nazism, which likewise sought to establish the rule of a single empire on earth. All of these imperialist movements were, of course, prolific in the hatred they inspired in their adherents. This is because universalist ideals tend to give rise to hatred as soon as they encounter determined opposition. Determined opposition is, for them, unwanted evidence that the ideal in question may not be as universal as had been previously supposed.

We can therefore recognize two different kinds of hatred: There is the kind of hatred that is found in nationalist movements, which is the hatred of one clan, tribe, or nation for another that is in competition with it. And there is the kind of hatred that is found in imperialist movements, which is the hatred that a universal ideal bears against those nations or tribes that refuse to accept its claim of universality. The question is whether liberals, who believe they have largely freed themselves of the hatred found in nationalist movements, are also free of the enduring hatred, at times genocidal, that all previous universalist ideologies have displayed from the moment they had to contend with genuine, deep-seated opposition to their doctrines.

Experience suggests that a hatred of the nationalist, the particularist, and the dissident is found among imperialists of every stripe. The supposition that imperialists have a greater capacity for love or for tolerance, is, it would appear, a myth promoted by these same imperialists. In this part of the book, I want to look more closely at the hatred found among liberal advocates of a new universal political order. I will begin with the well-known antipathy toward the national state that is my home, Israel. I will then enlarge the scope of my discussion to include parallel phenomena—including the hatred directed against British and American nationalism, and against other national states—that are increasingly inseparable from the liberal universalism in our time.

XX: The Shaming Campaigns Against Israel

EVERY FEW MONTHS, ISRAEL is publicly pilloried in international bodies, in the media, and on university campuses around the world for an alleged violation of human rights, whether real or imagined. The particular case that first caused me to think carefully about this phenomenon was a raid on a Turkish ship trying to penetrate an Israeli naval blockade on Gaza, which left nine dead after the ship resisted seizure. But a great many other incidents have also resulted in such campaigns, including Israeli actions against the radical Islamic regime in

Gaza, the Israeli strike against the Iraqi nuclear program, the visit of an Israeli public figure to the Temple Mount, the purchase and occupancy by Jews of a building in East Jerusalem, and many others.

But whatever the ostensible subject, and regardless of whether Israel's political leaders, soldiers, and spokesmen have executed their duties in an appropriate fashion, the result is another campaign of vilification in the media and on campuses and in the corridors of power—a shaming campaign of a kind that few nations have historically experienced on a regular basis. In each such campaign, we Israelis must again see our nation treated not as a democracy doing its duty to defend its people and its freedom, but as some kind of a scourge. We again see everything that is precious to us, and everything we consider just, trampled before our eyes. We again have to experience former friends turning their backs on us, and Jewish students running to dissociate themselves from Israel, even from Judaism, in a vain effort to retain the favor of digusted peers. And we again feel the bite of the rising anti-Semitic tide, returned after a hiatus following the Second World War.

All this has happened repeatedly, and we know it will happen again. Indeed, these outbursts have grown more vicious and effective with each passing year for decades now. And there is every reason to think this trend will continue.

As to the reactions of Jews and other friends of Israel to these shaming campaigns, their responses have not really changed in recent decades either: My liberal friends always seem to think that a change of Israeli policy could prevent these campaigns of vilification, or at least lessen their reach. My conservative friends always seem to say that what we need is "better public relations."

No doubt, Israel could always stand to have better policies and better public relations. But my own view is that neither of these otherwise sensible reactions can help improve things, because neither really gets to the heart of what has been happening to Israel's legitimacy. Israel's policies have fluctuated radically in recent decades, being sometimes better, sometimes worse. And the adroitness with which Israel presents its case in the media and through diplomatic channels has, likewise, been sometimes better, sometimes worse. Yet the international efforts to smear Israel, to corner Israel, to delegitimize Israel and drive it from the family of nations, have proceeded and advanced and grown ever more potent despite the many upturns and downturns in Israeli policy and Israeli public relations.

Nothing could make this more evident than the Jewish withdrawal from Gaza and the subsequent establishment there of an independent and belligerent Islamic republic forty miles from downtown Tel Aviv. Israelis and friends of Israel can reasonably be divided on the question of whether the withdrawal from Gaza in 2005, or the parallel withdrawal from the Security Zone in South Lebanon in 2000, was really in Israel's interests, and whether the Jewish state is today better off because of them. But it is hard to say that these withdrawals have contributed much to stemming the tide of hatred and vilification being poured on Israel's head internationally. Those who hate Israel have moved on to pointing to other Israeli policies that inflame their anger not a whit less. Whatever is driving the trend toward the progressive delegitimization of Israel, it is something that operates to a great degree without reference to the details of particular Israeli policies at a given moment.

To put this in slightly different terms, it is not the maintenance of a security zone in South Lebanon, or Israeli control of the Gaza Strip, or the raid on a Turkish blockade runners' boat that is reponsible for what is happening to the way in which Israel is perceived on the world stage. These specific instances of Israeli policy are, for Israel's detractors, largely symbols of something deeper and more hateful that they see revealed time and again when they look upon the state of Israel and its deeds.

The philosopher Thomas Kuhn has suggested that we are trained to see the world in terms of a certain framework of concepts, which he called a *paradigm*. The paradigm determines not only the interpretation that a scientist gives the facts, but also what facts there are to be interpreted: The "facts" that scientists consider admissible for discussion are those that easily conform to the dominant paradigm, or that can be made to conform to it by extending the paradigm or introducing minor repairs into it. Those that cannot be made to conform are overlooked entirely or dismissed as unimportant. Even a mountain of facts, Kuhn suggests, will not change the mind of a scientist who has been trained in a given paradigm, because the conceptual framework through which he views the world is fundamentally incapable of assimilating them. How, then, do scientists come to change their minds? Kuhn argues that in many cases, they never do. The prejudices of the old guard run too deep, and it takes a new generation of scientists, whose commitments are not quite so dogmatic, to be able to consider a new theory fairly.[1]

Kuhn's ideas have had an immense impact on the way the scientific enterprise is understood. But the revolution in how scholars think about facts, arguments, and truth has not yet had much of an impact on the way debates are conducted in the public arena. With respect to the way hatred of Israel is treated in public discourse, for instance, most writers are still convinced that if only certain facts were better known—or better presented—Israel's standing in the eyes of public opinion, and particularly among the liberals who are Israel's harshest detractors in Europe and America, could be improved dramatically.

Unfortunately, I do not believe this is so. While media battles such as the one surrounding the Turkish ship off Gaza may be an unavoidable necessity, Kuhn's argument makes it clear that the outcomes of these contests won't have any real impact on the overall trajectory of Israel's standing among educated people in the West. This standing has been deteriorating for the past generation, not because of this or that set of facts, but because the paradigm through which educated Westerners are looking at Israel has shifted. We've been watching the transition from one paradigm to another in everything having to do with Israel's legitimacy as an independent national state.

XXI: Immanuel Kant and the Anti-Nationalist Paradigm

WHAT IS THE OLD PARADIGM? And what is the new one to which the international arena has been shifting?

I will begin with the old paradigm, which is the one that granted Israel its legitimacy in the first place. The modern state of Israel was founded, both constitutionally and in terms of the understanding of the international community, as a national state, the state of the Jewish nation. This is to say that it is the offspring of an early modern political theory that recognized the freedom of nations to assert and defend their independence against the predations of international empires.[2] There had always been national states, of course.[3] But the modern ideal of the national state was consolidated during the long struggle of nations such as England, the Netherlands, and France to liberate themselves from the pretensions to universal empire of the German and Spanish Habsburgs (that is, the "Holy Roman Empire"). What made the defeat of the Spanish armada by Elizabeth in 1588 a turning point in history was precisely the fact that in repelling Philip II's bid to rule England, she made solid the freedom of nations from the Austro-Spanish claim to a right to rule over all mankind.

The defeat of the universalist ideal in the Thirty Years' War in 1648 led to the establishment of a new paradigm for European politics—one in which a revitalized concept of the national state offered freedom to peoples across the continent. By the 1800s, this idea of national liberty had been extended to the point that some conceived of it as an ordering principle for the entire world. The institution of the independent national state would free the nations, allowing them to determine their own course, each determining its own form of government and laws, religion and language. Greece declared itself an independent national state in 1822. Italy was unified and won independence in a series of wars beginning in 1848. And dozens of other national states followed. Theodor Herzl's Zionist Organization, which proposed an independent national state for the Jewish people, fit into this same political understanding. In 1947, a few months after India gained its independence, the United Nations voted by a two-thirds majority for the establishment of what UN documents called a "Jewish State" in Palestine.

But the idea of the national state has not flourished in the period since the establishment of Israel. On the contrary, it has largely collapsed. With their drive to establish a European Union, the nations of Europe established a new paradigm in which the independent national state is no longer seen as holding the key to the well-being of humanity. On the contrary, the independent national state is now seen by many political and intellectual figures in Europe as a source of incalculable evil, while the multinational empire—which Mill singled out as the very epitome of despotism—is mentioned time and again with fondness as a model for a post-national humanity. Moreover, this new paradigm is aggressively advancing into mainstream political discourse in other nations as well, including countries such as the United States and Israel that had long seemed immune to it.

How is it that so many Europeans are now willing to lend a hand in dismantling the states in which they live, and exchanging them for the rule of an international regime?

I have already mentioned that unifying the nations under a German Holy Roman Emperor and a universal church is an old European dream. Enlightenment philosophy, while turning away from Christianity, nevertheless maintained much the same dream, which was given its best-known modern formulation in a 1795 manifesto by Immanuel Kant called *Perpetual Peace: A Philosophical Sketch*. In it, Kant launched a famous attack on the ideal of the national state, comparing national self-determination to the lawless freedom of savages, which, he said, is rightly detested as "barbarism" and a "brutish debasement of humanity." As he wrote:

We look with profound contempt upon the way in which savages cling to their lawless freedom. They would rather engage in incessant strife than to submit to legal constraint. . . . We regard this as barbarism, coarseness, and brutish debasement of humanity. We might thus expect civilized peoples, each united within itself as a [national] state, would hasten to abandon so degrading a condition as soon as possible. But instead of doing so, each state sees its own majesty . . . precisely in not having to submit to any external legal constraint, and the glory of its ruler consists in his power to order thousands of people to immolate themselves.[4]

According to this view, political independence is a form of life in which "savages cling to their lawless freedom." Civilized people, if they will only exercise reason, will "hasten to abandon so degrading a condition as soon as possible." This is true of the individual, who submits to the lawful order of the state. And it is true of nations as well, which must in the same way give up any right to independence, submitting to an "international state" that will establish "public coercive laws" over them, growing until it brings into submission "all the people of the earth":

There is only one rational way in which states co-existing with other states can emerge from the lawless condition of pure warfare. . . . They must renounce their savage and lawless freedom, adapt themselves to public coercive laws, and thus form an *international state*, which would necessarily continue to grow until it embraced all the people of the earth.[5]

In *Perpetual Peace,* then, Kant argues that the establishment of an international or imperial state is the only possible dictate of reason. Those who do not agree to subordinate their national interests to the directives of the imperial state are regarded as opposing the historic march of humanity toward the reign of reason. Those who insist on their national freedom are supporting a violent egoism on a national scale, which is as much an abdication of sound morals as the insistence on violent egoism would be in our personal lives.

For many years, the Kantian paradigm, which imputed an intrinsic immorality to the institution of the national state, found few takers in Europe, where progressive opinion was firmly on the side of dismantling empire and permitting the nations their independence. But after the Second World War, when Nazism was added to the list of crimes attributed to the national state, the result was very different. Nazism was portrayed as the rotten fruit of the German national state, and Kant looked to have been right all along. For the nations to arm themselves, and to determine for themselves when to use their arms, was now seen as barbarism and a brutish debasement of humanity.

I have already discussed this argument in Chapter V, where I emphasized that the order of national states regards the world as governed best when nations are able to chart their own independent course. The Nazi viewpoint was precisely the opposite of this: Hitler saw his Third Reich as an improved incarnation of what he referred to as the "First Reich"—which was none other than the Holy Roman Empire of the Habsburgs. Hitler's dream was to build his empire on the ruin of the order of national states in Europe.

Many Europeans, however, declined to see things this way, accepting the view that Nazism was, more or less, the national state taken to its ugly conclusion. The Marxists' condemnation of the Western national state was joined by a liberal anti-nationalism, which eagerly sought an end to the old order in the name of Kant's march toward Enlightenment. As the philosopher Jürgen Habermas, perhaps the leading theoretician of a post-national Europe, pointed out, this transition was particularly easy for Germans—given Germany's role in the Second World War and the fact that postwar Germany was in any case under occupation and no longer an independent state.[6] He might have added that unlike the British, French, and Dutch, the German-speaking peoples of central Europe had historically never lived under a unified national state, so that the hope represented by such a state was perhaps somewhat less important to them in any case.

Be this as it may, this post-national vision found takers all over Europe. A mere generation later, in 1992, European leaders signed the Treaty of Maastricht establishing the European Union as an international government, and depriving member states of many of the powers associated historically with national independence. Of course, there are Europeans who have not accepted this course. But the impact of the new paradigm, the engine driving the movement toward European Union, has nevertheless been overwhelming. Both in Europe and America, we are watching the growth of a generation of young people that, for the first time in four hundred years, does not recognize the national state as the foundation of our freedoms. Indeed, there is a powerful new paradigm abroad that sees us doing without such states. And it has unleashed a tidal wave of consequences, for those who embrace it and for those who do not.

XXII: Two Lessons of Auschwitz

I HAVE ALWAYS BEEN troubled by the prospect that a nation such as Britain, which has so often been a light to others in politics, philosophy, and science, should some day soon step down from the stage of world history forever. I see Britain, America, the Netherlands, and others as forming part of a family of nations whose continued independent existence is meaningful to me personally. Nevertheless, my first concern is for Israel, and I would like now to try to understand what my country looks like when seen through European eyes—or rather, through the eyes of the new paradigm that provides an understanding of Israel to so many in Europe, and now also to increasing numbers of educated people in America and elsewhere.

Consider the Auschwitz concentration camp. For most Jews, Auschwitz has a very particular meaning. It was not Herzl's Zionist Organization that persuaded nearly all Jews the world over that there could be no other way but to establish an independent Jewish state in our day. It was Auschwitz, and the deaths of six million Jews at the hands of the Germans and their sympathizers that accomplished this. From the horror and humiliation of Auschwitz, this one inescapable lesson emerged: that it was Jewish dependence on the military protection of others that had brought this about. This message was articulated with perfect clarity by David Ben-Gurion in the National Assembly of the Jews of Palestine in November 1942:

We do not know exactly what goes on in the Nazi valley of death, or how many Jews have already been slaugh-

tered. . . . We do not know whether the victory of democracy and freedom and justice will not find Europe a vast
Jewish cemetery in which the bones of our people are
scattered. . . . We are the only people in the world whose
blood, as a nation, is allowed to be shed. . . . Only our children, our women . . . and our aged are set apart for special
treatment, to be buried alive in graves dug by them, to be
cremated in crematoriums, to be strangled and to be murdered by machine guns . . . for but one sin: . . . Because
the Jews have no political standing, no Jewish army, no
Jewish independence, and no homeland. . . . Give us
the right to fight and die as Jews. . . . We demand the
right . . . to a homeland and independence. What has
happened to us in Poland, what God forbid, will happen
to us in the future, all our innocent victims, all the tens
of thousands, hundreds of thousands, and perhaps millions . . . are the sacrifices of a people without a homeland. . . . We demand . . . a homeland and independence.[7]

In these words, the tie between the Holocaust and what Ben-
Gurion calls the "sin" of Jewish powerlessness is powerfully
in evidence. The meaning of Auschwitz is that the Jews failed
in their efforts to find a way to defend their children. They
depended on others, decent men in power in America or
Britain, who, when the time came, did little to save European
Jewry. Today, most Jews continue to believe that the only thing
that has really changed since those millions of our people
perished—the only thing that stands as a bulwark against the
repetition of this chapter in the world's history—is Israel.

Jews, however, are not the only ones for whom Auschwitz
has become an important political symbol. Many Europeans,

too, see Auschwitz as being at the heart of the lesson of the Second World War. But the conclusions they draw are precisely the opposite of those drawn by Jews. Following Kant, they see Auschwitz as the ultimate expression of that barbarism, that brutal debasement of humanity, which is national particularism. From this point of view, the death camps provide the ultimate proof of the evil of permitting nations to decide for themselves how to dispose of the military power in their possession. The obvious conclusion is that it was wrong to give the German nation this power of life and death. If such evil is to be prevented from happening again and again, the answer must be in the dismantling of Germany and the other national states of Europe, and the yoking together of all the European peoples under a single international government: Eliminate the national state once and for all, and you have sealed off that dark road to Auschwitz.

Notice that according to this view, it is not Israel that is the answer to Auschwitz, but the European Union. A united Europe will make it impossible for Germany, or any other European nation, to rise up and persecute others once again. In this sense, it is European Union that stands as the guarantor of the future peace of the Jews, and indeed, of all humanity.

Here, then, are two competing paradigms concerning the meaning of Auschwitz. Each is looking at the same facts: Both paradigms take it as a given that millions were murdered in Auschwitz by the Germans and their collaborators, that the deeds done there were utterly evil, and that Jews and others who died there were the helpless victims of this evil. But at this point, agreement ends. Individuals looking at the same facts by way of these different paradigms see different things:

Paradigm A: Auschwitz represents the unspeakable horror of Jewish women and men standing empty-handed and naked, watching their children die for want of a rifle with which to protect them.

Paradigm B: Auschwitz represents the unspeakable horror of German soldiers using force against others, backed by nothing but their own government's views as to their national rights and interests.

It is important to recognize that these two views, which at first do not even seem to be talking about the same thing, are actually describing moral positions that are almost perfectly irreconcilable. In the one, it is the agency of the murderers that is seen as the source of the evil; in the other, it is the powerlessness of the victims—a seemingly subtle difference in perspective that opens up into a chasm when we turn these competing paradigms in another direction and look at Israel through their eyes.

Here are the same two paradigms, now with their attention turned to the independent state of Israel and what it represents:

Paradigm A: Israel represents Jewish women and men standing rifle in hand, watching over their own children and all other Jewish children and protecting them. *Israel is the opposite of Auschwitz.*

Paradigm B: Israel represents the unspeakable horror of Jewish soldiers using force against others, backed by nothing but their own government's views as to their national rights and interests. *Israel is Auschwitz.*

In both paradigms, the fact of Israel takes on an extraordinary significance because of the identity of the Jews as the victims of the Shoah. For Israel's founders, the fact that the survivors of the death camps and their children could be given weapons and permitted to train as soldiers under a Jewish flag seemed a decisive movement of the world toward what was just and right. It could in no sense make up for what had happened. But it was just nonetheless, granting the survivors precisely the empowerment that, had it come a few years earlier, would have saved their loved ones from death and worse. In this sense, *Israel is the opposite of Auschwitz.*

At the same time, Israel takes on extraordinary significance in the new European paradigm as well. For in Israel, the survivors and their children took up arms and set themselves on a course of determining their own fate. That is, this people, so close to the Kantian ideal of perfect self-renunciation only a few decades ago, have instead chosen what is now seen as the path of Hitler—the path of national self-determination. It is this that lies beneath the nearly boundless disgust so many feel toward Israel, and especially toward anything having to do with Israel's attempts to defend itself, regardless of whether these operations are successful or unsuccessful, irreproachable or morally flawed. In taking up arms in the name of their own national state and their own self-determination, the Jews, as many Europeans and others now see it, have simply taken up the same evil that led Germany to build the camps. The details may differ, but the principle, in their eyes, is the same: *Israel is Auschwitz.*

Try to see this through European eyes. Imagine being a proud Dutchman today, whose nation held high the torch of freedom in that hopeless uprising against Catholic Spain, a war of independence that lasted eighty years. "Yet I am willing to give this up," he says to himself, "to sacrifice this heritage with its dreams of past glory, and to say good-bye to the state founded by my forefathers, for the sake of something higher. I will make this painful sacrifice for the sake of an international political union that will ultimately embrace all humanity. Yes, I will do it for humanity." Yet who is it that stands against him? Who, among the civilized peoples, would dare turn their backs on this effort, blessed by morality and reason, to attain at last the salvation of mankind? Imagine his shock: "The Jews! Those Jews, who should have been the first to welcome the coming of the new order, the first to welcome the coming of mankind's salvation, instead establish themselves as its opponents, building up their own selfish little state, at war with the world. How dare they? Must they not make the same sacrifices as I in the name of Enlightenment and reason? Are they so debased they cannot remember their own parents in Auschwitz? No, they cannot remember—for they've been seduced and perverted by the same evil that had previously seized our neighbors in Germany. They have gone over to the side of Auschwitz."

Thus it is not just by coincidence that we constantly hear Israel and its soldiers being compared to the Nazis. We are not talking about just any old calumny, chosen arbitrarily or for its rhetorical value alone. In Europe, and wherever else the new paradigm has spread, the comparison with Nazism, absurd though it may be, is natural and inevitable.

This answers the question of how it can be that, at some very fundamental level, the facts do not seem to matter: How it can be that even where Israel should easily be recognized as having justice on its side—where it acts in self-defense, and with painstaking restraint—the country can be pilloried in campaigns of vilification that bite deeper and hit harder with every passing year. How it can be that after the destruction of the Israeli security zone in South Lebanon, and after Israeli withdrawal from the Gaza Strip, the hatred of Israel only grows more full-throated.

The answer is that while hatred for Israel may, at a given moment, be focused quite sincerely on certain facts about the security zone or the Gaza Strip or the Turkish blockade runners, the trajectory of international disgust or hatred for Israel is not driven by these facts. It is driven by the rapid advance of a new paradigm that understands Israel, and especially the independent Israeli use of force to defend itself, as illegitimate down to its foundations. If you believe that Israel is, in some important sense, a variant of Nazism, then you will not be very impressed by "improvements" in Israeli policies or public relations. An improved Auschwitz is still Auschwitz.

One may well ask: If this is right, and the comparison between Israel and the most odious political movement in European history is hardwired into the new paradigm of international politics that is quickly advancing upon us, then will not individuals who subscribe to this paradigm reach the conclusion that Israel has no right to exist and should be dismantled?

The answer to this question is plain. Of course this comparison leads to the conclusion that Israel has no right to exist and should be dismantled. And why not? If Germany and France have no right to exist as independent states, why should Israel? And if so many are prepared to remain dry-eyed on the day that Britain and the Netherlands are finally gone, why should they feel differently about Israel? On the contrary, while Jews and their friends continue to speak in dread of "Israel's destruction," this phrase is no longer feared among those who have embraced the new paradigm—some of whom are already permitting themselves to fantasize in public about political arrangements that will permit the Jewish state to cease to exist.[8]

XXIII: Why the Enormities of the Third World and Islam Go Unprotested

I HAVE SUGGESTED THAT the principal force driving the progressive delegitimization of Israel in international forums, media, and universities in recent years has been the advance of a new anti-nationalist paradigm in international relations emanating, first and foremost, from Europe. As I understand the matter, the drive to subordinate the national states of Europe to an international political organization, the European Union, has caused severe damage to the principle that originally granted legitimacy to Israel as an independent national state: the principle of national freedom and self-determination, which had allowed the Jewish state independent action where necessary to protect its people. Many in Europe increasingly see such national independence and self-help as illegitimate, and this is moving them toward a systematic rejection of Israel's legitimacy. Moreover this same view is quickly spreading in America and other countries as well.

This raises an important question: If the intensifying hostility toward Israel is being driven, to a great degree, by the collapse of support for the idea of the independent national state, why do so many of Israel's harshest critics support the establishment of an independent state for Palestinian Arabs? Why do they refrain from criticizing the use of force by states such as Iran, Turkey, and various Arab regimes, and by many other countries in the Third World? Many of these regimes use force far more aggressively than Israel does—in some cases committing atrocities on an unimagined scale. If the national-state paradigm has collapsed, why does there seem to be toler-ance, if not outright support, for independent action when it is exercised by such regimes?

As before, the beginning of an answer is to be found in the anti-nationalism of Kant. Recall that for Kant, human history should be seen as a progressive movement from barbarism to the eventual triumph of morality and reason, which he equates with the establishment of a universal state. According to this view, human individuals first give up their selfish, lawless free-dom by joining together in national states. Then these national states must do the same thing, giving up their selfish, lawless freedom by subordinating themselves to the coercive public law of the universal state. Unlike some, Kant is not certain that this movement of history is inevitable. But he does see it as the only historical development that can legitimately be consid-ered moral and in accord with reason. Any other view of history "would force us to turn away in revulsion."[9]

But this progressive interpretation of history does not mean that all nations are moving along the path from barbarism to reason at the same rate. On the contrary, Kant believes that there are different stages of achievement along this road, and that different peoples reach them at different times. As he ex-plains in an essay called "Idea for a Universal History with a Cosmopolitan Purpose" (1784), peoples leave the *savage state* and reach the level of *civilization* when they form themselves into national states, each one governed internally by the rule of law. But the order of national states is not the same as *moral*

maturity, which is the third and final stage—yet to be reached—
in the story of mankind. Attaining this last stage requires that
mankind "finally . . . take the step" that reason dictates, and
submit to a universal federal state. Kant explains that this
would be

> A federation of peoples in which every state, even the
> smallest, could expect to derive its security and rights not
> from its own power or its own legal judgment, but solely
> from this great federation, from a united power and the
> law-governed decisions of a united will.[10]

Here, "moral maturity" is equated with the renunciation of one's
own judgment as to what is right, and of one's own power to act
in the service of what is right. The judgment of the universal
state will determine what is right; the "united power" and "united
will" of the universal state will impose what is right.

Kant did not believe that in his own day any nation had yet
reached this level of "moral maturity." But he did believe that
Europe would probably attain it eventually, having been compelled to reach it by the pain and suffering induced by so many
wars.[11] The rest of the world, in the meantime, remained in a
condition of savagery, and had not yet taken even the initial step
of banding together in the form of national states. This they
would obviously have to do first, before they could rise higher.

Kant's three stages of human progress are reproduced more
or less exactly in the way in which European anti-nationalists
speak about international affairs. According to this view, there
is exactly one place in the world in which one can find nations
that have at long last reached the stage of "moral maturity": the
European Union. Only in Europe has it become perfectly clear

to many millions that the order of national states must now be transcended. Only there is the ideal of national independence well on its way to being discarded. From this point of view, it is evident what one is supposed to think of Iran, Turkey, the Arabs, and the Third World, which are all considered as being at a much more primitive stage in their history. These are said to be peoples who are still trying to escape savagery, still trying to consolidate national states governed under the domestic rule of law. Once they have arrived at this point, possibly centuries from now, they too will gradually begin to recognize the rationality of outgrowing their national states and reaching "moral maturity" under an international government.

The prevalence of this three-stage view of history explains much about the enthusiasm of many European leaders for establishing new states in the Middle East and the Third World, as well as their relative disinterest in the aggression and atrocities committed in these regions. In their eyes, these wars and atrocities are just a stage that the peoples of the "developing world" have to go through. Like children, they supposedly do not know any better—and they will continue not to know any better for some time.[12]

Nothing like this can be said about Israel, of course. Considered from the perspective of European liberalism, the Jews are no Muslim or Third World people. Jews are to be seen as a European people, and the standards applied to us are those that are supposed to apply to Europe, which has finally reached the stage of "moral maturity." Hence the disgust and rage leveled at Israelis and Jews for insisting on our national self-determination. Whenever we act unilaterally in military matters, or rely on our own independent judgment in legal and constitutional affairs, we are seen as former Europeans who have grotesquely turned our backs on the path to moral maturity. We are not like children, who cannot be held responsible because they do not know better. We are like adults, who do know better, and have nonetheless consciously chosen the path of unreason and immorality.

This explains why there is such an imbalance between the way many in Europe see Israel and the way they regard Iran, Turkey, the Arab states, and the Third World. The double standard arises directly from the Kantian interpretation of history. Wherever the new paradigm strikes root, there you will find that the moral demands made of Israel are ever more stringent, whereas public criticism of Israel's Muslim neighbors is soft-pedalled or does not take place at all. This for the simple reason that the Iranians, Turks, and Arabs are not considered to be at the right stage in their history to understand morality and reason. As Kant would say, with them "everything as a whole is made up of folly and childish vanity, and often of childish malice and destructiveness."[13]

Of course, it is neither polite nor politic to say that all these nations are no better than simple and violent children, and that for this reason little is to be expected of them. But scratch the polite surface, and you will find that this shocking condescension, on the border of racism, is everywhere. The insistence that Israelis must be held accountable to a higher moral standard than Arabs or Iranians because we are, after all, "Europeans," appears constantly in background conversations. Most who hold this view are, however, careful not to put it on the official record. Not so the Danish ambassador to Israel, who did recently make just this point during a public address, which reflects quite well what so many have told us so often in private:

> There is the allegation that Europe is applying double standards, discriminating. . . . I think Israel should insist that we discriminate you [*sic*]. That we apply double standards. This is because you are one of us. . . . Sometimes, the response on the part of some of the Israeli interlocutors is, 'Look what's going on in Syria. Look what's going on elsewhere.' Those are not the standards that you are being judged by. It's not the standards that Israel would want to be judged by. So I think you have the right to insist that we apply double standards, and put you to the same standards as all the rest of the countries in the European context.[14]

XXIV: Britain, America, and Other Deplorable Nations

THE TERRIBLE CAMPAIGNS OF vilification directed against Israel, then, would seem to have the following cause: The Jews, despite being perceived as a "European" people who should know better, nonetheless continue to act as an independent national state, pursuing their interests and aspirations according to their own understanding. And they do this rather than accepting a European conception of what it means to be a "morally mature" nation. If this is right, then we should be able to see cases in which other nations are similarly deplored for the same reason. Are there other examples of nations that have been subjected to comparable campaigns of vilification? And are these nations, too, examples of "European" nations that are held to a different standard because they should know better?

The answer to these questions is certainly yes. In the 1980s, the outstanding example of a nation subjected to such disgust and moral vilification was of course the apartheid regime in South Africa. In the 1990s, international horror was directed against Serbia. Today, with both of these countries out of the way as objects of opprobrium, the moral outrage that has long taken aim at Israel has been turned against the United States, against Britain after its vote to leave Europe, and against Eastern European nations such as Hungary, Poland, and Czechia that resist European standards of behavior on a number of fronts. In pointing to these examples, I do not mean to suggest that these very different nations belong in the same moral category. I think it is obvious that they do not. Yet they are all examples of nations that have been subjected to the kind of campaigns of vilification and shaming that have been most prominently associated with Israel in recent years. I would like to understand what it is, from the perspective of European liberalism, that makes these nations so deplorable, and what moves the revulsion against them.

I will begin with the American case. It is hard to miss the hatred that has been heaped upon American administrations for their own assertion of an independent political posture. This has certainly been true of the overtly nationalist themes of the Trump presidency. Yet in many respects, this is not something new. At least since the end of the Cold War, Europeans have been excoriating American administrations for their "refusal to join" international agreements that have won the favor of the "international community," from the Kyoto Protocol to the International Criminal Court. They have deplored America for its willingness to solve pressing security problems on its own, as in the case of the Second Gulf War, which was conducted without a mandate from the United Nations. Indeed, Europeans find it disturbing that Americans do not always view their own military as existing to serve "the international community," and that Americans are willing to disavow the United Nations as the world's "supreme decision-making authority." In other words, in addition to being troubled by the substance of this or that American policy, the European leadership has consistently found it disturbing that the United States sees itself as having a right to act unilaterally, according to its own judgment, in the service of its own people, values, and interests. Their problem is, in other words, that the United States acts as an independent nation.

The similarity to Israel's case is striking. As with Israel, the waves of disgust and anger always fix on a particular American decision or policy. But while the particular issues come and go, they are not what is driving the trajectory of ever-increasing disgust and anger. What is driving it is the insistence on the right, where necessary, to unilateral action—that is, the insistence on living under the old order of national states. And here, as in Israel's case, the consternation is in accordance with a systematic double standard: The Americans are reviled, and their behavior deplored, for exercising independent judgment in the pursuit of their interests as a nation, whereas no such scandal is attached to China or Iran exercising independent judgment and pursuing their own interests. Again, it is the national independence of a "European" people that should have reached moral maturity and should know better that is driving the anger and hatred.

This same outrage has been extended to Britain as well in the wake of its decision to return to a course of national independence and self-determination, and to nations such as Czechia, Hungary, and Poland that insist on maintaining an immigration policy of their own that does not conform to the European Union's theories concerning refugee resettlement. In these and other similar cases, the substantive objections are secondary to the anger over the very possibility of an independent policy by a European nation.[15] And as in Israel's case, these independent policies are compared with Nazism or fascism.[16]

Nor is the censure limited to mere talk. There are at least two cases in which such moral condemnation was followed by coercive action: the delegitimization campaigns conducted against South Africa and Serbia, ultimately resulting in the destruction of the apartheid regime in South Africa, and the forcible expulsion of Serbia from Kosovo. I do not doubt that the South African regime was morally repugnant, or that Serb forces were responsible for outrages after the collapse of Yugoslavia. But what is of interest for my purposes here is not the objective moral failings of these nations—a matter concerning which there can be little disagreement. Rather, I want to know why these two nations were singled out for vilification when so many other nations rivaled them in bloodshed, oppression, and torture, and yet were largely ignored. My proposal is that the hatred directed against these nations cannot be explained simply by referring to the wrongs they committed. For who can seriously say that the Serbs had a worse human rights record than North Korea, Iran, Turkey, Syria, Sudan, or the Congo? Or that the oppression of blacks in South Africa, dreadful though it surely was, was more reprehensible than the oppression of women in Saudi Arabia today?

The reason that these peoples were singled out for special hatred and disgust, and for special punishment, is that white South Africans and Serbs are seen as Europeans, and are held to a moral standard that is without any relation to what is expected of their African or Muslim neighbors. After all, why should two million Albanians in Kosovo be recognized as a second independent Albanian state while thirty million Kurds continue to suffer terror and persecution, year after year, at the hands of the Turks, Arabs, and Iranians for want of an independent homeland? The decisive difference between the two cases is, I submit, that the Serbs, who regard Kosovo as their own, are perceived as a European people who should know better; while the Turks, Iranians, and Arabs who continue to oppress and murder the Kurds are seen (from the perspective of the paradigm of the European liberals) as childish savages from whom one can expect, morally, virtually nothing.

The point is initially counterintuitive, but straightforward once you consider it. If a nation is European, or descended from European settlement, then what is expected of it is in accordance with European standards—which increasingly means the Kantian renunciation of a national right to independent judgment and action, especially with regard to the use of force. By contrast, Iran, Turkey, the Arabs, and the Third World are, in this view, considered primitive peoples that have not yet even arrived at the stage of the national state consolidated under the rule of law. In practice, this means that much of the time, no moral standards are seen as applying to them at all.

XXV: Why Imperialists Hate

"LIBERAL INTERNATIONALISM" IS NOT merely a positive agenda for the erasure of national boundaries and the dismantling of the national states in Europe and elsewhere. It is an imperialist ideology that incites against nationalism and nationalists, seeking their delegitimization wherever they appear in Europe, or among nations such as America and Israel that are regarded having emerged from European civilization.

Why has the hatred emanating from liberal circles been so little discussed? It seems that this is because the existence of such a hatred does not fit within the Kantian paradigm, according to which reason should be moving mankind toward the abandonment of the independent national state, along with the hatred and violence that characterized the era of independent nations. According to this view, the coming international state will arise together with reason and peace. But if it were to turn out that support for the liberal imperialist program produces not reason and peace, but hatred and violence, the claim that liberal empire is the only position available to reasonable people would be badly damaged.

There is, in other words, a blind spot in contemporary liberal discourse. Due to their commitment to a universal political order, liberal imperialists tend to attribute hatred to national and tribal particularism (or else to religion), while overlooking or downplaying the hate that is a direct consequence of the advance of their own aspiration of attaining universal political order.

None of this should be surprising. Historically, every imperial theory with which we are familiar—whether Egyptian or
Assyrian, Greek or Roman, Christian or Muslim, liberal or Marxist—has offered an ideology of universal salvation and peace.[17]
And each such imperialist ideology, as soon as it collides with
a determined rejection of the salvation it offers, responds to
this rejection with an intense and abiding hatred. The universal, it seems, can love all men and all nations only as long as
they are willing to allow themselves to be determined, in their
thoughts and actions, by this universal. The moment that particular nations and particular men insist on self-determination,
everything changes. We then find that the universal hates the
particular, is appalled and disgusted by it. And this hate and
disgust only grow more inflamed as the resistance of the particular proves itself resilient and enduring.

This is the story of Christianity's hatred for the Jews, who
rejected the Gospel's message of salvation and peace. And it is
the story of Europe's hatred for modern-day Israel, which has
rejected the European Union's message of salvation and peace.
Kant's proposal to dismantle the national states of Europe and
bring them under the rule of an international federation is,
in other words, an Enlightenment recapitulation of an ancient
Christian trope. The anger that advocates of liberal empire
feel in confronting Israel's refusal to accept their program of
perpetual peace is very much akin to what some of their forefathers must have felt in confronting the Jews' refusal of the
Gospel.[18] And the Jews, too, when they find this hatred bearing
down upon them once again, experience feelings akin to what
their forefathers must have felt.

Once this is said, we must consider again Hitler's hatred of
the Jews, which is so often identified as an archetypal case of a

national or tribal hatred, the hatred of one nation for another. The Germans, however, have never cultivated an Old Testament conception of themselves as an independent national state, as the English, the Dutch, and the Americans did. The Catholic-German dream of *Austriae est imperare orbi universo,* the Nazi German dream of becoming "lord of the earth," and the Enlightenment German dream of "an *international state,* which would necessarily continue to grow until it embraced all the people of the earth," are all transformations of a single ideal and passion, that of emperors and imperialists, who dream of extinguishing all nations that are self-determining and free upon this earth, and suffusing them with a universal will bearing a single, universal salvation to all.

This is an ideal and passion that has found the Jews, with their irreducible concern for their unique cause and covenant, to be an insufferable impediment.[19] For this reason, German hatred of the Jews has indeed become a byword and an archetype. But it is not an archetype of the hatred of one nation for another with which it competes. It is an archetype of the hatred of emperors and imperialists, whose universal will cannot abide even a single, obstinately dissenting people, no matter how small. One must take time to consider this, so that it is understood well: To those in the grip of universalist delusions, there is no truth unless it is pure, without exceptions. And so the salvation they offer cannot be true unless it is pure, without exceptions—meaning that it must hold good for all nations, for every woman and every man, in every age. To allow even this one small dissent, to *tolerate* this one small dissent, would mean that the universal salvation that has been offered to mankind is false. And yet the Jews insist on dissenting.

This horror for the national and the particular has waned somewhat among Christians. Where Hebrew Scripture is firmly embraced, we now meet many Christians who are able to love the particularity of a unique national purpose and perspective. This is why so many devout Christians, both Protestant and Catholic, remain nationalists in America and Britain, even as the commitment to national independence has fallen into deep disrepute. They identify personally with ancient Israel, and it is this affinity that teaches them to love the particularity of a unique national purpose. It is also why so many in these countries love Israel, a love that has no source except in their personal identification with the ancient Israelite nation in the Old Testament.

But the horror for the national and the particular, the hatred of emperors and imperialists, burns bright today among "liberal internationalists." They have taken up the yearning for universal empire, believing in it as Christians once believed, and as Marxists once believed. The Jews will remain an object of special outrage for proponents of liberal empire, just as they were to their predecessors. The heart of the liberal imperialists is, however, capacious. And their hatred for the particular that will not submit, which has at times been directed almost exclusively against Israel, has in recent years discovered that there are many others who wish obstinately to defend their own unique cause and perspective. These holdouts against universal liberalism are to be found these days in America and Britain; in France, the Netherlands, and Denmark; in Czechia, Poland, Hungary, and Greece; in India and Japan; and in many other countries as well. And they will, all of them, in turn, be hated as the Jews have been hated, for wishing to chart an independent course that is their own.

Ironically, in the eyes of liberal imperialists, every dissident and every dissent look the same.[20] But these dissident movements and nations do not and never will possess a single worldview that they seek to advance. They share no universal doctrine that they offer for the salvation of all mankind. In some countries, the opposition to liberal empire is rooted in aspirations that I cannot help finding attractive and admirable, whereas in others it is in the name of things that I find distasteful or worse. What these very different peoples and movements have in common is only a desire to see their nation set its own course, for good or for ill. I cannot defend all of the particularist movements that will arise from this desire for national freedom, nor should anyone be asked to do so. Free nations cannot always make the right choices. They advance by trial and error, by pursuing what they perceive to be their own interests according to their own national traditions and their own unique point of vantage. Humanity's interest lies not in suppressing these views in the name of some fixed doctrine that will enthrone yet another world empire. Our interest is, rather, to allow the nations, insofar as this is possible, to pursue aspirations that are original to them. We will not be enamored with what every nation does with this freedom. But in tolerating the ways of other nations, we will be released from the old imperialist hatred of the different and diverse. And we may even come to see that a world of experiment and innovation will bring a greater blessing to the families of the earth than any universal design that we ourselves might have chosen.

Conclusion

―――――

THE VIRTUE OF NATIONALISM

IT IS REMARKABLE THAT Moses, who speaks with the Lord of heaven and earth, nonetheless initiates no universal conquest, and presents himself as legislating for Israel alone. The prophets of Israel certainly understood that the *tora* had been given for the betterment of all mankind. And yet Hebrew Scripture maintains a permanent distinction between the national state sanctioned by Moses in Deuteronomy, which is to govern within prescribed borders; and the aspiration to teach God's word to the nations of the world, which takes place when the nations come to Jerusalem to learn Israel's ways, and is associated with no conquest. How different is this biblical sensibility from what we find among the empires of antiquity, which always have their eye set on conquest, and seek to impose their vision of peace and prosperity on the nations at whatever cost!

In this book, I have sought to understand what stands behind the biblical preference for a political order based on the national state, a preference that in modern times became a pillar of the Protestant construction of Western civilization. The institution of the national state, I have suggested, offers a number of advantages over the alternative forms of political order that are known to us: The national state, like empire, drives war to the borders of a large, politically ordered region, establishing a protected space in which peace and prosperity can take hold. But unlike empire, the independent national state inculcates an aversion to adventures of conquest in distant lands. Moreover, an order of national states offers the greatest possibility for the collective self-determination. It establishes a life of productive competition among nations, each striving to attain the maximal development of its abilities and those of its individual members. And it provides the state with the only known basis for the development of free institutions and individual liberties. These are considerable advantages, and in light of them I conclude that the best political order known to mankind is, in fact, an order of independent national states.

This suggests that one should be a nationalist. I do not mean only that one should be a patriot, loyal to his or her own nation and concerned to advance its interests. Rather, what I propose is a broader view, one that recognizes the larger interest that all mankind share in a world of independent and self-determining nations, each pursuing interests and aspirations that are uniquely its own. Such a view is far from advocating a utopian universal right to national independence. But it does provide a much-needed aim or end for politics among the nations, pointing beyond the mere accumulation of power toward life and the good. Such a view can be beneficial in foreign affairs, in which a nationalist will be on his guard against imperial projects, coercive international institutions, and theories of actionable universal rights—all of which turn the minds

of statesmen from the needs and aspirations of the actual people they govern, and toward intrigue in foreign lands that they
invariably understand far less than they believe. And it can be
beneficial in domestic affairs, where a nationalist will have his
eyes constantly on what must be done to maintain and build up
the material well-being of his own nation, its internal cohesiveness, and its unique cultural inheritance—all of which must be
diligently tended to if the nation is to grow strong, becoming a
blessing to its own and a model and inspiration to others.

I have nowhere sought to deny or justify the many injustices
that have been done by nationalists of various countries. Nor
do I believe that an order of national states will make angels
of us in the future. But I do believe that to be devoted to the
cause of empire, and to the ideal of bringing the world under
a single authority and a single doctrine, is to advocate something far worse. I have pointed out more than once that it is just
such imperialism that has produced the greatest destroyers the
earth has known, with moderns such as Napoleon, Hitler, and
Stalin not least among them. Of course, my liberal friends can
explain at length how their own imperialism will be different
from all others that have come before, how they have developed new conceptual tools and new methods of governance,
and how these will finally bring us peace and prosperity. Past
experience, however, urges against trusting in these theories,
even if we appreciate those promoting them as well-intentioned
persons. The truth is that they are nearly all utopians, bursting
with love for the abstract theory they see before their eyes. In
the end, they will be consumed by the hatred of the universal
for the particular that will not submit, just as their predecessors
were. In the end, they will conclude that there is no alternative but to coerce the dissenters—dissenting individuals and

dissenting nations—making them conform to the universal theory by force, for their own good.

This means that the question of whether nationalism is desirable makes its presence felt on two very different levels. In the first place, there is the great theoretical question of what is the best political order. I have said that an order of national states is the best form of political order. But I have also emphasized that such an order is not to be regarded as a utopia, a blueprint for establishing a perfect political world, since it cannot be made perfect in the world, and the world cannot be perfected by it. Rather, nationalism should be regarded as a virtue in the political order—by which is meant that the conditions under which mankind live are improved as we advance toward a world of independent national states.

In the second place, there is the more personal question of whether nationalism is a virtue or a vice in the individual. All my life, I have heard it said that nationalism corrupts the human personality and makes it vicious. This is an opinion that I have heard from Christians and Muslims, liberals and Marxists, all of whom have found it congenial to cultivate visions of the earth as a political unity, governed by the one political perspective that happens to be their own. For all of them, nationalism is a vice because they believe, as Herzl was told in proposing a Jewish national state in the 1890s, "that we should not create new distinctions between people, that we ought not to raise fresh barriers, but make the old ones disappear instead."[1] Of course, each of them means that once the barriers have been torn down, it will be his own point of view that prevails on this new borderless earth and not someone else's—hardly a generous or a gracious offer, when you think about it. And yet it is the nationalist, who prefers to leave the barriers in place, and who believes that good fences make good neighbors, that is, in their eyes, vicious.

My own understanding is different. I have always thought that to be a nationalist is a virtue. This is not only because the order of national states is the best political order, and it is an admirable thing to devote oneself to moving this old earth a step closer to such a political order. Besides this, I believe that orienting oneself toward an order of independent national states paves the way for certain positive traits of character that are more difficult, if not impossible, to attain so long as one remains committed to the dream of empire. I will say a few more words about this.

As I have suggested, the desire for imperial conquest has a long history of being fueled by universal theories of mankind's salvation. Christianity, Islam, liberalism, Marxism, and Nazism have all served, in the recent past, as engines for the construction of empire. And what all of them have in common is the assertion that the truths that will bring deliverance to the families of the earth have at last been found, and that what is needed now is for all to embrace the one doctrine that can usher in the longed-for redemption.

Human beings are intolerant by nature, and it would be foolish to attribute this intolerance entirely to one or another political or religious standpoint. Nevertheless, if one wishes to inflame this innate intolerance, making it harsh and poisonous to the greatest degree possible, one could hardly do better than to disseminate a worldview according to which there is but one true doctrine, and mankind's salvation depends on the entire world submitting to it. Such beliefs are the fuel of empire because of the kind of men and women they create: imperialists who are at the same time revolutionaries. Regarding the universal ideal before their eyes as true for all, these are individuals who will not hesitate to overthrow whatever particularist tribal or national traditions stand in the way of the deliverance they see at hand. One can have no better destroyer than an individual ablaze with the love of a universal truth. And there is something of the destroyer, intellectually if not yet physically, in everyone who embraces universal salvation doctrines and the empires they call into being.

The order of tribes and clans also cultivates a certain kind of character, namely that of the loyalist to a particular clan or tribe. Members of an independent tribe or clan tend to be keenly aware of how the viability of the political community rests almost entirely on bonds of mutual loyalty. For this reason, clansmen and tribesmen cultivate a love of great deeds and self-sacrifice accomplished in the name of such loyalty, and an understanding of honor that prizes loyalty above all else. But they are also concerned for the authority and honor of their inherited tribal traditions, which they defend fiercely and even with physical violence, yet with remarkably little concern for whether these traditions in fact direct them toward what is true or right. Such men and women are quite able to countenance the ruin of a neighboring clan or tribe if they feel that it is necessary for the survival of their own and the preservation of their customary beliefs. However, since they harbor no universal aspiration, the evils they do are local and not general in scope, and one can bring them to make peace if they are convinced that their clan or tribe is not threatened.

At the midpoint between these two types of character—the universalist revolutionary and the tribal loyalist—one finds the type which is most compatible with nationalism. The nationalist is a particularist, like the tribesman, and his loyalty to the national state reminds us of the loyalties of the order of tribes and clans. Nevertheless, the nationalist also reminds us of the imperialist in his commitment to an ideal that is greater than the well-being of his own clan or tribe, which is the order of independent national states. He thus takes part in a political endeavor that is quite different both from the indefinite expansion of empire and from the petty warfare of anarchy. And this endeavor encourages in him a different cast of mind, in two respects:

First, the order of national states is an ideal that is premised upon a measure of humility with respect to the wisdom and achievements of the nations. The nationalist, we may say, knows two very large things, and maintains them both in his soul at the same time: He knows that there is great truth and beauty in his own national traditions and in his own loyalty to them; and yet he also knows that they are not the sum of human knowledge, for there is also truth and beauty to be found elsewhere, which his own nation does not possess. This balance of factors permits a moderating skepticism with respect to one's own national inheritance, which is recognized as a product of a particular history and circumstances. And it gives rise to a willingness to consider, on an empirical basis, the advantages of the institutions and customs of other nations. As we find it, for example, in the writings of Selden or Burke, such a moderate skepticism does not preclude an intense loyalty to one's own national traditions, but encourages a desire to repair and improve them where necessary. Nor does such a view collapse into a relativistic unwillingness to generalize from experience, as is often said. Rather, it cultivates a wariness of over-extending such generalizations, which may fail to hold good when applied to a given nation at a given time, for reasons that may not yet be visible to us.

Second, the free national state, as we know, comes into being and is maintained through the alliance of diverse tribes and clans, each of which exists thanks to the loyalty of its people to their own tribal leadership and traditions. The nationalist, while remaining loyal to the interests and perspectives of his own tribe and clan, nevertheless recognizes the immense value that is found in the unity of these diverse tribes and the peace that exists among them. This point of vantage changes his character, making it something quite different from that of the independent tribesmen or clansmen of earlier days. For while the nationalist will at times take sides in the disputes among the tribes that still constitute the nation, he tends to view their claims with a measure of detachment that grows out of his concern for the nation as a whole. In this way, the nationalist learns a moderate skepticism regarding the point of view of his own tribe, and is better able to see the merits of the views being advanced by other tribes. He thus becomes more alert to the advantages of an empirical and pragmatic politics that takes the respective views of the different tribes into account—an approach that leads, in many cases, to a better understanding of the good of the nation than what the perspective of any one tribe can afford.

In the soul of the nationalist, then, one often finds a gratifying tension between his intense loyalty to the inherited traditions of his own nation and tribe; and the skepticism and empiricism that result from his awareness of the diversity of traditions, both within the tribes of his own nation and among foreign nations. I say that this tension is a very great virtue in any individual, and that the fruits that are born of it in terms of political and moral understanding are not to be exceeded by those that arise from any other disposition.

I do not, of course, mean to say that every nationalist will succeed in overcoming a narrow attachment to his own tribe. Certainly, many do not. Much less do I suppose that skeptical and tolerant individuals cannot exist among the imperialists. It has been my pleasure to know more than a few such men and women, who have succeeded in escaping the rationalist rigidity of their colleagues. Rather, my point is that universal salvation theories—of which the pursuit of a universal liberal empire is today the most influential—work relentlessly to establish conformity and break down the effects of countervailing considerations, not only among the nations that are subjected to them, but also in the soul of the individual. It is nationalism, alone among the political dispositions that are known to us, that offers a consistent counterweight to this fanaticism of the universal, establishing the diversity of independent nations as a virtue of the political order, and the tolerance and appreciation of such diversity as a virtue in the individual.

———

IT IS SAID THAT when God calls Abraham, he tells him that he will "make of you a great nation . . . and in you will all the families of the earth be blessed."[2] Yet nowhere are the patriarchs offered an empire over the earth, only a kingdom over Israel. The other nations that will one day find their way to God and his teachings will do so in their own time and according to their own understanding. Each nation judges in accordance with a perspective that is its own. There is no human being, and no nation, that can claim to have captured the entire truth for all the others.

This Mosaic view is diametrically opposed to that offered by Kant's supposedly enlightened imperialism, which asserts that moral maturity arrives with the renunciation of national independence and the embrace of a single universal empire. But there is no moral maturity in the yearning for a benevolent empire to rule the earth and take care of us, judging for us and enforcing its judgments upon us. It is in fact nothing but a plea to return to the dependency of childhood, when our parents took care of us and judged for us in all important matters. True moral maturity is attained only when we stand on our own feet, learning to govern ourselves and defend ourselves without needlessly harming those around us, and where possible also extending assistance to neighbors and friends. And the same is true for nations, which reach a genuine moral maturity when they can live in freedom and determine their own course, benefiting others where this is feasible, yet with no aspiration to impose their rule and their laws on other nations by force.

Wishing to attain maturity, we should shoulder the burdens of national freedom and independence that we have received as an inheritance from our forefathers. Let us do everything in our power to ensure that this precious gift is still intact when the time comes to pass this national freedom on to our children.

ACKNOWLEDGMENTS

THIS BOOK WAS WRITTEN at the suggestion of Steven Grosby, whose own work on nationalism and its relationship with the Jewish Bible has long been an inspiration to me. Steven has guided me in this and in numerous other matters for many years now. I am pleased to have the opportunity to express my gratitude for his mentorship, collaboration, and friendship.

The kernel of the book is a theory of the national state that I developed in conversation with Ofir Haivry during the first decade of our partnership at the Shalem Center beginning in 1994. We have been through much together since. I could not have written such a book without his many contributions to my thinking, which are felt throughout these pages.

My treatment of Locke and his relationship with the Bible has been informed by Jonathan Silver's insights on the subject. My view of political life as founded upon relations of mutual loyalty has likewise come to maturity in light of discussions with my daughter Avital Hazony Levi. My presentation owes much to both of them.

I would like to thank those scholars who have devoted precious time to commenting on parts of the manuscript, including

Randy Barnett, Raphael Ben-Levi, Peter Berkowitz, R. Rafi Eis, Steven Grosby, Ofir Haivry, Yael Hazony, Michael Kochin, Neal Kozodoy, Julius Krein, Walter Russell Mead, Joshua Mitchell, Glenn Moots, Paul Rahe, R.R. Reno, R. Mitch Rocklin, Eric Schliesser, Jerry Unterman, Joshua Weinstein, and Jonathan Yudelman.

The last few years have been trying ones for me and my family. I have been blessed with friends who have extended all manner of support and assistance, which has made it possible for me to reach this point whole and in good spirit. I would like to thank, especially, Barry and Lainie Klein, Seth and Nealy Fischer, Roger and Susan Hertog, David and Hila Brog, R. Arnold Scheinberg, Michael Murray, John Churchill and Alex Arnold of the John Templeton Foundation, R. Jay Marcus, R. Menachem Zupnik, Bart Baum, Jack Berger, Stephanie Dishal, Ron Hersh, Nicholas Khuri, Fern Baker, and Meirav Jones.

I am fortunate to have found both inspiration and skill in Andrew Stuart, my agent. Lara Heimert, publisher at Basic Books, provided wise counsel and enthusiastic support at every stage. Dan Gerstle of Basic invested his great sensitivity and intelligence in improving the book in every way. Keith Urbahn, Jonathan Bronitsky, and Frank Schembari of Javelin and Betsy DeJesu and Carrie Majer of Basic designed an exceptional marketing campaign, and Melissa Veronesi deftly handled production. I am grateful for their efforts, which made this project something more significant than I believed it would be in setting out.

I have dedicated the book to the members of my tribe, the children that my wife, Yael, and I have brought into the world and raised together. In seeking to teach them, I have learned much. Some of what I have learned has been captured here.

NOTES

INTRODUCTION: A RETURN TO NATIONALISM

1. On Reagan's "new nationalism," see Norman Podhoretz, "The New American Majority," *Commentary* (January 1981); Irving Kristol, "The Emergence of Two Republican Parties," *Reflections of a Neo-Conservative* (New York: Basic Books, 1983), 111.

2. For my views on Jewish nationalism, see Yoram Hazony, *The Jewish State* (New York: Basic Books, 2000); "Did Herzl Want a Jewish State?" *Azure* 9 (Spring 2000); "The Guardian of the Jews," *Azure* 13 (Summer 2003); "Character," *Azure* 14 (Winter 2003).

3. My definition of nationalism draws on a tradition of political thought exemplified by Mill, who argued that it is "in general a necessary condition of free institutions that the boundaries of government should coincide in the main with those of nationalities." John Stuart Mill, *Representative Government*, in *Utilitarianism, on Liberty, and Considerations on Representative Government*, ed. Geraint Williams (London: Everyman, 1993 [1861]), 394. Similarly, Mazzini argued that "with the exception of England and France, there is perhaps not a single country whose present borders correspond to [God's] design. . . . Natural divisions and the innate, spontaneous tendencies of the peoples will replace the arbitrary divisions sanctioned by evil governments. The map of Europe will be redrawn. Free nations . . . will arise." Guiseppe Mazzini, "The Duties of Man," in *A Cosmopolitanism of Nations*, eds. Stefano Recchia and Nadia Urbiniti, trans. Stefano Recchia (Princeton: Princeton University Press, 2009 [1859]), 93. The traditional association of nationalism with views

of this kind has been confused by the proliferation of new definitions advanced in academia. Of these, perhaps closest to the traditional view is that of Ernst Gellner, who suggests that nationalism is a "political principle, which holds that the political and the national unit should be congruent." Gellner, *Nations and Nationalism* (Oxford, UK: Blackwell, 1983), 1.

4. Charles Krauthammer, "Universal Dominion: Toward a Unipolar World," *The National Interest* (Winter 1989–1990), 46–49. Krauthammer explains that he does not refer to the United States as an empire because "we do not hunger for territory." Charles Krauthammer, "Democratic Realism: American Foreign Policy in a Unipolar World," Irving Kristol Annual Lecture, American Enterprise Institute, February 10, 2004. It is a mistake, however, to suppose that imperialism expresses a hunger for territory. It is rather the expression of a hunger to control other nations—something that many analysts seem to believe can be attained today using aerial bombardment and other methods that do not require annexation of territory. A similar view appears in William Kristol and Robert Kagan, "Toward a Neo-Reaganite Foreign Policy," *Foreign Affairs* 75:4 (July–August 1996), 18–32, which proposes "benevolent global hegemony," where hegemony is defined as "preponderant influence and authority over all others in its domain" (p. 20).

5. For Thatcher's views, see her Speech to the College of Europe ("The Bruges Speech"), September 20, 1988; Margaret Thatcher, *Statecraft* (New York: HarperCollins, 2002), 320–411.

6. Regarding the hesitation among imperialists to use this term, Thomas Donnelly remarks, "There's not all that many people who will talk about it openly. . . . It's discomforting to a lot of Americans. So they use code phrases like 'America is the sole superpower.'" Thomas E. Ricks, "Empire or Not?" *Washington Post*, August 21, 2001. Nevertheless, after the al-Qaida attack on the United States on September 11, 2001, both proponents and opponents began to speak more emphatically of empire. See Max Boot, "The Case for American Empire," *Weekly Standard*, October 15, 2001; Stephen Peter Rosen, "An Empire If You Can Keep It," *National Interest* (Spring 2002); Stanley Kurtz, "Democratic Imperialism: A Blueprint," *Policy Review* (May 2003); Herfried Münkler, *Empires*, trans. Patrick Camiller (Malden, MA: Polity, 2007 [2005]); Niall Ferguson, "America as Empire, Now and in the Future," *The National Interest* (June 23, 2008). More critical approaches were offered by Andrew Bacevich, *American Empire* (Cambridge, MA: Harvard University Press, 2002); Michael Ignatieff, "The American Empire," *New York Times Magazine*, January 5, 2003; John Judis, *The Folly of Empire* (New York: Scribner,

2004). For formulations of a universal political order that do not use the term "empire," see, among others, Alexander Wendt, "Why a World State Is Inevitable," *European Journal of International Relations* 9 (2003), 491–542; Anne-Marie Slaughter and John Ikenberry, *Forging a World of Liberty Under Law* (Princeton, NJ: Woodrow Wilson School, Princeton University, September 27, 2006).

7. Recent authors defending an order of independent national states, or aspects of such an order, include Roger Scruton, "In Defense of the Nation," in *The Philosopher on Dover Beach* (New York: St. Martin's Press, 1990), 299–328; David Miller, *Nationality* (Oxford, UK: Oxford University Press, 1992); Gertrude Himmelfarb, "The Dark and Bloody Crossroads: Where Nationalism and Religion Meet," *The National Interest* 32 (Summer 1993), 53–61; Margaret Canovan, *Nationhood and Political Theory* (Northampton, MA: Edward Elgar, 1996); Lenn Goodman, "The Rights and Wrongs of Nations," in *Judaism, Human Rights, and Human Values* (Oxford, UK: Oxford University Press, 1998), 137–161; John Bolton, "Should We Take Global Governance Seriously?" *Chicago Journal of International Law* 1 (2000); David Conway, *In Defense of the Realm* (Hampshire, UK: Ashgate, 2004); Jeremy Rabkin, *Law Without Nations?* (Princeton, NJ: Princeton University Press, 2005); Pierre Manent, *A World Beyond Politics?* (Princeton, NJ: Princeton University Press, 2006); Natan Sharansky, *Defending Identity* (New York: PublicAffairs, 2008); John Fonte, *Sovereignty or Submission* (New York: Encounter, 2011); Dani Rodrik, *The Globalization Paradox* (New York: Norton, 2011); Bernard Yack, *Nationalism and the Moral Psychology of Community* (Chicago: University of Chicago Press, 2012); Amitai Etzioni, "The Democratisation Mirage," *Survival: Global Politics and Strategy* 57 (July 2015), 139–156.

8. See John Breuilly, *Nationalism and the State* (Chicago: University of Chicago Press, 1982), 8.

9. I have avoided the term "nation-state," which is often understood to mean that the nation consists of those individuals living in a given state. For the relationship between the nation and the state, see Chapters IX and X.

10. Here and throughout the book, I take *liberalism* to be a rationalist political theory based on the assumption that human beings are free and equal by nature, and that obligation to the state and other institutions arises through the consent of individuals. Since liberalism is a rationalist theory, its precepts are supposed to be universal, applying in all times and places. It is sometimes useful to refer specifically to "classical liberalism," which, in addition, proposes that human political motivation is largely concerned with protecting life and property.

Part One: Nationalism and Western Freedom

1. The signatories of the 1957 Treaty Establishing the European Community assert that they are "determined to lay the foundations of an ever closer union among the peoples of Europe." In the Solemn Declaration on European Union of 1983 (the "Stuttgart Declaration"), ten European governments agreed to "an ever closer union among the peoples and Member States of the European Community." The 1992 Maastricht Treaty establishing the European Union also declares that "this Treaty marks a new stage in the process of creating an ever closer union among the peoples of Europe" (Title I, Article A).

2. The idea of the United States as an empire with overseas possessions was briefly taken up by the American political leadership in the 1890s, but quickly fell into disrepute. On America's constitutional standing as an independent national state, and the effect of this status on its foreign relations, see Rabkin, *Law Without Nations?*, 98–129.

3. Yoram Hazony, *The Philosophy of Hebrew Scripture* (Cambridge, UK: Cambridge University Press, 2012), 103–160; Rabkin, *Law Without Nations?*, 9–11.

4. See Part One, note 23, below.

5. Quoted in Harold Nicolson, *Monarchy* (London: Weidenfeld and Nicolson, 1962), 20.

6. G. R. Driver and John C. Miles, trans., *The Code of Hammurabi* (Oxford, UK: Clarendon, 1955); James B. Pritchard, ed., *Ancient Near Eastern Texts* (Princeton, NJ: Princeton University Press, 1969), 163.

7. For "house of bondage," see Exodus 13.3, 20.2; Deuteronomy 5.6.

8. In this book, I distinguish between the *nation* and the *tribes* and *clans* that together constitute the nation. I will use the word *people* more loosely to refer to national, tribal, or clan groupings without reference to their scale. For discussion, see Chapter IX.

9. On the ancient Israelite kingdom as a classical national state, see Hans Kohn, *The Idea of Nationalism* (Toronto: Collier, 1944), 27–30; Steven Grosby, *Biblical Ideas of Nationality* (Winona Lake, IN: Eisenbrauns, 2002); Anthony Smith, *Chosen Peoples* (Oxford, UK: Oxford University Press, 2003); Aviel Roshwald, *The Endurance of Nationalism* (Cambridge, UK: Cambridge University Press, 2006), 14–22; David Goodblatt, *Elements of Ancient Jewish Nationalism* (Cambridge, UK: Cambridge University Press, 2006), 21–26; Doron Mendels, *The Rise and Fall of Jewish Nationalism* (New York: Doubleday, 1992). The biblical History of Israel does not, in fact, depict the national state as ideal. God's initial preference is that

Israelite national unity be achieved under the order of tribes and clans and without a standing government. It is the failure of this order in the book of Judges that brings God to acquiesce in the establishment of the state. See Judges, esp. 17–21, and Samuel 1.8; Hazony, *The Philosophy of Hebrew Scripture*, 144–154.

10. For the king, see Deuteronomy 17.15; Jeremiah 30.21. For the prophets, see Deuteronomy 18.15, 18. Regarding priests teaching the king, see Deuteronomy 17.18–20. All translations from the Hebrew Bible are my own.

11. Deuteronomy 2.4–6, 9, 19.

12. Calls for the unification of the divided tribes of Israel under their own government include Isaiah 11.13–14; Jeremiah 3.18, 30.21, 50.4; Ezekiel 34.23, 37.15–24; Hoshea 2.2. Compare Isaiah 9.21; Jeremiah 33.24. Regarding the freedom of other nations, see Jeremiah's call for the restoration of Moav (48.47), Ammon (49.6), and Elam (49.39); see also Daniel 11.41. Notice, too, the grief expressed for Moav at Isaiah 15.5, 16.11. The restoration of Israel is described as being in friendship with Egypt and Assyria at Isaiah 19.23–25.

13. Deuteronomy 17.14–20.

14. The term "race" did not take on its present strictly biological meaning until the late nineteenth century. After the Second World War, terms such as "ethnicity" and "ethnic group" were coined to replace this term, which had become tainted through its association with Nazi race theories. Azar Gat, *Nations* (Cambridge, UK: Cambridge University Press, 2013), 27.

15. Non-Jews are said to have joined Israel during the departure from Egypt at Exodus 12.38, Numbers 11.4. For Jethro, see Numbers 10.29; and Ruth at 1.16. The Mosaic punishment of *karet*, being "cut off" from the people, is especially aimed at those who do not participate in the most basic aspects of Israelite nationhood: circumcision (Genesis 17.14); fasting on Yom Kippur (Exodus 12.15, 19); and maintaining sexual purity (Leviticus 18.1–29). See also Numbers 15.31; Mishna Keritot 1.1; Maimonides, *Commentary on the Mishna* for Keritot 1.1, which offers a more extensive list, including keeping the sabbath and Pesah.

16. Polybius, *Histories*, 5.104. By contrast, he reports that Philip of Macedon contemptuously declared, "What is this Greece which you demand that I evacuate?" (18.5). Expressions of loyalty to the Greek nation as a whole can also be found in Herodotus and Isocrates, among others. See Roshwald, *The Endurance of Nationalism*, 26–30. But neither a Greek national state nor a philosophical or literary work describing such a united national state seems to have ever come into being. For a

discussion of the national states of ancient Edom, Aram, and Armenia, see Grosby, *Biblical Ideas of Nationality*, 120–165. A broader survey of ancient national states in the Middle East and Asia is Azar Gat, *Nations*, 89–110.

17. As Cicero, Roman statesman and philosopher, expresses it, "There will not be different laws at Rome or Athens, or different laws now and in the future, but one eternal and unchangeable law will be valid for all nations and for all times." *On the Commonwealth*, 3.33. Stoicism is closely related to the idea of "world citizenship," or cosmopolitanism, descended from Diogenes the Cynic. See Malcolm Schofield, *The Stoic Idea of the City* (Cambridge, UK: Cambridge University Press, 1991); Julia Annas, *The Morality of Happiness* (Oxford, UK: Oxford University Press, 1993), 159–179.

18. On the Roman pursuit of universal empire and the adoption of this Roman imperial aim by Christianity, see Anthony Pagden, *Lords of All the World* (New Haven, CT: Yale University Press, 1995), 11–62. On the Christian order in Europe and its pursuit of a "Christian peace," see Garrett Mattingly, *Renaissance Diplomacy* (New York: Dover, 1988).

19. As the Ottoman Sultan Mehmed the Conqueror put it, apparently after capturing Constantinople for Islam in 1453, "There must be only one empire, one faith, and one sovereignty in the world." Franz Babinger, *Mehmed the Conqueror and His Time*, trans. Ralph Manheim (Princeton, NJ: Princeton University Press, 1978 [1953]), 112. After the fall of Constantinople, Russia took up claims to be the "Third Rome" and protector of all of Christianity, which likewise gave birth to a long tradition of Russian universal empire. See Smith, *Chosen Peoples*, 98–106; Henry Kissinger, *World Order* (New York: Penguin, 2014), 51–59.

20. On the development of national states in Christian Europe and the absence of such states under Islam, see Grosby, *Biblical Ideas of Nationality*, 6, n. 17.

21. As Hastings writes, "The Old Testament provided the paradigm. Nation after nation applied it to themselves, reinforcing their identity in the process." Hastings, *The Construction of Nationhood*, 196. On France, see Joseph Strayer, "France: The Holy Land, the Chosen People, and the Most Christian King," in *Medieval Statecraft and Perspectives of History*, eds. John Benton and Thomas Bisson (Princeton, NJ: Princeton University Press, 1971), 300–314. For the Czechs, see Howard Kaminsky, *A History of the Hussite Revolution* (Berkeley: University of California Press, 1967); Derek Sayer, *The Coasts of Bohemia* (Princeton, NJ: Princeton University Press, 1998).

22. Writing of Henry VIII's Act of Supremacy, Robert Jackson emphasizes that this was "not merely a conflict between . . . Henry and the pope. It was more fundamental: A conflict between a conception of public life organized on a cosmopolitan theological-political basis, versus another constructed on the foundations of a separate kingdom, the intimation of a national state." Robert Jackson, *Sovereignty* (Malden, MA: Polity Press, 2007), 44–48, esp. 47. For England as a model for all subsequent European nationalism, see Hastings, *The Construction of Nationhood*, 35–65, 96–97; Liah Greenfield, *Nationalism* (Cambridge, MA: Harvard University Press, 1992).

23. The effect of the Hebrew Bible on the independent national states of Western Europe has been discussed in a series of important studies, including Hastings, *The Construction of Nationhood*; Philip Gorski, "The Mosaic Moment," *American Journal of Sociology* 105 (2000), 1428–1468; Grosby, *Biblical Ideas of Nationality*, passim, esp. 217–231; Fania Oz-Salzberger, "The Jewish Roots of Western Freedom," *Azure* 13 (Summer 2002), 88–132; Smith, *Chosen Peoples*; Anthony Smith, "Nation and Covenant," *Proceedings of the British Academy* 151 (2006), 213–255; Arthur Eyffinger, "Introduction" to Petrus Cunaeus, *The Hebrew Republic*, trans. Peter Wyetzner (Jerusalem: Shalem Press, 2006); Arthur Eyffinger, "How Wondrously Moses Goes Along with the House of Orange! Hugo Grotius' 'De Republica Emendanda' in the Context of the Dutch Revolt," in *Political Hebraism*, eds. Gordon Schochet, Fania Oz-Salzberger, and Meirav Jones (Jerusalem: Shalem Press, 2008), 57–71; Eric Nelson, *The Hebrew Republic* (Cambridge, MA: Harvard University Press, 2010); Glenn Moots, *Politics Reformed* (Columbia: University of Missouri Press, 2010); Diana Muir Appelbaum, "Biblical Nationalism and the Sixteenth Century States," *National Identities* (New York: Routledge, 2013), 1–16; Meirav Jones, "Philo Judaeus and Hugo Grotius's Modern Natural Law," *Journal of the History of Ideas* 74 (July 2013), 339–359; Ofir Haivry, *John Selden and the Western Political Tradition*; Yechiel Leiter, *John Locke's Political Hebraism* (Cambridge, UK: Cambridge University Press, forthcoming); as well as various essays in the journal *Hebraic Political Studies*, available at www.hpstudies.org/20/Issue.aspx.

24. None of which prevented Louis IV, the French "Sun King," from seeking a universal empire of his own in the aftermath. See Franz Bosbach, "The European Debate on Universal Monarchy," in David Armitage, ed., *Theories of Empire, 1450–1800* (New York: Routledge, 1998), 81–98.

25. Papal decree Zelo Domus Dei, November 26, 1648. Translation mine.

26. The three Westphalia treaties do not announce a new political order. They still refer to Europe as a universal *respublica Christiana*—a world Christian republic. This point is discussed at length by Croxton, who suggests that the interpretation of the treaties as having been responsible for giving birth to a "Westphalian" system of sovereign states goes unnoticed in the international-relations literature until Pierre-Joseph Proudhon points it out in 1863. Derek Croxton, *Westphalia* (New York: Palgrave MacMillan, 2013 ed.), 339–362. Of course Vattel was already writing about a system of putatively "equal" and "sovereign" states in Europe in 1758, a century after the Westphalia treaties, but Croxton's point is basically right: What is later called the Westphalian system is hardly the only possible view of the order emerging during the Thirty Years' War.

27. The English common lawyer Matthew Hale, a disciple of Selden, writes that although God gave the Ten Precepts "to one particular nation, the Jewish church, yet he made that nation signal and eminent and conspicuous to all the world by signs, wonders, and observable providence, that they might be like a beacon upon a hill, like a mighty and stately pillar set up in the middle of the world to hang upon it those tables of natural righteousness, which might be conspicuous and legible to the greatest part even of the gentile world of many ages." Matthew Hale, *Treatise of the Nature of Laws in General*, quoted in Richard Tuck, *Natural Rights Theories* (Cambridge, UK: Cambridge University Press, 1979), 163.

28. European national states waged war over territory, but "they did not extinguish each other's sovereignty." See Jackson, *Sovereignty*, 66.

29. Honorius of Augsburg's *Summa Gloria*, written in the wake of the Investiture Controversy in 1123, argued that the right of the Catholic Church to oppose unjust actions of the state stems from the prophet Samuel's creation of the kingdom of Saul, whose rule was not absolute, but limited by divine justice even after Israel was ruled by an anointed king. See R. W. Carlyle and A. J. Carlyle, *A History of Medieval Political Theory in the West* (Edinburgh: William Blackwood, 1950), 4:286–289. In 1159, John of Salisbury invoked the limitations imposed on Jewish rulers in the book of Deuteronomy, and argued that all should "attend to the law which is imposed upon princes by the Greatest King who is an object of fear over all the earth. . . . Certainly this [law] is divine and cannot be dismissed with impunity." John of Salisbury, *Policraticus*, ed. and trans. Cary Nederman (Cambridge, UK: Cambridge University Press, 1990), 35–36.

30. John Fortescue, *In Praise of the Laws of England*, in *On the Laws and Governance of England*, ed. Shelley Lockwood (Cambridge, UK: Cambridge University Press, 1997); Ofir Haivry and Yoram Hazony, "What Is

Conservatism?," *American Affairs* (Summer 2017), 221–225. Fortescue's work was written around 1470 and published undated in 1543 or thereabouts, during the reign of Henry VIII.

31. The phrase "ancient customs and privileges" appears in the Dutch Declaration of Independence, the Act of Abjuration, of 1581. Oliver J. Thatcher, ed., *The Library of Original Sources* (Milwaukee, WI: University Research Extension Co., 1907), 5:190. Similarly, the English Petition of Right of 1628 speaks of the "rights and liberties of the subjects" as these appear in the "laws and free custom of the realm."

32. On Selden, see Haivry, *John Selden and the Western Political Tradition*; Haivry and Hazony, "What Is Conservatism?," esp. 225–230.

33. Hazony, *The Philosophy of Hebrew Scripture*, 151–152.

34. In the charter, Roosevelt and Churchill declared, "They respect the right of all peoples to choose the form of Government under which they will live; and they wish to see sovereign rights and self-government restored to those who have been forcibly deprived of them" (Article 3). However, it is also possible to see the Atlantic Charter as the beginning of the end of the order of independent national states, with its reference to the "pending . . . establishment of a wider and permanent system of general security" (Article 8). Like Woodrow Wilson, Roosevelt tended to suppose that old-style imperialism could be replaced by a form of "collective security" that would somehow evade establishing a new imperial order. Churchill, for his part, was a frank defender of Britain's empire outside of Europe, so the notion of a world security system fit easily with his views. For Roosevelt on Christianity, see Franklin Roosevelt, "Radio Address on the President's Sixtieth Birthday," January 30, 1942.

35. The entire *Second Treatise* can be read as a commentary on the Hebrew Bible. For a discussion of Locke's biblicism, see Joshua Mitchell, *Not by Reason Alone* (Chicago: University of Chicago Press, 1993), 73–97; Leiter, *John Locke's Political Hebraism*. Liberal social-contract theory is, in particular, an interpretation of the covenants of the Hebrew Bible. See Roshwald, *The Endurance of Nationalism*, 16; Michael Walzer, *Exodus and Revolution* (New York: Basic Books, 1985), 83–84. None of this is to say that the liberal social contract is an especially sound interpretation of the biblical teaching.

36. Locke is known as an empiricist, but this view of his thought is based largely on his *Essay Concerning Human Understanding* (Oxford, UK: Oxford University Press, 1975 [1789]), which is an influential exercise in empirical psychology. His *Second Treatise on Government* is not, however, a similar effort to bring an empirical standpoint to the theory of the state. Locke was one of the few political writers of his time who did not

argue on the basis of historical experience (Trevor Colbourn, *The Lamp of Experience* [Indianapolis, IN: Liberty Fund, 1998], 5–6), and the *Second Treatise* begins with a series of axioms without any evident connection to what can be known from the historical and empirical study of the state, asserting that (i) prior to the establishment of government, men exist in a "state of nature," in which (ii) "all men are naturally in a state of perfect freedom," as well as in (iii) a "state of perfect equality, where naturally there is no superiority or jurisdiction of one over another." Moreover, (iv) this state of nature "has a law of nature to govern it"; and (v) this law of nature is, as it happens, nothing other than human "reason" itself, which "teaches all mankind, who will but consult it." It is this universal reason that leads human beings to (vi) terminate the state of nature, "agreeing together mutually to enter into . . . one body politic" by an act of free consent. (See John Locke, *Second Treatise,* sections 4, 6–7, 15.) From these axioms, Locke proceeds to deduce the proper character of the political order for all nations on earth. Concerning Locke's rationalism, Quinton correctly concludes, "In Locke, an empiricist account of knowledge in general is combined with a rationalist theory of our knowledge of morality, the basis of Locke's theory of self-evident natural rights. 'Moral knowledge,' says Locke, 'is as capable of real certainty as mathematics.' Moral truths, like geometrical theorems, he regards as demonstrable necessities. By the time he reaches Book IV of his *Essay on Human Understanding* [see esp. 4.3.18], in which this position is taken, and argued for in a startlingly feeble way, Locke has altogether forgotten the moral fallibilism that is intimated by his rejection in Book I of 'innate practical principles.' It is this ethical rationalism that is fundamental to Locke's political theory, being an apt support for passionately dogmatic liberalism." Anthony Quinton, *The Politics of Imperfection* (London: Faber and Faber, 1978), 41.

37. "Every man being . . . naturally free, . . . nothing [can] put him into subjugation to any earthly power but only his own consent." Locke, *Second Treatise,* section 119.

38. Locke, *Second Treatise,* sections 55–69. Locke is likewise unable to justify obligations between parents and children after the children have reached maturity, and he must resort to the Mosaic instruction to "Honor your father and your mother" (Exodus 20.11; Deuteronomy 5.16) to make his system of obligation work (section 66).

39. "The great and chief end of men's uniting into commonwealths, and putting themselves under government, is the preservation of their property." By "property," Locke says he means the "lives, liberties and estates" of the individuals who join in the government. Locke, *Second*

Treatise, sections 123–124. See also 87, 173, 222. Locke recognizes the existence of no clans, tribes, or nations prior to the establishment of the state. The only collective of interest to him is the people or nation created "wherever any number of men, in the state of nature, enter into society *to make one people,* one body politic under one supreme government" (section 89, emphasis added). This is another way of saying that for Locke, as opposed to empiricists such as Selden and Burke, the political concept of the nation is entirely absent. This point is emphasized by Uday Singh Mehta, "Edmund Burke on Empire, Self-Understanding and Sympathy," in *Empire and Modern Political Thought,* ed. Sankar Muthu (Cambridge, UK: Cambridge University Press, 2012), 181; Ethan Alexander Davey, "Constitutional Self-Government and Nationalism," *History of Political Thought* 35 (Autumn 2014), 458–484.

40. As reported in the *Morning Chronicle,* April 18, 1794. Quoted in Richard Bourke, *Empire and Revolution* (Princeton, NJ: Princeton University Press, 2015), 683. Burke's relationship to Locke is exhaustively treated in Ofir Haivry, *The "Politick Personality,"* doctoral dissertation at University College London, 2005.

41. Jean-Jacques Rousseau, *On the Social Contract* (1762); Immanuel Kant, "Perpetual Peace," in *Political Writings,* ed. H. S. Reiss, trans. H. N. Nisbet (Cambridge, UK: Cambridge University Press, 1991 [1795]), 93–130; Ayn Rand, *Atlas Shrugged* (New York, Signet, 1996 [1957]); John Rawls, *A Theory of Justice* (Cambridge, MA: Harvard University Press, 1972). My account diverges from that of Leo Strauss and others who present Rousseau as a critic of Locke. True, Rousseau argues for a return to certain virtues required to maintain social cohesion and wage war in defense of the community. But it is a great exaggeration to see this as such a break with Hobbes and Locke that it initiates "the first crisis of modernity," as Strauss asserts in *Natural Right and History* (Chicago: University of Chicago Press, 1953), 252. What is now regarded as political modernity in fact emerges from the English conservative tradition of Fortescue, Coke, and Selden and its struggle against the absolutist theories of both absolutists and Puritans in England (Quinton, *The Politics of Imperfection,* 21). The first crisis of modern political thought is that which is initiated by the rationalist political theories of Hobbes, Locke, and Rousseau against this conservative tradition (Quinton, *The Politics of Imperfection,* 29–31). Rousseau's adherence to Locke's axiom system as a point of departure for political thought places him squarely within the rationalist tradition. His suggestion that a "people" does not exist until it is established by the state, and his proposed "civil religion" defined by the needs of the state (Rousseau, *Social Contract,* 1.6, 4.8) are

ersatz creations of the Lockean rationalist universe, in which Rousseau's thought remains imprisoned.

42. Locke writes that, according to the law of nature, "mankind are one community," making up "one society distinct from all other creatures." Indeed, men are divided into nations only by their wickedness: "Were it not for the corruption and viciousness of degenerate men, there would be no need . . . that men should separate from this great and natural community, and by positive agreements combine into smaller and divided associations" (Locke, *Second Treatise,* section 128). Locke thus distinguishes between the natural community of all mankind and the "smaller and divided" associations made by positive agreement to protect life and property. These smaller associations to enter into government can be made by "any number of men," because "it injures not the freedom of the rest" (Locke, *Second Treatise,* section 95; see also 89). As far as Locke's political theory is concerned, then, there is nothing inherently beneficial or desirable about the division of mankind into independent nations, and the way in which governments divide the human community and set up boundaries between them is a matter of indifference. State boundaries can be drawn anywhere or nowhere—thus the inherently unbounded character of the Lockean state. On the relationship between social-contract theory and the unboundedness of the state, see Scruton, "In Defense of the Nation," 320.

43. Liberal writers have never taken much notice of the nationalism of England, Scotland, the Netherlands, and France during the period between Henry VIII and the American Revolution—a period of 240 years. Liberal historiography awakens to take notice of nationalism only in the wake of the American and French revolutions at the end of the eighteenth century. This literature often regards these revolutions as heralding the end of all traditional national constitutions, and turning to a universal constitution dictated by reason, by which is meant a liberal constitution. The resulting combination of liberalism and nationalism, perhaps most familiar from Mazzini, is popular during much of the nineteenth century and into the twentieth. Writing in the 1930s, however, Hayek sees "historical accidents" as having caused this association between nationalism and liberalism: "That liberalism became first allied with nationalism was due to the historical coincidence that, during the nineteenth century, it was nationalism which, in Ireland, Greece, Belgium, and Poland, and later in Italy and Austro-Hungary, fought against the same sort of oppression which liberalism opposed." Friedrich Hayek, "The Economic Conditions of Interstate Federalism," *New Commonwealth Quarterly* 5 (September 1939), 131–149.

44. This tendency to dispense with national states was evident to Montesquieu, who observed that as far as commerce is concerned, "the whole world . . . comprises but a single state, of which all societies are members." Montesquieu, *The Spirit of the Laws*, 20.23.

45. Mises advocates "a world super-state really deserving of the name . . . that would be capable of assuring the nations the peace they require." Ludwig von Mises, *Liberalism in the Classical Tradition*, trans. Ralph Raico (San Francisco: Cobden Press, 1985 [1927]), 150.

46. According to Hayek, "The abrogation of national sovereignties and the creation of an effective international order of law is a necessary complement and the logical consummation of the liberal program. . . . The idea of interstate federation [is] the consistent development of the liberal point of view." Friedrich Hayek, "The Economic Conditions of Interstate Federalism."

47. I have in mind debates such as those in political theory between John Rawls's *A Theory of Justice* and Robert Nozick's *Anarchy, State and Utopia* (New York: Basic Books, 1974); or in economics between John Maynard Keynes, *General Theory of Employment, Interest and Money* (New York: Houghton Mifflin Harcourt, 1964 [1936]), and Friedrich Hayek, *The Constitution of Liberty* (Chicago: University of Chicago Press, 1960); or those in jurisprudence between Herbert Hart, *The Concept of Law* (Oxford, UK: Oxford University Press, 1961), and Ronald Dworkin, *Taking Rights Seriously* (New York: Gerald Duckworth, 1977). It is especially remarkable that universities present contemporary political theory as an argument between Rawls and Nozick, since both base their theories on Locke's free and equal individuals in a state of nature, and on the social contract that supposedly emerges from their free consent. See Russell Kirk, *Rights and Duties* (Dallas, TX: Spence, 1997), 98.

48. This view of the liberal construction as the "right side of history" was popularized by Bill Clinton. See Bacevich, *American Empire*, 32–38; David Graham, "The Wrong Side of the 'Right Side of History,'" *Atlantic*, December 21, 2015. Clinton's successors George W. Bush and Barack Obama embraced this rhetoric, with Bush, for instance, declaring, "We believe that liberty is the direction of history." Address at the National Endowment of Democracy, Washington, DC, November 6, 2003.

49. See my discussion, Chapter XIV, section 2.

50. Kaiser Wilhelm II, "Order of the Day," found in possession of captured soldiers. Charles Andler, *Pan-Germanism* (Paris: Armand Colin, 1915), 81.

51. Hitler explicitly rejects both the liberal social-contract state and the national state built by unifying disparate tribes on the basis of language

and history, calling such states "misbegotten monstrosities." The state, in Hitler's view, had an entirely different purpose from the national state, which was first, the "preservation and advancement of a community of physically and psychically homogenous creatures" by "assembling and preserving the most valuable stocks of basic racial elements"; and then, beyond this, to raise this race to a "dominant position," until it becomes a "master people" and "mistress of the globe." Adolf Hitler, *Mein Kampf,* trans. Ralph Manheim (New York: Houghton Mifflin, 1971 [1925]), 393, 396, 398. Thus if the Germans dealt firmly with the "racial poisoning" that afflicted them, they "must someday become lord of the earth." Hitler, *Mein Kampf,* 688.

52. Anthony Smith correctly sees a "fundamental divergence" of Hitler's Nazism from nationalism due to its embrace of a "biological imperialism" incompatible with the existence of a plurality of independent national states. Anthony Smith, *Nationalism in the Twentieth Century* (Oxford, UK: Martin Robertson, 1979), 78–80. As one German scholar writes, Hitler's entire purpose was "to destroy the nation-state system and to return to an imperial order." Münkler, *Empires,* 144. Indeed, to the extent that Hitler admired anything about Britain, it was its empire. See Niall Ferguson, *Empire* (New York: Basic Books, 2002), 279–282.

53. Konrad Adenauer, *World Indivisible with Liberty and Justice for All,* trans. Richard and Clara Winston (New York: Harper and Brothers, 1955), 6–10. See also Jean Monnet, *Memoirs* (London: Collins, 1978), 285–286. Compare Helmut Kohl, chancellor of Germany, forty years later: "European integration is in reality the question of war and peace in the Twenty-First Century. . . . We have no desire to return to the nation state of old." *The Times,* February 3, 1996, quoted in David Conway, *With Friends like These* (London: Civitas, 2014), 105.

54. As Margaret Thatcher put this shortly after being ousted as prime minister, "Germany's preponderance within the [European] Community is such that no major decision can really be taken against German wishes. In these circumstances, the Community augments German power rather than containing it." Margaret Thatcher, *The Path to Power* (New York: HarperCollins, 1995), 614.

55. See my discussion, Chapters XXI and XXIII.

56. A careful examination of the similarities between liberalism and Marxism, without losing sight of the moral distinctions between them, is provided by Ryszard Legutko, *The Demon in Democracy* (New York: Encounter, 2016). Increasingly relevant, as well, are studies examining the historical connections between liberalism and imperialism, including Uday Singh Mehta, *Liberalism and Empire* (Chicago: University of Chicago

Press, 1999); Jennifer Pitts, *A Turn to Empire* (Princeton, NJ: Princeton University Press, 2006).

57. Bush described the new world order in fantastic terms: "A hundred generations have searched for this elusive path to peace. . . . Today that new world is struggling to be born, a world quite different from the one we've known. A world where the rule of law supplants the rule of the jungle." George H. W. Bush, "Address to a Joint Session of Congress on the Persian Gulf Crisis and the Federal Budget Deficit," September 11, 1990.

58. Jürgen Habermas describes such "transnationalism" as "a global domestic politics without a world government . . . embedded within the framework of a world organization with the power to impose peace and implement human rights." Habermas, *The Divided West* (Malden, MA: Polity Press, 2006), 136. See also Rabkin, *Law Without Nations?*, 41–43.

59. Ludwig von Mises, *Liberalism in the Classical Tradition*, 150.

60. João Carlos Espada observes that "democracy in Europe is mainly perceived as an expression of a dogmatic rationalist project" detached from its Anglo-American association with empiricism, traditionalism, and common sense. For this reason, he writes, education in Europe largely ignores the English and American tradition, seeing them as incomplete manifestations of liberal-democratic government "whose first full formulation would only occur in the 1789 French Revolution." João Carlos Espada, *The Anglo-American Tradition of Liberty* (New York: Routledge, 2016), 10, 109, 187–188. However, this European view has increasingly been adopted in Britain and America as well.

61. See discussion in Part Three.

62. On the pluralism of the early modern European order, see Kissinger, *World Order*, 35.

63. On American global policy after the end of the Cold War, see Bacevich, *American Empire*. Bacevich concludes, "Holding sway in not one but several regions of pivotal geopolitical importance, disdaining the legitimacy of political and economic principles other than its own, declaring the existing order to be sacrosanct, asserting unquestioned military supremacy with a globally deployed force configured not for self-defense but for coercion: These are the actions of a nation engaged in the governance of empire. . . . Like it or not, America today *is* Rome" (p. 244). As Tom Friedman put it, "The emerging global order needs an enforcer. That's America's new burden." Thomas Friedman, "A Manifesto for a Fast World," *New York Times Magazine*, March 28, 1999. See also Thomas Friedman, *The Lexus and the Olive Tree* (New York: Picador, 1999), 465–468; Francis Fukuyama, *The End of History and the Last Man*

(New York: Free Press, 1992); and Shimon Peres, *The New Middle East* (New York: Henry Holt, 1995), among many other such works.

64. On the conservative (or "traditionalist") school in English political theory, see Quinton, *The Politics of Imperfection*; J. G. A. Pocock, *The Ancient Constitution and the Feudal Law* (Cambridge, UK: Cambridge University Press, 1987 ed.), esp. 30–55, 148–181; Harold J. Berman, "The Origins of Historical Jurisprudence: Coke, Selden, Hale," *Yale Law Journal* 103 (May 1994), 1652–1738; Colbourn, *The Lamp of Experience*; Kirk, *Rights and Duties*; Ethan Alexander-Davey, "Restoring Lost Liberty: François Hotman and the Nationalist Origins of Constitutional Self-Government," *Constitutional Studies* 1 (2016), 37–66; Haivry, *John Selden and the Western Political Tradition*; Haivry and Hazony, "What Is Conservatism?"

65. Long after the Enlightenment made it unfashionable for political theorists to cite passages from the Bible, biblical ideas continue to be handed down from one generation to the next, just without the citations. As Michael Lind writes concerning the contemporary United States, "Calvinism and the common law together have produced what is perhaps the most biblicist national culture in the world." Michael Lind, *The Next American Nation* (New York: Free Press, 1996), 272.

PART TWO:
THE CASE FOR THE NATIONAL STATE

1. Individuals frequently act out of mixed motives as well. For example, it is common for parents to act to increase their own property in part out of a desire to benefit their children; and a soldier may act out of a desire to enhance his own reputation as well as to be of service to his country. But this important fact does not affect the argument I have made here, which is that human motivation is much of the time concerned with action on behalf of one collective or another.

2. This extension of the self is described by Hume, who argues that we feel pride and shame with respect to things that are "parts of ourselves, or something nearly related to us" (*A Treatise of Human Nature*, 2.1.5), including pride in one's family and country (2.1.9). He then concludes that such pride is in fact love (2.2.1). For a similar theory in light of recent research in psychology, see Jonathan Haidt, *The Righteous Mind* (New York: Vintage, 2012), 256–318.

3. On the moral significance of such bonds of mutual loyalty, see David Miller, *Nationality* (Oxford, UK: Oxford University Press, 1992),

65–80; Bernard Yack, *Nationalism and the Moral Psychology of Community* (Chicago: University of Chicago Press, 2012), 169–183.

4. Other small-scale institutions that are resilient in the face of duress due to bonds of mutual loyalty among members who know each other personally include small towns or villages, churches, local political factions and unions, and street gangs.

5. This transmission of family, clan, tribal, or national loyalty to the children growing up in a given family does not happen automatically or in a uniform way. The intensity with which these loyalties are felt varies with the presence or absence of circumstances of danger to the family, clan, tribe, or nation in question. It depends, too, on the intensity with which the parents experience the challenges to their family, tribe, and nation, and the sensitivity of each child. Some children resist the loyalties of their parents and are more strongly influenced by those of a teacher, clergyman, or military commander who becomes, as it were, a second father or mother to them. And of course, even childhood loyalties can be broken or weakened when the trust implied by them is betrayed.

6. This use of the term "cohesion" comes from John Stuart Mill, *Representative Government*, in *Utilitarianism, on Liberty, and Considerations on Representative Government,* ed. Geraint Williams (London: Everyman, 1993 [1861]), 241; Henry Sidgwick, *The Elements of Politics* (n.p.: Elibron Classics, 2005 [1891]), 233, 276. As Sidgwick writes, "What is really essential . . . to a nation is . . . that the persons composing it should have a consciousness of belonging to one another, of being members of one body, over and above what they derive from the mere fact of being under one government; so that, if their government were destroyed by war or revolution, they would still hold firmly together" (202). It refers to the same phenomenon that Mill also calls "fellow-feeling" (392); which appears as "bonds of sentiment" in J. G. Herder, *Ideas for a Philosophy of the History of Mankind,* in *Herder on Social and Political Culture,* ed. and trans. F. M. Barnard (Cambridge, UK: Cambridge University Press, 1969 [1784–1791]), 324; and as the "sentiment of solidarity in the face of other groups" in Max Weber, "The Nation," in *From Max Weber,* trans. and eds. H. H. Gerth and C. Wright Mills (Oxford, UK: Oxford University Press, 1946 [1921]), 172.

7. Accessible discussions of the order of tribes and clans appear in Mark Weiner, *The Rule of the Clan* (New York: Farrar, Straus and Giroux, 2013); Azar Gat, *Nations* (Cambridge, UK: Cambridge University Press, 2013), 29–66. See also Adam Ferguson, *An Essay on the History of Civil Society,* ed. Fania Oz-Salzberger (Cambridge, UK: Cambridge University

Press, 1995 [1767]), 85. Steven Grosby points out that in the Bible, the clan (*mishpaha*) is clearly described as a subdivision of the tribe (*shevet*), and the family (*beit av*) is a subdivision of the clan. The twelve tribes are subdivisions of the Israelites as a people (*am*). Steven Grosby, *Biblical Ideas of Nationality* (Winona Lake, IN: Eisenbrauns, 2002), 15–22.

8. A common view among academic scholars regards the nation as a fiction or a recent invention. Among others, see Hans Kohn, *The Idea of Nationalism* (New York: Macmillan, 1948); Elie Kedourie, *Nationalism* (Oxford, UK: Blackwell, 1960); Ernst Gellner, *Nations and Nationalism* (Ithaca, NY: Cornell University Press, 2006 [1983]); Eric Hobsbawm, *Nations and Nationalism Since 1780* (Cambridge, UK: Cambridge University Press, 1990); Benedict Anderson, *Imagined Communities* (New York: Verso, 1991). For critical discussion of the thesis that nations are an invention of modernity, see Anthony Smith, "The Myth of the 'Modern Nation' and the Myths of Nations," *Ethnic and Racial Studies,* January 1988, 1–26; Azar Gat, *Nations,* 214–220; Susan Reynolds, *Kingdoms and Communities in Western Europe, 900–1300* (Oxford, UK: Oxford University Press, 1984), 255–256; Len Scales and Oliver Zimmer, eds., *Power and the Nation in European History* (Cambridge, UK: Cambridge University Press, 2005).

9. Jeremiah 32.39; Ezekiel 11.19; Chronicles 2.30.12.

10. This model of political society rejects the dichotomy between traditionalist, community-oriented societies (*gemeinschaft*) and modern, individualist societies (*gesellschaft*) that has been so prominent in the academic literature. For a parallel discussion offering a somewhat different approach, see Bernard Yack, *Nationalism and the Moral Psychology of Community,* 44–67. Recent works on loyalty worthy of attention include Andrew Oldenquist, "Loyalties," *Journal of Philosophy* 79 (1982), 173–193; George Fletcher, *Loyalty* (Oxford, UK: Oxford University Press, 1995); Richard Rorty, "Justice as Loyalty," *Ethical Perspectives* 4 (1997), 139–149; Anna Stilz, *Liberal Loyalty* (Princeton, NJ: Princeton University Press, 2009); John Kleinig, *On Loyalty and Loyalties* (Oxford, UK: Oxford University Press, 2014). For discussion of the problem collective attachments pose for liberal political thought, see Alisdair MacIntyre, *After Virtue* (Notre Dame, IN: Notre Dame University Press, 1981); Michael Sandel, *Liberalism and the Limits of Justice* (Cambridge, UK: Cambridge University Press, 1982); Charles Taylor, *Sources of the Self* (Cambridge, UK: Cambridge University Press, 1989); Amitai Etzioni, *The Spirit of Community* (New York: Simon and Schuster, 1993); Will Kymlicka, *Multicultural Citizenship* (Oxford, UK: Oxford University Press, 1995); Patrick Deneen, *Why Liberalism Failed* (New Haven, CT: Yale University Press, 2018).

11. The basis for such family-feeling among nations is in a shared language, religion, or law. But these are often insufficient to prevent nations from warring against one another, as in the case of America's wars with Britain. More powerful is a history of having fought together against common enemies in the past, which is the record of ancient mutual loyalties that can at times be revived by conditions of joint adversity and triumph.

12. None of this is meant to deny the possibility of sympathy toward other human beings, or toward other living things in general. The inclination to identify with others, or to be of assistance to others, is certainly very widespread, and is not limited to the collectives to which we are loyal. On the other hand, such feelings of sympathy are in most cases able to motivate only short-term acts of kindness, which may be significant in context but establish no lasting commitment of the kind that mutual loyalty provides. Because of the relatively weak and unreliable character of feelings of sympathy, such sentiments do not play an important role in creating and maintaining political order. Where we find that assistance is provided on an ongoing basis, or where the assistance offered requires great sacrifice, the mutual loyalties of the collective are almost always found to be responsible. For a careful exploration, see Eric Schliesser ed., *Sympathy* (Oxford: Oxford University Press, 2015).

13. See David Miller, *Nationality*, 42–45.

14. Some nations, including the English, French, and many others, preserve explicit traditions of their mixed national origins.

15. On the erosion of the ability to think in terms of human collectives in liberal societies, see Jonathan Haidt, *The Righteous Mind*, 111–133.

16. It is often said that a great variety of factors can contribute to human identity. However, the different "identities" in question, even where they reflect a novel content unfamiliar from earlier human history, merely establish new clans and new tribes.

17. Such a cultural inheritance is of course never uniform. A national tradition has many strands, and each tribe, clan, and family emphasizes and develops different strands within the tradition, often in the context of a conscious competition with the others.

18. Such discussion typically invokes Thomas Hobbes, *Leviathan* 1.13–14; John Locke, *Second Treatise on Government*, section 97; or Jean-Jacques Rousseau, *On the Social Contract*, 1.6.

19. As Hume writes, "Nothing is a clearer proof that a theory . . . is erroneous, than to find that it leads to paradoxes repugnant to the common sentiments of mankind, and to the practice and opinion of all nations and ages. The doctrine which founds all lawful government on an original contract . . . is plainly of this kind." David Hume, "Of the Original

Contract," in *Essays,* ed. Eugene F. Miller (Indianapolis, IN: Liberty Fund, 1985 [1753]), 465–487, esp. 486. Rejection of the social contract as the basis for the state also appears in Adam Smith, *Lectures on Jurisprudence* (Indianapolis, IN: Liberty Fund, 1982 [1766]), 402–404; Ferguson, *An Essay on the History of Civil Society,* 24–29, 118–120; Edmund Burke, *Reflections on the Revolution in France,* in *Revolutionary Writings,* ed. Iain Hampsher-Monk (Cambridge, UK: Cambridge University Press, 2014), 32–33, 100–101; Benjamin Constant, "Principles of Politics," in *Political Writings,* ed. Biancamaria Fontana (Cambridge, UK: Cambridge University Press, 1988 [1815]), 176–178; G. F. W. Hegel, *Philosophy of Right,* trans. T. M. Knox (New York: Oxford University Press, 1967 [1820]), 156–167; Mill, *Representative Government,* 212; Theodor Herzl, *The Jewish State,* trans. Harry Zohn (New York: Herzl Press, 1970 [1896]), 91–94.

20. This brief discussion of political order in tribes and clans is necessarily incomplete. In particular, one cannot understand such a political order without appreciating the place of *kavod* in holding these political forms together. The Hebrew term *kavod* (often translated as "honor" or "piety") refers to the weight and significance that is attributed to the older and more powerful members of the collective, and to their ways of behaving and looking at the world. It is not only mutual loyalty that characterizes human collectives, but also the hierarchy within each collective that is established by the recognition of differences of *kavod* among its respective members. But I will have to leave an examination of this matter for another time. In this regard, see Roger Scruton, *The Meaning of Conservatism* (New York: Palgrave, 2001 [1980]), 23–25.

21. As portrayed in the biblical books of Joshua, Judges, and Samuel, which trace the initial success of the Israelite tribes as a voluntary alliance, and the decay of their common endeavors into civil war and defenselessness against foreigners. When their tribal military organization proves to be no match for the standing armies of neighboring states, they too cry out for a national government—or, in other words, for a king. For discussion, see Yoram Hazony, *The Philosophy of Hebrew Scripture* (Cambridge, UK: Cambridge University Press, 2012), 144–150.

22. This willingness to contribute to the national state is the result of a basic trust in others that is possible only where the community in question is regarded as one's own. See Sidgwick, *The Elements of Politics,* 201–203, 276; Miller, *Nationality,* 90–98; Roger Scruton, *England and the Need for Nations* (London: Civitas, 2004), 6–12, 24–25.

23. The national state does not rule over every member of the nation that establishes it, nor does it rule over only members of this nation. But as Yack correctly points out, nationalists tend to be more concerned

that borders should permit national freedom and self-determination than that there should be a perfect congruence between political and national boundaries. Yack, *Nationalism and the Moral Psychology of Community*, 122–123. See my discussion of national freedom in Chapter XIII.

24. On the awareness in Athens and other city-states of a broader Greek-speaking Hellenic nation, see Aviel Roshwald, *The Endurance of Nationalism* (Cambridge, UK: Cambridge University Press, 2006), 26–30; Jonathan Hall, *Hellenicity* (Chicago: University of Chicago Press, 2002). It has been proposed that the Athenians were a "nation," as in Edward Cohen, *The Athenian Nation* (Princeton, NJ: Princeton University Press, 2000), but it is needlessly confusing to speak of Athens as a nation when this term so well describes the broader Greek nation, whose city-states were tribal states that failed to unite under a single national state.

25. My discussion elaborates on Burke's famous comparison between the contract established "in a partnership agreement in a trade of pepper and coffee, callico or tobacco" and the partnership engaged in maintaining society. See Edmund Burke, *Reflections on the Revolution in France*, 100–101. On the "foreswearing of the calculation of transient benefits" in partnerships, see Michael Kochin, "The Constitution of Nations," *The Good Society* 14 (2005), 68–76.

26. Genesis 12.3; Amos 3.2. Compare Genesis 10.31, 22.18, 26.4.

27. Marc van de Mieroop, *Cuneiform Texts and the Writing of History* (New York: Routledge, 1999), 70.

28. In Manent's apt slogan: "The city signified war and liberty. The empire signified peace . . . and property." Pierre Manent, *A World Beyond Politics?* (Princeton, NJ: Princeton University Press, 2006), 48.

29. The "feudal" orders of medieval Europe and Japan were highly developed versions of the order of tribes and clans. As Brierly emphasizes, discussion of the "state" with reference to these and many other periods in human history is anachronistic. James Brierly, *The Law of Nations*, 2nd ed. (Oxford, UK: Oxford University Press, 1936), 3. A contemporary argument for anarchical or feudal political order is Hedley Bull, *The Anarchical Society*, 4th ed. (New York: Columbia University Press, 2012). On the transition from feudalism to the national state, see Hendrik Spruyt, *The Sovereign State and Its Competitors* (Princeton, NJ: Princeton University Press, 1994).

30. Many emperors have gone to great trouble to make their personal traits known to their subjects so they may feel they are loyal to the emperor as an individual. The result is nonetheless far removed from loyalty to an actual, familiar person.

31. On human unity as the ordering principle of imperial states, see Michael Walzer, "Nation and Universe," in *Tanner Lectures on Human Values* (Salt Lake City: University of Utah Press, 1990), 11:538–542.

32. See Theodor Herzl, "Judaism," in *Zionist Writings,* trans. Harry Zohn (New York: Herzl Press, 1973), 51.

33. Adam Ferguson, *An Essay on the History of Civil Society,* 29.

34. See Part Two, note 12, above.

35. Azar Gat, *Nations,* 111–131.

36. Historians often describe this threat of rebellion by subjugated peoples as if it is motivated by resentment of economic oppression. Economic exploitation is no doubt present in most instances of imperial conquest. But the emphasis on this fact obscures the fundamental similarity between the conflicts of neighboring, independent nations and those that arise within the imperial state, in which a revolt is almost always that of a conquered nation against the alien nation that has subjugated it.

37. As a rule, advocates of the imperial state do not see themselves as having set out only to exploit the other nations of the world. There are, of course, exceptions, and Niall Ferguson describes the rise of the British Empire in just these terms. Niall Ferguson, *Empire* (New York: Basic Books, 2002). For a more balanced account, see Anthony Pagden, *Lords of All the World* (New Haven, CT: Yale University Press, 1995); David Armitage, *The Ideological Origins of the British Empire* (Cambridge, UK: Cambridge University Press, 2000).

38. Genesis 6.5–8.14, 11.1–9.

39. The three-way distinction between city-states, national states, and empires is treated in Grosby, *Biblical Ideas of Nationality,* 29–39, 121–122; Yoram Hazony, "Empire and Anarchy," *Azure* 12 (Winter 2002), 27–70; Azar Gat, *Nations,* 3, 83.

40. Mill regards the shared heritage of the nation as creating a portion of mankind "united among themselves by common sympathies which do not exist between them and any others." These common sympathies are based on "identity of political antecedents; the possession of national history and the consequent community of recollections; collective pride and humiliation, pleasure and regret, connected with the same incidents in the past." Mill, *Representative Government,* 391. On religion as a principal factor in defining nationality, see Gertrude Himmelfarb, "The Dark and Bloody Crossroads: Where Nationalism and Religion Meet," *The National Interest* 32 (Summer 1993), 53–61. A bounded land or territory is typically a part of this national heritage. But notice that a bounded land receives its identity from the nation that lives on it, and not the nation

from the land, as is often claimed. For discussion, see Steven Grosby's essay on "Territoriality" in *Biblical Ideas of Nationality*, 191–212.

41. Miller, *Nationality*, 19–27; Gat, *Nations*, 23. I have avoided using the term "ethnicity," now popular in the academic literature, because it seems only to contribute to an unnecessary multiplication of terms, the Greek word *ethnos* traditionally being translated as "nation" or "people."

42. Thus a nationalist is one who supports not only independence for the nation, but also its unification. It is in this sense that Joseph Ellis writes that George Washington was "the most nationalistic of the nationalists," because of his unwavering support for unification under a strong central government during and after the Revolutionary War. Joseph Ellis, *The Quartet* (New York: Vintage, 2015), 109.

43. Micah 4.4. Compare Kings 1.4.25.

44. Exodus 15.20–21.

45. Milton and Rose Friedman, *Free to Choose* (New York: Harcourt Brace, 1979).

46. One may wish to say that "pain" is used metaphorically when speaking of the pain of a family, because what is meant by the pain of the family is not precisely the same as the pain of the individual. This is acceptable so long as we understand that the pain of the family, although it is something different from that of the individual, is no less real. Thinking in this way requires us to use the term "metaphor" in a manner that is at odds with the customary Aristotelian usage.

47. See Lenn Goodman, "The Rights and Wrongs of Nations," in *Judaism, Human Rights, and Human Values* (Oxford, UK: Oxford University Press, 1998), 143. Academic scholarship has tended to emphasize the impact of modern means of communication on such collective experiences. But as Gat emphasizes, illiterate societies have their own means of wide-scale cultural transmission, including a network of religious centers around the country, the gathering of the public on market days to hear news, and traveling musicians, poets, storytellers, and readers. See Gat, *Nations*, 12–13.

48. On "collective autonomy," see Miller, *Nationality*, 88–89.

49. On violence in the order of tribes and clans, see Steven Pinker, *The Better Angels of Our Nature* (New York: Penguin, 2012), especially 47–55.

50. In a federal or similar regime, there will be local courts and local police, and even local laws. But these are still answerable to the national government, which oversees them. See Chapter XV.

51. J. G. Herder, *Ideas for a Philosophy of the History of Mankind*, 324. Hume argues similarly, pointing to the lack of interest that much of

the nation has in wars fought at great distances from home. As a consequence, he writes of empires that "their downfall . . . never can be very distant from their establishment." David Hume, "Of the Balance of Power," *Essays,* ed. Eugene F. Miller (Indianapolis, IN: Liberty Fund, 1985 [1753]), 340–341. Montesquieu, Burke, and Adam Smith likewise expressed disapproval of empire. Their views are discussed in essays by Michael Mosher, Uday Singh Mehta, and Emma Rothschild in *Empire and Modern Political Thought,* ed. Sankar Muthu (Cambridge, UK: Cambridge University Press, 2012).

52. As Mill says of the English in India, their interference was "almost always in the wrong place. The real causes which determine the prosperity and the wretchedness, the improvement or deterioration, of the Hindus are too far off to be within their ken. They have not the knowledge necessary for suspecting the existence of those causes, much less for judging of their operation. The most essential interest of the country may be . . . mismanaged to almost any excess without attracting their notice." Mill, *Representative Government,* 418.

53. This is not an insignificant achievement considering that from 1337 to 1453, five English kings spent the best of their people's resources on a fruitless effort to conquer France. For a more recent example of such an eliminationist politics, one need only look at the partition of Poland, which snuffed out that nation's independent existence in 1795. None of the parties to the partition—Austria, Russia, and Prussia—were national states.

54. A comparable account framed in different terms is Henry Kissinger, *World Order* (New York: Penguin, 2014), 37, 41–44.

55. Thus Hitler declared that the Slavic peoples would be to Germany what India was to the British. Ferguson, *Empire,* 279.

56. The debate over Fritz Fischer's *Germany's War Aims in the First World War* (New York: Norton, 1968) has largely been shaped by Fischer's thesis that Germany must shoulder much of the blame for the First World War. But one does not have to accept this conclusion to recognize the power of Fischer's argument that the Germans were motivated by an imperialist strategy on the continent, had been preparing to implement this strategy for years, and apparently welcomed the Serbia crisis as an opportunity to pursue it. These facts succeed in pinning blame for the war on Germany only if one assumes that British and French imperialism played little or no role in provoking the crisis and prolonging the war once it was under way. Books such as Christopher Clark, *The Sleepwalkers* (New York: HarperCollins, 2012), which see the First World War as having been started almost by accident, tend to ignore or downplay

the decades of imperialist competition that brought Germany to confront Britain over the character of the world order it sought to impose (thereby conveniently leaving the Serb nationalists, whose machinations were the immediate cause of the war, as the only real "bad guys" in the story). For an overview of the dispute regarding Fischer's thesis, see John C. G. Röhl, "Goodbye to All That (Again)? The Fischer Thesis, the New Revisionism, and the Meaning of the First World War," *International Affairs* 91 (2015). On German imperial aspirations, see also Vejas Gabriel Liulevicius, *War Land on the Eastern Front* (Cambridge, UK: Cambridge University Press, 2005); Pierre Manent, *A World Beyond Politics?*, 83–84.

57. Not long before this, the avoidance of overseas possessions had been a consistent American policy. President Grover Cleveland, for example, argued in 1893 that the annexation of Hawaii was "a perversion of our nation's mission. The mission of our nation is to build up and make a greater country out of what we have instead of annexing islands." Quoted in John Judis, *The Folly of Empire* (New York: Scribner, 2003), 26.

58. Stuart Creighton Miller, *Benevolent Assimilation* (New Haven, CT: Yale University Press, 1984). For a pungent example of the imperialist aspirations of the day, see Theodore Roosevelt, "Expansion and Peace," *The Independent*, December 21, 1899, in *The Strenuous Life* (Mineola, NY: Dover, 2009 [1910]), 11–18.

59. Teddy Roosevelt, himself originally one of the most outspoken advocates of American empire, switched sides, attacking "professional internationalists" and "faddists of all types that vitiate sound nationalism." Quoted in Judis, *The Folly of Empire*, 113. In fact, American presidents were unable to interest their nation in overseas wars again until the Japanese attacked Pearl Harbor in 1941.

60. The perversity of this duality is perhaps best expressed in the fact that England, whose common-law tradition forbade slavery on its own soil, was also a major slave-trading power, its ships transporting millions of African slaves to the Americas. Eventually, at the end of the eighteenth century, Christian agitation succeeded in turning the British government into an active agent working for the abolition of slavery worldwide. (See David Brog, *In Defense of Faith* [New York: Encounter, 2010], 125–156.) But even this change of heart did not prevent Britain from pursuing the expansion of its empire in the belief that it was bringing Christianity and civilized institutions to mankind.

61. American support for an order of independent national states was not unequivocal, however. Woodrow Wilson's enthusiastic support for national self-determination did not prevent him from working to establish the League of Nations as a form of coercive international

government. His aim was to establish a court-adjudicated international law "as the actual rule of conduct among governments"—precisely the opposite of self-determination for its member nations (League of Nations Covenant, Preamble and Articles 10–17). During the Second World War, Franklin Roosevelt likewise combined a commitment to national self-determination with the belief in a "permanent system of world security" (Atlantic Charter, Article 8). Such views were openly anti-imperialist, but also sought to establish a new world order that itself required the establishment of a form of empire.

62. Emer de Vattel, *The Law of Nations*, 3.47–48. Translation mine. For a more general discussion of freedom as requiring the "diversification and decentralization of power in society," see Robert Nisbet, "The Contexts of Democracy," in *The March of Freedom*, ed. E. J. Feulner Jr. (Washington, DC: Heritage Foundation, 2003), 223; Michael Oakeshott, "The Political Economy of Freedom," in *Rationalism in Politics and Other Essays* (Indianapolis, IN: Liberty Fund, 1991 [1962]), 388–389.

63. Goodman, "The Rights and Wrongs of Nations," 154–155.

64. In both India and Israel, many Muslims also serve in the military and in positions of authority in government. But the extent to which these Muslim communities can be fully integrated remains an open question.

65. Napoleon's views were derived from the French Republic of which he was an agent. His destruction of Venice took place even before he assumed rule over France. See R. R. Palmer, *The Age of the Democratic Revolution* (Princeton, NJ: Princeton University Press, 1959).

66. Moses Hess, *Rome and Jerusalem*, trans. Meyer Waxman (New York: Bloch, 1918 [1862]).

67. For a famous critique of rationalist speculation in political philosophy, see Michael Oakeshott, "Rationalism in Politics," *Rationalism in Politics and Other Essays*. On rationalism and empiricism in political thought, see Thomas Sowell, *A Conflict of Visions*, rev. ed. (New York: Basic Books, 2007); Gertrude Himmelfarb, *The Roads to Modernity* (New York: Vintage Books, 2005); Yuval Levin, *The Great Debate* (New York: Basic Books, 2014); João Carlos Espada, *The Anglo-American Tradition of Liberty* (New York: Routledge, 2016); Haivry and Hazony, "What Is Conservatism?," *American Affairs* (Summer 2017). On rationalism and empiricism in science, see Yoram Hazony, "Newtonian Explanatory Reduction and Hume's System of the Sciences," in *Newton and Empiricism*, eds. Zvi Biener and Eric Schliesser (Oxford, UK: Oxford University Press, 2014), 138–170. As Quinton emphasizes, the conservative objection to "abstract" theorizing is not an objection to generalization from experience, without which reasoning would be impossible. The empiricist does allow

"very general" principles derived from experience, but the derivation is considered fallible, and the general principles themselves are potentially limited in the extent of their application. Anthony Quinton, *The Politics of Imperfection* (London: Faber and Faber, 1978), 13.

68. Mill, *Representative Government*, 140–141. Similar arguments in favor of systems of multiple, competing states appear in David Hume, "The Rise of Arts and Sciences," in *Essays*, 118–123; Adam Ferguson, *An Essay on the History of Civil Society*, 59–62; William McDougall, *Ethics and Some World Problems* (London: Methuen, 1924), 46–48; Anthony D. Smith, *The Ethnic Origins of Nations* (Cambridge, MA: Blackwell, 1986), 218; Pierre Manent, "Democracy Without Nations?," in *Modern Liberty and Its Discontents,* eds. Daniel Mahoney and Paul Seaton (New York: Rowman and Littlefield, 1998), 195. This empiricist regard for the diversity of national perspectives is not to be confused with that of German romanticism or French "postmodernism," which deny the possibility of attaining truth in politics or morals. The empiricist standpoint regards the diversity of national perspectives as an advantage in the pursuit of truth.

69. It was this lethargy of empire that de Gaulle had in mind in predicting that a unified Europe would become "a materialist, soulless mass, with no idealism left." Quoted in Margaret Thatcher, *Statecraft* (New York: HarperCollins, 2002), 365.

70. Friedrich Hayek, "The Economic Conditions of Interstate Federalism," *New Commonwealth Quarterly* 5 (September 1939), 131–149.

71. Thatcher, *Statecraft*, 374–376, 420. A similar argument is made at length in Dani Rodrik, *The Globalization Paradox* (New York: Norton, 2011).

72. In the case of Britain's delegation of decision-making powers to the European Union, Thatcher concludes that the British were naïve. She describes how European bodies were granted decision-making powers that were then, inevitably, expanded by the decision of European institutions in which Britain had a say but no effective power. Thatcher, *Statecraft*, 368.

73. The principle of national self-determination does not, in and of itself, require a democratic form of government or a tradition of concern for individual liberties. Miller, *Nationality*, 90; John Plamenatz, *On Alien Rule and Self-Government* (London: Longmans, 1960).

74. As Miller emphasizes, the concern for the universal protection of individual rights, if embraced to the exclusion of other considerations, leads inexorably to "benevolent imperialism." Miller, *Nationality*, 77. This dynamic stands, for example, behind Sidgwick's argument for

the expansion of liberal empire (what he calls the "beneficent exercise of dominion") over nations that are "markedly inferior in civilization." Henry Sidgwick, *The Elements of Politics*, 278–279.

75. Mill, *Representative Government*, 394. Mill is an awkward fit within the principal liberal tradition descended from rationalist theorists such as Hobbes and Locke. On many issues, his empiricism means that his argument is more similar to that of other empiricists such as Hume and Burke. Mill's nationalism is of a piece with this larger pattern.

76. In the original American Constitution, only the House of Representatives was selected by direct public election. Even today, the Supreme Court is still an unelected body.

77. Mill's argument on this point is well known. "Free institutions are next to impossible in a country made up of different nationalities. Among a people without fellow-feeling, especially if they read and speak different languages, the united public opinion necessary to the working of representative government cannot exist. . . . An army composed of various nationalities has no other patriotism than devotion to the flag. Such armies have been the executioners of liberty through the whole duration of modern history." Mill, *Representative Government*, 392–394. Less known is Mill's conclusion, in which he argues that Britain will never know enough about India to be able to govern it appropriately. See Part Two, note 52, above.

78. Raymond Aron, for example, proposes an international federal regime as a compromise between a homogenous national state and a universal imperial state. See *The Dawn of Universal History* (New York: Basic Books, 2002 [1996]), 5.

79. Kant's position is stated unequivocally in "Idea for a Universal History with a Cosmopolitan Purpose," in Immanuel Kant, *Political Writings*, ed. Hans Reiss, trans. H. B. Nisbet (New York: Cambridge University Press, 1970 [1784]): "A federation of peoples in which every state, even the smallest, could expect to derive its security and rights not from its own power or its own legal judgment, but solely from this great federation, from a united power and the law-governed decisions of a united will" (47). Or, as he writes, "A system of united power, hence a system of general political security" (49). And: "A great political body of the future . . . , the highest purpose of nature, a universal cosmopolitan existence . . . within which all the original capacities of the human race may develop" (51). A similar view is presented in Kant's later essay, "Perpetual Peace: A Philosophical Sketch," in *Political Writings*, 102–105, in which an "international state," apparently without federal divisions, is presented

as an ideal, and an international federation is described as an intermediate aim. See Chapters XXI, XXIII.

80. See August Heckscher, *Woodrow Wilson* (New York: Scribner, 1993), 551. Wilson's proposed League of Nations committed all members to "preserve as against external aggression the territorial integrity and existing political independence of all Members of the League" in accordance with a complex mechanism of international governance. See the League of Nations Charter, Articles 10–17. This prompted the Republican Henry Cabot Lodge's famous call for the American people to be "now and ever for Americanism and nationalism, and against internationalism." Official Proceedings of the Seventeenth Republican National Convention, quoted in William Widenor, *Henry Cabot Lodge and the Search for an American Foreign Policy* (Berkeley: University of California Press, 1980), 347–348.

81. Friedrich Hayek, "The Economic Conditions of Interstate Federalism." See also Sidgwick, *The Elements of Politics*, 268–269; Ludwig von Mises, *Liberalism in the Classical Tradition,* trans. Ralph Raico (San Francisco: Cobden Press, 1985 [1927]), 150. See also Chapter IV (Part One), notes 55–56 in this book.

82. Isaiah 2.4; Micah 4.3; Psalms 46.9.

83. See especially the Ninth and Tenth Amendments to the Constitution of the United States.

84. Philip Hamburger, *Separation of Church and State* (Cambridge, MA: Harvard University Press, 2002), 147–189.

85. Despite Lincoln's well-known position that he was fighting to preserve the Union rather than to eradicate slavery, I see little sense in separating the two issues. It was the slaving cultural inheritance of the South and its unwillingness to part with it that was the cause of secession. Moreover, once the war was under way, the federal government moved to abolish all slavery in the United States and did so between 1863 and 1865, including in states that did not secede. Had the war been fought only over the formal matter of secession, it would not have resulted in such an immediate and total abolition of slavery. See Eric Foner, *The Fiery Trial* (New York: Norton, 2011).

86. A significant event in this story was the ratification of the Fourteenth Amendment to the American Constitution. Passed in 1868, after the Civil War, this amendment explicitly subordinated the laws of the respective states to the supervision of the federal government in all things related to the privileges and immunities of citizens, stating that "No State shall make or enforce any law which shall abridge the privileges or

immunities of citizens of the United States; nor shall any State deprive any person of life, liberty, or property, without due process of law; nor deny to any person within its jurisdiction the equal protection of the laws." Fourteenth Amendment to the US Constitution.

87. On the biblical origins of federalism, see Daniel Elazar, *Covenant and Polity in Biblical Israel* (New Brunswick, NJ: Transaction, 1995).

88. The signatories to the treaty, including Germany, France, and Britain, resolve "to continue the process of creating an ever closer union among the peoples of Europe, in which decisions are taken as closely as possible to the citizen in accordance with the principle of subsidiarity" (Preamble). For the passage quoted, see Article B and Article G, section 5.

89. See Jeremy Rabkin, *Law Without Nations?* (Princeton, NJ: Princeton University Press, 2005), 43. The right of the citizens of European states to appeal to European Community law against the laws of their own national governments was established by the European Court of Justice in 1963. Case 26/62, *Van Gend en Loos v. Nederlandse Administratie der Belastingen* (1963) ECR 1; John Fonte, *Sovereignty or Submission* (New York: Encounter, 2011), 132–133.

90. EU laws have to be ratified by appointed and elected bodies, and national legislatures also have limited powers to intervene. But in any case, decision-making authority remains with the European federal courts. Estimates suggest that perhaps half of new legislation in European states is imposed by the EU bureaucracy according to this procedure, and upheld by the judicial hierarchy. For an overview of the curtailment of national-state authority in the European Union, see Fonte, *Sovereignty or Submission*, 121–158.

91. For an overview of this subject, see Will Kymlicka, *Politics in the Vernacular* (Oxford, UK: Oxford University Press, 2001), 23–24. The advantages of the civic or neutral state are emphasized, especially, by Lord Acton in John Emerich Dalbert-Acton, "Nationality," *Essays on Freedom and Power*, ed. Gertrude Himmelfarb (Boston: Beacon Press, 1949 [1862]), 166–195. It became a guiding normative principle in the academic study of nationalism in the wake of works such as Kohn, *The Idea of Nationalism,* and Kedourie, *Nationalism.*

92. For criticism of the myth of the "civic nation," see Yack, *Nationalism and the Moral Psychology of Community,* 23–43; Roshwald, *The Endurance of Nationalism,* 253–295; Taras Kuzio, "The Myth of the Civic Nation: A Critical Survey of Hans Kohn's Framework for Understanding Nationalism," *Ethnic and Racial Studies* 25 (January 2002), 20–39; Stephen Shulman, "Challenging the Civic/Ethnic and West/East Dichotomies in the Study

of Nationalism," *Comparative Political Studies* 35 (June 2002), 554–585; Will Kymlicka, *Politics in the Vernacular,* 23–27.

93. Michael Walzer, for example, describes the United States as characterized by a "sharp divorce of state and ethnicity," although he admits that "American Indians and blacks have mostly been excluded from this unity." See his "Pluralism in Political Perspective," in *The Politics of Ethnicity,* eds. Michael Walzer et al. (Cambridge, MA: Harvard University Press, 1982), 17–18. The desirability of separating nationality from the state appears repeatedly in German-Jewish political thought, notably in the writings of Hermann Cohen, Martin Buber, and their followers. See my discussion in Yoram Hazony, *The Jewish State* (Basic Books, 2000), 181–264. A contemporary elaboration of this tradition is Yael Tamir, *Liberal Nationalism* (Princeton, NJ: Princeton University Press, 1993).

94. On the theory of "constitutional patriotism" as an alternative to nationalism in a "post-national" Germany, see Jürgen Habermas, "The European Nation-State" and "Does Europe Need a Constitution?" in *The Inclusion of the Other,* eds. Ciaran Cronin and Pablo De Greiff (Cambridge: Massachusetts Institute of Technology Press, 1998), 117–120, 160–161. Some proponents emphasize that it is not the constitutional documents themselves, but rather the principles that are enshrined in them, which should be the object of loyalty. My argument is the same, however, whether it is the document or the principles described in the document that are supposed to be the object of loyalty.

95. On the religious awe of the American flag cultivated after the Civil War in the United States, see Samuel Huntington, *Who Are We?* (New York: Simon and Schuster, 2004), 127–128.

96. I have referred here to the largest nation within a free national state as the *majority nation.* However, there can also be a free national state in which the largest nation does not enjoy a majority, but only a plurality, while the rest of the population consists of a number of smaller national minorities. In the interests of avoiding unnecessary jargon, I will continue to speak of the "majority nation," which term I understand to include nations in a plurality position of this kind as well. Of course, there do exist occasional states in which two nations or tribes, each overwhelmingly dominant within its own territory, balance one another within a single federal state. Well-known examples are Canada, Belgium, and Czechoslovakia (dissolved 1993).

97. As John Jay wrote in the *Federalist Papers:* "Providence has been pleased to give this one connected country to one united people—a people descended from the same ancestors, speaking the same language,

professing the same religion, attached to the same principles of government, very similar in their manners and customs, and who, by joint counsels, arms, and efforts, fighting side by side throughout a long and bloody war, have nobly established general liberty and independence." John Jay, *Federalist* 2. See also Gregory Jusdanis, *The Necessary Nation* (Princeton, NJ: Princeton University Press, 2001), 155–162.

98. The American public-school system was established in the 1830s with the aim of maintaining a public culture based on Protestantism and American nationalism. Carl Kaestle, *Pillars of the Republic* (New York: Hill and Wang, 1983), 75–103. On policies by schools and other institutions aimed at "Americanizing" immigrants during the twentieth century, see Huntington, *Who Are We?*, 131–136.

99. The effort to preserve German culture through German-speaking schools in Wisconsin was likewise stamped out by the legislature in 1889. James Morone, "The Struggle for American Culture," *PS: Political Science and Politics* 29 (1996), 424–430. New territories have generally been brought into the traditional Anglo-American legal framework wherever English-speaking majorities have existed. In Louisiana, where a legal code modeled on the French civil law was permitted, the federal government stipulated that both the code and court proceedings must be in the English language. Rabkin, *Law Without Nations?*, 109–111, 306–307nn19, 22.

100. Native Americans were granted status as American citizens in 1924, and many of the rights guaranteed by the US Constitution in 1968. A relevant discussion of the destruction of the Crow nation is Jonathan Lear, *Radical Hope* (Cambridge, MA: Harvard University Press, 2008).

101. Gat, *Nations*, 260–264; Anthony Marx, *Faith in Nation* (Oxford, UK: Oxford University Press, 2003); Eugen Weber, *Peasants into Frenchmen* (Stanford, CA: Stanford University Press, 1976); Linda Colley, *Britons* (New Haven, CT: Yale University Press, 1992).

102. Sidgwick refers to national states as "organic states"; whereas an "inorganic state" is "one in which the rule is that of an alien element supported by an army divorced in feeling from the rest of the population. The community thus artificially held together lacks the kind of cohesion that constitutes a nation." Henry Sidgwick, *The Elements of Politics*, 236; also 277.

103. On Israel as a Jewish national state, see Hazony, *The Jewish State*, 267–275.

104. In Eastern Europe, India, and the Middle East, many of the more successful national states have been established as a result of population exchanges, often accompanied by violence. As Roshwald writes,

"Pluralistic values, it seems, are much easier to embrace in the absence of diversity." Roshwald, *The Endurance of Nationalism*, 264. Where these national states have nevertheless found themselves faced with protracted internal conflict, it has been in those regions in which a national minority forms a strong local majority: in Muslim Kashmir in India, in the Kurdish southeastern provinces of Turkey, in Arab-majority territories held by Israel, and so on.

105. As Margaret Canovan writes, "The problem of maintaining unity and stability has . . . historically been harder to solve on democratic than on non-democratic terms. . . . The more democratic the state is to be, the more need there is for the people to have some bond of unity other than that provided by common subjection." Canovan, *Nationhood and Political Theory* (Northampton, MA: Edward Elgar, 1996), 22. These conclusions are supported by Dorina Bekoe in her survey of internally divided African states, "Democracy and African Conflicts: Inciting, Mitigating, or Reducing Violence?," in *Democratization in Africa* (conference report of the National Intelligence Council, 2008), 30. See also Anthony Smith, *The Ethnic Origins of Nations*, 146.

106. See Chapter XIV, section 5.

107. Woodrow Wilson, in declaring the war aims of the United States during the First World War, asserts that in the postwar settlement, "National aspirations must be respected. Peoples may now be dominated and governed only by their own consent. 'Self-determination' is not a mere phrase. It is an imperative principle of actions which statesmen will henceforth ignore at their peril." Woodrow Wilson, "Address to a Joint Session of Congress Analyzing German and Austrian Peace Utterances," February 11, 1918. The supposition that such a universal imperative could be implemented stems from Wilson's belief that he was witnessing the birth of a "new world" in which "the day of conquest and aggrandizement is gone"—and that "this happy fact [is] now clear to the view of every public man whose thoughts do not still linger in an age that is dead and gone." In the context of this messianic view of the political world, he declared his Fourteen Points to be "the moral climax of . . . the culminating and final war for human liberty," after which "all peoples and nationalities" would have a "right to live on equal terms . . . with one another." Woodrow Wilson, "An Address to a Joint Session of Congress on the Conditions of Peace," January 8, 1918.

108. Himmelfarb suggests that the transition from Mill to Wilson marks a shift from realistic to utopian modes of thinking about nations. Himmelfarb, "The Dark and Bloody Crossroads," 60. Compare Gellner, *Nations and Nationalism*, 1–3; Yack, *Nationalism and the Moral Psychology of*

Community, 233–252. See also Tamar Meisels's study, *Territorial Rights,* 2nd ed. (Dordrecht, Netherlands: Springer, 2009).

109. Many are described in James Minahan, ed., *The Encyclopedia of Stateless Nations* (Westport, CT: Greenwood Press, 2002).

110. A wretched summary of this matter was made by Wilson in a meeting with Edward Dunne and Frank Walsh at the President's House, Paris, June 11, 1919, in which they had come to plead the cause of Ireland. Describing his experience at Versailles following his suggestion that all peoples have a right to self-determination, Wilson told them, "When I gave utterance to those words, I said them without the knowledge that nationalities existed, which are coming to us day after day. . . . You do not know and cannot appreciate the anxieties that I have experienced as a result of many millions of people having their hopes raised by what I have said. . . . No one knows the feelings that are inside of me. . . . It distresses me." Reprinted in the *Hearings of the Committee of Foreign Relations, U.S. Senate,* no. 106 (1919), 835–838, esp. 838. The secondary literature describing Wilson's statement as part of a speech before the Senate is mistaken.

111. Woodrow Wilson, "Address to a Joint Session of Congress on the Conditions of Peace," January 8, 1918; Henry Kissinger, *Diplomacy* (New York: Simon and Schuster, 1994), 242–243.

112. Michael Doran, *Ike's Gamble* (New York: Free Press, 2016).

113. As Sidgwick suggests, the principles often described as "international law" are properly called "international morality." Sidgwick, *The Elements of Politics,* 256. The "natural laws" (or "natural obligations") of nations to which I refer here are principles or obligations that are known from experience, and so are open to revision, as in the natural sciences. These are to be distinguished from rationalist assertions of natural law or natural right, which are derived from supposedly self-evident axioms.

114. The terms *right* and *sovereignty* can be useful only if intended in a restricted sense. The term "sovereignty" is problematic due to its origin in absolutist doctrines maintaining that the will of the king is inviolable in his realm. In fact, neither the will of the king, nor that of parliament, nor that of the people (as in "popular sovereignty") can be regarded as absolute. The people are not infallible any more than the king or parliament is, as the popular election of the Nazis in 1933 confirms. In certain extreme cases, then, individuals, tribal or national groups, and foreign actors may have cause to violate the laws or policies of a national government on its soil. The will of no human individual or institution can properly be said to be inviolable. Sovereignty, for this reason, properly belongs only to God. On "popular sovereignty," see Edmund Morgan,

Inventing the People (New York: Norton, 1988). In the same way, the term "right," which is today often used to suggest a derivation a priori from universal reason, can have no such meaning here. Rights under international law, like rights under domestic national law, can be derived only empirically, as norms that have been shown to uphold a given moral or legal system and to benefit those living under it.

115. The Anglo-American constitutional tradition also recognizes a right of the individual to carry arms for self-defense, rather than an absolute government monopoly of the use of force. For this reason, I have referred to the state's monopoly of the organized use of force.

116. On demographics and national decline, see David Goldman, *How Civilizations Die* (New York: Regnery, 2011). Kissinger emphasizes that the purpose of the Concert of Europe was not to freeze borders, but to ensure that changes occurred "as a matter of evolution." Kissinger, *World Order,* 66. This is more realistic than attempting to maintain virtually all borders fixed in perpetuity, which is, in effect, the position of many political and intellectual figures in our day.

117. Miller, *Nationality,* 114–115.

118. Some nations or tribes continue to prefer even today to be governed by a much stronger national state, as a protectorate under one or another type of federative arrangement. America's government in Puerto Rico, a Spanish-speaking country with a population of nearly four million, is a well-known example. America, Britain, France, and other countries continue to govern dozens of such protectorates, although their populations are usually smaller.

119. On the World Trade Organization, see Rabkin, *Law Without Nations?,* 193–232. On the "globalization" of domestic politics under the rubric of the pursuit of universal human rights, see Rabkin, *Law Without Nations?,* 158–192; Fonte, *Sovereignty or Submission,* 201–278.

Part Three:
Anti-Nationalism and Hate

1. Thomas Kuhn, *The Structure of Scientific Revolutions* (Chicago: University of Chicago Press, 1996 [1962]), esp. 148–151.

2. See Chapter III.

3. See Chapter II, esp. note 16 (Part One).

4. Immanuel Kant, "Perpetual Peace," in *Political Writings,* ed. Hans Reiss, trans. H. B. Nisbet (Cambridge, UK: Cambridge University Press, 1970), 102–103. Emphasis removed.

5. Ibid., 105. Emphasis in the original. When Kant uses the term "international state" here, he apparently means a non-federal state with a single jurisdiction ("a world republic"). He recognizes that such a state is not yet feasible and so proposes "an enduring and gradually expanding federation" as a practical alternative (105). A universal federation is still, however, a universal imperial state, and not something to be desired. See my discussion in Chapter XV.

6. Jürgen Habermas, "The European Nation-State," in *The Inclusion of the Other,* eds. Ciaran Cronin and Pablo De Greiff (Cambridge: Massachusetts Institute of Technology Press, 1998), 118.

7. Speech by Ben-Gurion before a special session of the National Assembly, November 30, 1942, file J/1366, Central Zionist Archives, Jerusalem.

8. See, for example, Tony Judt, "Israel: The Alternative," *The New York Review of Books,* October 23, 2003.

9. Immanuel Kant, "Idea for a Universal History with a Cosmopolitan Purpose," in *Political Writings,* 53.

10. Ibid., 47.

11. Ibid., 47–49. Moreover, Europe "will probably legislate eventually for all other continents" (52).

12. Kant repeatedly compares the moral immaturity of mankind to the immaturity of children, as in "Idea for a Universal History," 42.

13. Ibid., 42.

14. Ambassador Jesper Var, speaking at the Jerusalem Post Diplomatic Conference, December 11, 2014. Video of his comments available at www.youtube.com/watch?v=AYojm0TRGPg.

15. In one especially striking incident in 2010, the Arizona legislature empowered state law officers to restrict illegal immigration. In response, the Obama administration inserted a legal challenge to the state's action in a report filed with the United Nations Human Rights Council. Far from defending the freedom of Americans against foreign encroachment, the US government joined forces with an international body in an effort to tar Arizona with the stigma of moral illegitimacy. See "Report of the United States of America Submitted to the U.N. High Commissioner for Human Rights in Conjunction with the Universal Periodic Review," available at www.state.gov/documents/organization/146379.pdf; "State Department Stands by Decision to Include Arizona in U.N. Human Rights Report," Fox News, August 30, 2010; "Reporting Arizona Law to UN Was Correct," Chandra S. Bhatnagar and Alessandra Soler Meetze, CNN, September 4, 2010.

16. Justin Welby, Archbishop of Canterbury, for example, regards the vote for British independence as being "in a nationalist, populist or even fascist tradition of politics." *The Guardian,* February 13, 2017.

17. Even Nazi imperialism was a salvationist creed scattering promises of world peace. As Hitler writes in *Mein Kampf,* the triumph of the German race might attain "what so many pacifists today hope to gain" albeit in the wrong way: "a peace, supported not by . . . tearful, pacifist, female mourners, but based on the victorious sword of a master people." Adolf Hitler, *Mein Kampf,* trans. Ralph Manheim (New York: Houghton Mifflin, 1971 [1925]), 396. Compare Anthony Smith, who emphasizes that Nazism is a salvationist creed, waging "a war of 'world salvation'" to "annihilate inferior polluting slave-races." See *Nationalism in the Twentieth Century* (Oxford, UK: Martin Robertson, 1979), 80.

18. See Matti Friedman, "An Insider's Guide to the Most Important Story on Earth," *Tablet,* August 26, 2014.

19. See Michael Mack's discussion of Kant's philosophical anti-Semitism in *German Idealism and the Jew* (Chicago: University of Chicago Press, 2003), 1–41.

20. See Yoram Hazony, "There's No Such Thing as an 'Illiberal,'" *Wall Street Journal,* August 4, 2017.

CONCLUSION:
THE VIRTUE OF NATIONALISM

1. Theodor Herzl, *The Jewish State,* trans. Harry Zohn (New York: Herzl Press, 1970), 107.

2. Genesis 12.2–3.

INDEX

YORAM HAZONY is President of the Herzl Institute in Jerusalem and Director of the John Templeton Foundation's Project in Jewish Philosophical Theology. His previous books include *The Jewish State: The Struggle for Israel's Soul* and *The Philosophy of Hebrew Scripture*. His essays have appeared in the *Wall Street Journal*, the *New York Times*, the *New Republic*, *Commentary*, *American Affairs*, and *First Things*, among other publications.